AF539025

Traditions of Women Culture

Traditions of Women Culture

Edited by

P. Kumar

GLOBAL PUBLICATIONS
NEW DELHI-110 002 (INDIA)

GLOBAL PUBLICATIONS
4378/4B, G-4 JMD House
Murari Lal Street, Ansari Road
Daryaganj, New Delhi - 110 002
Phone : 23278062 (Off.)
e-mail : omega_publications@yahoo.com

Head Office :
79/23, Laxmi Garden
Near Satya Jyoti School,
Gurgaon (Haryana)
Mob : 9213562438

Traditions of Women Culture

First Published : 2011

ISBN : 978-93-80833-47-7

PRINTED IN INDIA

Published by Ishwari Prasad Garg for Global Publications, New Delhi-110002 and Printed at Suman Printers, Delhi

Preface

Missionary magazines give glimpses here and there of the thoughts and feelings and homes of the "Women of India;" persons interested in their education tell us of the schools that exist or do not exist for them; those devoted to the hospital question dilate upon the errors of native medicine, and the want of proper attendance and accommodation for women in sickness; while people of taste, and with a love of art, tell us of the beautiful dresses, the Oriental colouring, and, alas ! of the corruption of native taste by European models.

Some books give us lives of distinguished Indian women, and show us how talent will make its way through every obstacle; others appeal to our sympathy with tales of woe; we weep with the writers over the unhappy child-widow, or grieve at the strict rules of the purdah; but it requires time and. patience to find and to look through all the tracts, magazines, and publications that deal with these subjects separately, and it is a satisfaction to find one volume in which an attempt is made to trace the career of Indian women from the cradle to the grave, and to give some account of their customs, their occupations, their pleasures, their religion, and their dress.

Specialists and academical students of Indian lore will not expect to find in so small a compass all the data they require; they must naturally dig deeper, and make more profound researches into dictionaries and encyclopaedias for the knowledge which they seek. A work of this kind does not pretend to exhaust the subject with which it deals, or to settle the many questions referred to in its pages, and the writer of this one would probably be the first to admit that there are nooks and crannies in the vast continent of India which she has been unable to explore, curious customs which she has not discovered, mines of information which she has not reached.

The major topics dealt in this book are : *The Woman's Movement in the Past; Evolution of Sex and Significance; Birth and Infancy; Education of Women; Marriage System in Society; Widow-Remarriage and Divorce; Female Life in Field and Factory; Medical Aid and Assistance for Sick; Embroidery and Needlecraft; Jewellery and Ornament; Amusements and Pleasures; Anglo-Indian Society; The Sphere of Woman; Economics and Biology; Confusion of Thought of Times; Female Crimes and Criminals in the Past; Death and Funeral Customs; etc.*

No doubt, these will serve the purpose of trainees and trainers, professional and policy planners in the field. Since the sources of information are all secondary, we express our gratitude to the scholars whose works are cited or substantially made use of. We are thankful to all those who rendered ready help and cooperation while working on this project.

I express my gratitude to various scholars, teachers and friends for their assistance and guidance. Finally, I thank the publishers for bringing out this book in very limited time.

—***Editor***

Contents

1

The Woman's Movement in the Past

I ask for nothing else than this—that woman should recognise her own individuality, and that man should recognise it also in education, vocation, domestic life, and national representation.

The study of sex is primarily a human one, firstly because sex has in all forms of animal existence only a physical value, lacking both the individual and the social importance that it possesses in man; secondly—what is really a necessary biological corollary to the first reason—sex specialisation and intensity have reached a higher stage in the human species than elsewhere.

Woman's position can only be said to have been a matter for serious discussion in recent times, for although primitive man and woman had certain grievances that they each felt against the other, yet there can be little doubt that these were settled by individuals as individuals, and were not taken up by the one sex as a sex question and rejected by the other. In point of fact woman was physically in too undifferentiated a condition in early pre-civilised life, and she was mentally and physically so much more man-like that it is probable that the idea of mental differences of sex had hardly occurred to either the man or the woman at this time. Woman was regarded by man and regarded herself also as simply an inferior copy of himself.

There is also ample evidence to prove that, although the virago such as Socrates' Xantippe has always, except possibly among the Spartans, excited derision and annoyance in the mind of man, there was not in the older civilisations any tendency for women of that time to assert themselves as women and as a distinctive sex state force. The feeling of *injustice*, of *limitation* felt so acutely by the modern woman manifested itself first in Renaissance times, and has grown and intensified slowly in the fifteenth, sixteenth, and seventeenth centuries, and then rapidly from the close of the eighteenth century to the present time. It is, therefore, pre-eminently a modern movement, and has excited greatest feeling only in the more progressive and more masculine countries of the modern civilised world.

I do not wish my point to be misunderstood. No movement is, of course, ever really new. Many primitive races are not free from some discontent of women. The Amazon myth and certain Greek and Roman examples might be quoted, but these were not large lasting movements. There was, of course, also besides woman's political movement a well-known Renaissance of woman's influence, and this was perhaps most marked in the two feminine countries, Italy and France. But the active discontent to which I allude appeared first in England, and spread from England to the United States and Germany; and although it is true that other countries, such as Hungary and France, were also affected, yet it was only in Germany and Anglo-Saxon lands that definite movements were established which gave origin to definite schools of thought.

For some reason the German Empire was and is hostile to woman's development, and the Anglo-Saxon countries favourable, and as both have misunderstood woman's requirements, it may be a matter of some interest to push the inquiry a little further.

The Anglo-Saxon Movement

Mary Astell, at the close of the seventeenth century, published (in 1696) a small volume on woman's position, which is probably the first of its kind in any country or any language. It passed through several editions, so that it may fairly be said to have been read with an interest that proved the subject was already exciting considerable attention. Richard Mulcaster, as early as 1581, supported a higher ideal of education for women, and he refers to public opinion as supporting him in this view. The question of sex emancipation must have been discussed in some slight degree, therefore, previous to his statement, but the movement, such as it was, came from the man's side, and there is no hint that woman felt in any conscious degree any bondage at the time he wrote on the subject. Mary Astell's work is, therefore, the first to point out clearly that women as women objected to the limitations imposed upon them. It is also to be noted that in her view woman was an inferior kind of man, having unlike sexual functions, and her work, which is quaintly written, pleads for higher education for women, on the ground of it making her more interesting to man quite as much as for her feminine functions and her own life. So that the first stage of the woman's movement began by a denial of woman's womanhood ; woman was from this early aspect simply a female man, and as such it was expedient, even with her own inferior powers, to educate her. After an attempt to prove that there is no difference of sex in the soul, she continues : "Neither can it be in the body (if I may credit the report of learned physicians), for there is no difference in the organisation of those parts which have any relation to or influence over the mind; but the brain and all other parts (which I am not anatomist enough to mention) are contrived as well for the plentiful conveyance of spirits which are held to be the immediate instruments of sensation, in women as in men."

To a man this unconsciousness of the sexual differences of the mind on the part of a woman is remarkable. That a man of this period, who scarcely troubled himself about woman's real nature, should have passed them over is not surprising; but that a woman, writing for the first time about a new subject, with her thoughts turned freshly in her own direction, should have passed over certain obvious differences, and assumed that the minds of men and women were alike, is indeed puzzling, and what is even more curious is that in some quarters the idea still persists. This persistence is surely itself strong evidence of one unlikeness that more than one student of sexual psychology has pointed out, namely, woman's less intense analytic consciousness of her own personality. Possibly also of a reticence to lay bare what is there.

The next defence of the woman's claim for wider opportunities took up a transitional attitude. It assumed that the minds of men and women were different, but considered that these differences were due to different habits of life and training, forgetful of the obvious fact that mental differences are marked in higher birds and mammals who are not differently trained nor differently environed in early life, forgetful, too, of the unquestionable influence that male and female reproductive glands exert on the individual as a whole. Emasculated animals develop feminine characteristics, the more marked the earlier the operation has been performed. Female birds whose plumage has been typical, when they cease to lay eggs at times acquire the plumage of a cock. Crowing hens that never lay, and women whose attributes change "at the change of life," and who may at this period acquire masculine characters, and even a thin beard, are well-known phenomena, with the mental characteristics that accompany them. Such are only a few common facts that have long been recognised, which prove, quite apart from other scientific evidence, that sex is of biological, of mental and bodily significance.

Mary Wollstonecraft and John Stuart Mill both assumed that woman's mind differed because woman had been prevented from using it; and Helen Thompson, an American authoress, after establishing by experiment mental differences between men and women, follows in Mill's footsteps, and attempts to reason away her results. Woman is, of course, not a mere female man, but a woman possessed of womanliness; and though there are manly women and womanly men, and men with female minds and women with male ones, yet womanliness is a broad characteristic of woman and manliness of man.

The first stage of the woman's movement, based upon woman's likeness to man, was erroneous, and the second stage, that thought the unlikeness existed but was acquired and was unnatural proves also to be untrue.

There is yet a third line of argument that Mary Wollstonecraft ("Rights of Woman," 1792) and Mill ("Subjection of Woman," 1869) attempted to justify, namely, that a woman had certain ethical rights in the state, and that these were not respected. This ethical issue became the one that dominated the whole of the Anglo-Saxon movement, permeated our education system when women were given larger opportunities, and has, in the opinion of many, led to some serious dangers in modern life.

That the rights of woman might be equal in value to the rights of man and yet not be identical never occurred to English or American men and women. That it might be granted that women had been treated badly, be admitted that there was need of reform, and yet that people should disagree with the aim of the emancipationists to give the woman the *same* educational and occupational opportunities as the man, was a position that was summarily dismissed. The whole question of woman's nature was disregarded. The spirit of the age was against woman's development, though it favoured in extreme quarters her emancipation, and it may be that woman has been sacrificed to an extent that after-ages are likely to regret.

It was a misfortune that in England the two pioneers who were accepted by the nation were precisely those who from experience knew little or nothing of the higher aspects either of womanhood or of manhood, their knowledge being mainly confined to one sex.

Mary Wollstonecraft had an unfortunate example of manhood in her father, and there was almost constant misery in the home of her early years. And Mill, by a curious and regrettable coincidence, was trained on an asexual system by his father, being almost exclusively deprived of womanly influences in his surroundings. The ignorance of man's higher nature that exists in the woman leader's writings, and the ignorance of woman's in the man's, is thus partially accounted for. But the people of England must themselves have acquiesced in this faulty position, otherwise other leaders would have been found. One such possible man certainly existed.

That the identical rights argument proved itself a fallacious one subsequent events have established.

As no one in the movement tried to discover what woman's powers were, men soon took their own standard of -comparison. If women were as fitted as men, why was it that in art, which she had had some practical knowledge of for centuries, no great woman artist had been produced ? Why was there not a woman Michael Angelo ? why not a woman Titian or a Raphael? Raphael had painted motherhood even, yet no woman had equalled him. Music, too, had been her study, yet there had been no woman Mozart, no woman Beethoven. And then it was remembered that there was a time when reading was more cultivated by women than men, when, in the early Middle Ages, men looked with contempt on the study of things mental, yet no recognised woman authoress of this time has been discovered. And up to the present time in dress, furnishing, cookery, and domestic life, inventions and designs have been mainly by men (as, for example, Chippendale and Sheraton in furniture, Worth in dress, Liebig in food preparations). So, as men still wished to deal justly by women, and women still expressed the desire to be freed from unjust restrictions that hampered them, a new kind of argument to meet this difficulty of woman's failure grew up.

It began to be tacitly assumed that woman was inferior to man, and Huxley only voiced the tendency of the time he wrote in when he asserted that women and the lower races must both be emancipated, if not entirely for their own sakes, at least for those who held them enslaved. He asserted and with truth, that emancipation benefited the emancipator more than the emancipated. And, as a result of this persistent effort, woman has attained some kind of emancipation. But the added freedom has not satisfied her. Why ? Is it not because it has not been founded on her natural capacity ?

She has largely obtained economic independence, with the result that she has depreciated man's wage-earning value, and in many industries is displacing him entirely.

Where before the unmarried woman had difficulty in obtaining employment, now the married man with wife and family has partly the difficulty that the single woman had to face. The lazy married man, too, has found out that it is useful for his wife to be able to work, and so he stops at home, or rather at the corner of the nearest public-house, and the wife, thus fettered, neglects her home, neglects her duties to her children, puts her babies out to be bottle-fed, and suffer illness and death while she often performs the man's work at a woman's current wage, A type of woman has meanwhile grown up almost without domestic education, who prefers public life to the home under any conditions.

What prompted woman to feel dissatisfied was never discovered, and has not been discovered at the present time. What dissatisfied her in her individual life, what dissatisfied her in her public life, remains unrecognised. She has been merely treated as a sexless being, as a man with female functions, or as an inferior human being having a subordinate social value, and precisely what the value was remained unknown.

Why women were fairly satisfied with their lives till two hundred years ago ; why this dissatisfaction broke out only in the cultured parts of the world, and there only in the more cultured classes, has never been studied.

Our movement, though a sincere and sympathetic one, and this is to its credit, supported by men as well as women, has miscarried, and woman's nature and the origin of her discontent remains now, as before, unknown. This is lamentable.

Germany

The writers in Germany who have written on woman's nature have shown themselves to have knowledge and sympathy mainly for those elements which are merely common to all females, and are not characteristically woman's at all, and have asserted from this knowledge that woman is therefore man's inferior. It would, of course, be as logical for woman to retort that taking a general estimate of the made elements in man, he could not compare with woman on her human side, and that the womanly promptings of her being were always lowered by his male assertiveness. One would have expected, had there not been such indisputable evidence to the contrary, that it would be unnecessary to point out that all investigations into the nature of woman must take note of woman's whole nature, and not inaccurately assume that, while man has a human individuality that is man's prerogative, woman has no individuality beyond that which she shares with all higher female life Yet this axiomatic assumption, which alone car make a study on this subject valuable, has been wholly disregarded.

It is true that poets like Schiller have written sympathetically about woman, but these have not been students of her nature, nor have they been specially associated with the question of her development. Of the names that are so associated almost all are hostile, and to some degree unhealthy in their tone, and all profoundly selfish.

I shall not, therefore, attempt to seriously criticise the German position, because it is self-condemned by its disregard of what is essentially womanly. It will only be necessary to point out the leading assumptions that have given the movement its characteristic tone.

Schopenhauer's writings on woman and on love may be dismissed, because in reality he neither writes of woman nor of love, but only of one and that the lower aspect of woman's nature. He should dissatisfy men no less than women by his assumptions, as, for instance, his contention that fidelity is impossible to man, which is in flagrant opposition to historic facts, which prove that the tendency of progressive civilised life is increasingly towards monogamy and mind comradeship in marriage, and that domestic ideals as shown in poetry and fiction favour more and more positively mutual sex purity of living; and his assertion that man's form is artistically superior to the woman's is contrary to all expert knowledge on the subject. A man so prejudiced in favour of man cannot be accepted seriously.

Von Hartmann's comparison of the sexes is simply an endeavour to prove that chastity in the man is unnecessary and unnatural, while it is an essential quality in woman. He asserts that "physiological shortcomings" are the basis of man's morality, assuming without one word of proof and without one single fact in support of his contention, that self-control in -man is associated with weak sexual impulse.

Marriage on this basis is solely on the man's side a matter of sensuality; he states that "if man wanted nothing, then woman would have nothing valuable to give him, in which case the influence of the gentler sex over the male would diminish to vanishing point." He fails to realise that man would be gross indeed if daily contact with a womanly mind had no influence on his own.

Recently a work on "Sex and Character" has been published, the work of a young man who wrote his book before reaching his twenty-first year, and who committed suicide before his twenty-fourth. It is ill-informed and unsupported by evidence, but it is shrewdly written. There is, however, little evidence of impartiality in his criticism of women; and although he does not wholly lack intuitive insight, this, such as it is, is limited to one aspect of the female character, namely, the influence of brute strength on physical weakness and fragility.

There is a similar disposition in German sex psychologists, which is, unfortunately, shared by some French and English scientists, to treat the psychology of sex from the physical point of view. So far has this unwholesome tendency gone that many writers for the general public have published larger volumes "for its benefit" than is allotted to such matters in medical text-books for the medical man acting as trained adviser. This fact alone is sufficient condemnation of the movement.

Exceptions

I have tried to give a fair impression of the general trend of the movement in the two countries. I have shown that in England men were sympathetic but lacking in intuitive power, that they acted as if woman must dewomanise herself and become manlike in order to be free, and that woman felt this position to be a true one herself. This attempt, as was to be expected, inevitably failed. In Germany also the same lack of intuitive power is apparent, but the Germans were led to a belief that woman's womanly qualities were only feminine and could be studied as such.

Of course, in both countries there were women and men who did not share these feelings; women happily married, as men when vocationally well satisfied, seldom express their feelings. It was mainly those men and women who were dissatisfied with woman's position who asserted themselves. Nevertheless, there could be little doubt that a general dissatisfaction did exist, and that in England it was popular and supported by the general feeling, while in Germany it was disliked and overborne.

Two writers, however, one an Englishman, the other a German woman, have taken this problem as it deserved to be taken, seriously and respectfully, and have each given important contributions to the study.

In the October number of the "National Review" for the year 1858, already referred to, appeared an unsigned article on "Woman," which, though nominally a review of some works on the subject, is in reality an original essay, far the most original one I have ever had ,the pleasure of reading. In it every argument of real strength for and against the woman's movement, that has been used in the fifty odd years that followed its publication, will be found summarised. That so able a statement excited so little comment is truly remarkable.

The writer is free alike from the follies of German and English schools of thought. He starts from the only scientific position possible under the circumstances, that woman has an individuality of her own, and that this needs interpreting before her nature can be understood.

At a time when it was being asserted in England that woman's mind was not less original than man's, and a decade before Mill's "Subjection of Women " urged the same untenable belief, he emphasised the fact of man's clear and undisputed predominance in the following words: "Society ever since the world began has received its characteristic nature and distinctive impress, not from the women, but from the men who helped to compose it." This is shown by the predominance of the masculine and manly elements in all terms of thought and expression, "and the world's history confirms it, that the collective body of men are in their nature more strong, more vigorous, more comprehensive, more complete in themselves than women." He here carefully guards himself against exceptions by the use of the words "collective body" of men as compared with a like "collective body" of women. To the argument that women have not had fair opportunities he replies by pointing out that had they had the mental ability they would have discovered them. He urges that woman's influence is now less than it was before the advent of "The Scientific Age," and states, as recent writers have since admitted, that this lessening influence has created "a sort of chasm between men and women." He connects woman's subordination with the growth of "material industry," and he urges woman to base her just claims to a larger life not upon the false basis of a non-existent equality, but upon the "unexpugnable position of her real nature."

Where writers, governed by a desire to assert the claim of man's superiority over woman, have characterised her intuitions as mere instincts, and placed her, as some German writers have done for this reason, with animals generally, he justly points out that these intuitions of women are due to greater delicacy of perceptive powers, and that woman's intellect is complementary to man's, offering suggestions to his, that in his brain become material for original thought.

He insists on the obvious but neglected fact, that is supported by our knowledge of the power of appetites in man, that woman is better in her nature but less noble in her power of self-control and in-dependent responsibility, and in a fine comparison of the two natures he states of woman that" her nature is higher than man's, but man is set above his nature."

He points out that woman, by this fineness of her character and by her weaker will-power, is less fitted for the coarser struggles of life, and that there are special considerations in her case which do not apply to man.

He pleads for a wider opportunity for mental culture, and asserts that the assumed objection to cultured women is unfounded. "Lieutenant Smith, skilled only in horses, does not like a young lady to mention Dante; and Jones, who has contracted all he once knew into a familiarity with the prices of cotton, trembles to be asked what Kepler's laws are" ; but " it is an error to suppose that educated men prefer the society of uninformed women. Perhaps, indeed, there is no exercise so delightful, or so highly appreciated on either side, as the interchange of ideas between the cultured minds of the different sexes."

He denies the absurd assumption that to be womanly one must necessarily have a weak personality, for "a manly woman is a very feeble man, a feeble man is a manly woman, and a strong woman is a strong woman, and not the less a true woman, and very different from what we call a strong-minded one."

The following analysis of the cause of the friendship of sex that develops into love is truly touched with the insight of genius.

"There are two ways in which women and men approach and modify one another. The one is where *they are drawn together by the affections?* where mutual sympathies, moral and intellectual, are aroused. ... Yet, so far are they from being merged in one another by this union, that each sex acquires from it its most complete and characteristic development; each gains from the other and strengthens what it has best of its own; they approach not by abnegations but by additions, each from the other of what is necessary to raise either man or woman to the fullness of the perfect creature."

"The other mode of approach is the reverse of this, where men brought up apart from women, and women deterred more or less from the society of men? lose not only the benefit of what each can give the other, but something of the truest characteristics of their own sex, which are not developed in their fullness and beauty except when the affections and sympathies, aroused by free intercourse, have their full play. *These men and women approach on a sort of neutral ground. Such women are more of men than the others ; but it is because they are less of women ; the two grow like one another by respective loss, not by respective gain"*

Is society, he asks, prepared to sacrifice the former higher type for the latter lower ? It is the position of this lower neutral class that has attracted attention. Is it not possible for both types to be provided for, clearly, realising the claims of the higher? This is the whole central position of the woman's movement, and no other writer, before or since, has troubled to realise what accurate answers to these questions would mean.

Finally, to conclude my quotations with this warning, given before our factory legislation had acquired its strength, and which is still of transcendent social importance at the present time : Women tend, by the more easy disorganisation of their higher but more delicate minds, to acquire more readily than men the possible vices of occupational life.

Business women, he says, are harder, have less feeling, are more unscrupulous; fisher-women become worse than fishermen; female lodging-house keepers are worse than male, and the fallen woman more irretrievably fallen. The broad truth of this fact is undoubted, and it is confirmed from all recent sources. The woman drunkard and morph maniac carry to greater excesses than the man of like habits does the craving that has mastered them. And he asks a question that few will be prepared to pass over lightly: "Is not the whole position of antagonistic relations and contests for advantage with the other sex the most perilous to delicacy and simple-mindedness into which a woman can enter?" And, as I have already pointed out, he connects the separation of the sexes, their lessened harmony with each other, with this spirit of antagonism that commercial competition arouses.

No one will dispute the fact that the relations of married life should be entirely amicable, that in proportion as a spirit of antagonism is aroused in the home there will be just this amount of failure, firstly as regards husband and wife, secondly as regards children, should they become parents. A woman who has once acquired an irritable, bickering spirit, which she tends to acquire in the industrial struggle, is apt to carry it into the home, and just because she is by nature non-combative, so the alternatives in the struggle in which she is nearly always worsted are either this chronic irritability or a broken, wholly submissive spirit, instead of the natural, even disposition which is soothing and restful to all that the healthy woman comes in contact with. In some instances the man's spirit is broken, not the wife's, and this is, of course, as regrettable as the wife's failure. It is at least worth consideration, therefore, this view that both directly and indirectly certain occupations are undesirable for women, and we may not feel disposed to disagree with the "National Review" writer when he asserts "that there are many phases of the life of industry totally unfitted for woman to enter on;

and that so far from its being to be desired that she should mingle in and understand by experience the difficulties with which many men have to contend, it is to be wished that her atmosphere should be as serene and her growth as unwarped as the conditions of humanity will allow." In this connection it may be interesting to observe that fifty years later, after bitter experience, this is precisely the conclusion that saner men and women are coming to. Factory life under any circumstances debases woman generally, and there are many callings unsuitable for girls and young women because they unfit them in future years for the possibilities of married life. The employment of married women outside the home (to which there are, obviously, justifiable exceptions, which I cannot dwell upon in this book, owing to lack of space) is now generally condemned from the home point of view, for the comfort, order, and homeliness of life is difficult when the wife works; from the child's standpoint, for the children are generally uncared for, and from the woman's own outlook, for the treble labour of industrial, domestic, and childbirth duties wear her out, and exhaust her to an unrealised degree. The more masculine her type, the better she can thus sterilise herself, but the womanly woman who influences the man and humanises his ideals, who becomes a mother to her children, and is not simply a bearer of them, is spoilt, distorted, and ruined by the strain which modern life conditions often impose.

> "On the other hand," he continues, "we yet more strongly deprecate anything in the nature of a cloisteral seclusion or an enforced idleness." He believes practical life employment" in affairs of some kind or other to be essential to the healthy condition and just development of every individual, male or female," but woman must follow those occupations "which are most in consonance with her nature as it is, and not as it is presumed it may become."

It is the study of what is consonant with the life of a true man and what with a true woman that will one day decide precisely what should be a man's field and what the woman's. It is not a matter for guess-work, nor for the industrial employer to discover after he has ruined thousands and thousands of lives, but for the scientist who shall take up such an investigation in a large-spirited and high-minded manner.

To me, therefore, this essay, with its wide grasp of facts, its modern outlook, after half a century has passed away, is far more deserving of preservation than any other that I am acquainted with. Here was the one clear-sighted Englishman who saw the dangers to which women would be exposed, who was fitted by nature and culture to lead the English movement, and to have left a world impression behind him, but who passed into oblivion because his work was drowned by the anti-social current that swept it by.

About thirty years later a German woman commenced writing a series of works on "Modern Women," "The Psychology of Woman," "We Women and our Authors," etc, which stand out in striking contrast to the general mass of inferior and unoriginal volumes on this subject that every year make their appearance.

In her preface to "Modern Women" she states that "a woman who seeks freedom by means of the modern method of independence is generally one who desires to escape from a woman's sufferings. She is anxious to avoid subjection, also motherhood, and the dependence and impersonality of an ordinary woman's life, but in doing so she unconsciously deprives herself of her womanliness," and there comes a time in the lives of all such women when they find themselves "standing at the door of the heart's innermost sanctuary," and realise that they are excluded. She remarks that these women are generally individualistic, and yet are not able to stand alone.

One may disagree, and I think justly, with her use of the word subjection, as if it were an unavoidable condition of womanhood; one may hold different views from the authoress in her assumption that the modern woman really does desire to escape womanhood, but there can be little doubt that there is a desire in this newer type to shake herself free of man's influences, that she is not satisfied with the old conception of motherhood, that dependence on the man is in some way unsatisfactory to her feelings, and that home life, which is, of course, extremely personal, and not impersonal as stated, is also distasteful to her. This writer's general outlook may be summarised, I hope not unfairly, as follows :

Woman is a much less independent and self-reliant being than man, and cannot achieve her own fulfilment alone; mentally and physically she requires his help to aid in her own development. "Woman, never, nowhere, and in nothing can make a starting-point," "all she does, performs, or suggests, represents always but a deviation, a connection with, or continuation of something already produced, existing, done." Mentally, even more than physically, she requires the stimulus of man, otherwise her life becomes vacant and wasted. "A woman has no destiny of her own ; she cannot have one, because she cannot exist alone. Neither can she become a destiny, except indirectly through the man. The more womanly she is, and the more richly endowed, all the more surely will her destiny be shaped by the man who takes her to be his wife. If, then, even in the case of the average woman, everything depends upon the man whom she marries, how much more true this must be in the case of the woman of genius, in whom not only her womanhood, but also her genius, needs calling to life by the embrace of a man. And if even the average woman cannot attain to the full consciousness of her womanhood without man, how much less can the woman of genius, in whom sex is the actual root of her being and the source from whence she derives her talent and her ego. If her womanhood remains unawakened, then however promising the beginning may be, her life will be nothing more than a gradual decay, and the stronger her vitality the more terrible will the death struggle be."

Dependence is natural to women, it is unnatural to men. "When man is no longer the supporter of woman, she becomes his oppressor," *as the woman always acts as an industrial parasite.* The underselling of man by woman, the necessary result of "emancipation," brings with it, as men are less able to marry, the equally inevitable accompaniment, "prostitution."

It is to be noted that it is of the modern womanly woman only, a product of modern times, that she writes, and in support of her contention she analyses very strikingly the life habits of several representative women of this class.

The woman of this type "knows nothing of her own powers until the man comes to reveal them." But these higher women, "unlike ordinary young girls, do not fall in love with mere outward qualities." "Physical maturity, which has hitherto been considered sufficient, has placed the need for intellectual maturity in the shade. Surely women want to be grown up in mind and soul before entering life." As their life development, and this implies a mental rather than a physical ideal, depends upon the men they choose for husbands, and it is this mental harmony *felt* between two individuals that attracts and is sought for, marriage for this reason becomes increasingly difficult to them, for though on a physical basis many men would be pleasing to many women, on a mental it requires an acquiescence of two whole individualities in each other, and this is rare. Since the reward of success is so great, and the price of failure so terrible, and the result for women so far-reaching, the withering of mind and body that results is tragic.

Finally, as this new life is, above all other things, womanly, so it is the manly, and, failing this, the male man that appeals to her. The big man and the little woman, the man of strength and courage, and the woman who feels the need and liking for protection, are grouped together. This new type of woman, a woman in her whole nature, has given up the combative element, which has always characterised man, to man entirely. She is no scold, no virago, and she would appeal to the man through one element, love. Such is Laura Marholm's (now Laura Hansson's) interpretation of women. A comparison of the essential positions of the two writers, a man who knew how to interpret a woman's nature and a woman not afraid to explain what in herself she felt to be truth, has not a little interest in showing how sincere workers on any problem tend to reach like results.

Neither of these studies are comprehensive enough, nor are they founded sufficiently securely upon scientific data to be of more than suggestive value to modern investigators, but they both help to give a fairly true picture of the subject, and in this make it more real and personal. Their agreements, as may be seen from the thirteen points taken from their works, is remarkable, with perhaps the exception of the fourth point, and where their views do not coincide they supplement. There can, I think, be no doubt that idtimately it is along the lines that are here laid down that future work will proceed.

It will be seen, I hope, from this analysis of the woman's emancipation that it has led inevitably to a consideration of man's. Woman's desire for emancipation was probably aroused by man's initiatory feeling that woman should have better educational opportunities; this and an upgrowth of a new type of womanhood have led cultured men in England to like cultured women, while the uncultured men and women have endeavoured to retard the development of woman's higher life. The question, therefore, is not exclusively a woman's question, but is really a sexual one. We have seen that woman is now desirous of becoming mentally mature before she undertakes the responsibilities of married life, and that she now is tending to apply a mental as well as a physical standard to man, and that her love is only given when her whole individuality is satisfied. Is it possible that woman's discontent is not so much dissatisfaction with her womanhood and its duties as with the prospect of defective self-realisation that is offered her ? Perhaps the assertion of men that women are neglecting their duties and shirking their burdens is only partially a just one. Perhaps woman is rightly dissatisfied with her relation to the man and the child. Does she object to maternity ? Is her creative feeling of motherhood declining ?

Of this, however, I am convinced, that the question of woman's distinctive individuality, mental and bodily alike being recognised, lies at the root of all fruitful investigation on the "woman's question" as regards her education, her social position and representation, and her own and man's relationship in the home.

In conclusion, I wish to make an appeal to women and men to take a broader and wiser view of this problem, and to feel earnestly enough about it to study what it really means. The majority of women are, and always will be, wives and mothers, and certain healthy individual and national needs of living are necessarily postulated by this fact. What are they ? All women have distinctive inherited qualities of mind and body which need healthy expression, as well as other qualities common to both sexes. Do we appreciate what these distinctive womanly attributes are ? Nearly all thoughtful men and women are extremely dissatisfied with the dominance of the lower commercialism over higher mind ideals. But this is not a sex, but a human question.

What is the cause of woman's discontent with modern womanly opportunities ? This is what we have to investigate, but which has never been investigated. The desire on the part of some women for franchise changes, of others for increased occupational facilities, of others for a wider domestic horizon, and yet others for the more or less complete abandonment of home life and the subordination or even rejection of maternal claims: these desires are but superficial expressions of a deeper feeling; and until we understand this governing feeling we cannot legislate without the gravest possibilities of disaster. When the young girl mind opens out into the womanly, why does a feeling of discontent with womanliness and its opportunities tend to arise ? Is this discontent biological or educational, healthy or unhealthy ? Until we can answer these preliminary inquiries the time will not have arrived for legislative action.

●●

2
Evolution of Sex and Significance

The word evolution has come to be used in several distinct ways, and therefore needs defining; if by evolution is meant a growth out of an antecedent condition, the word change would do equally well; but if evolution means, as it is usually taken to mean in the more popular use of the word, progressive change, then we should use this term more sparingly and scientifically than we do. From this outlook it is a misnomer to speak of the evolution of plants, because it cannot be said that any one type of plant is higher than another; some are more complex and some more specialised, but no plant form can be said to be higher than any other, a moss than a tree or a flower, or vice versa.

It is otherwise in the animal kingdom. Step by step as we rise from one order to later orders that follow it a real rise in type is discovered, single-celled are inferior to many-celled, and as we advance from sponge-like animals to worms, shell animals, insects, fishes, reptiles, birds, and mammals, up to man, it is seen that the later developing classes of animals have an increasing share of mind, that there is an evolution of animal life from lower to higher types, and mind is the test of what is low and high.

Is there, then, an evolution of sex ? Has sex any relation to this development of the higher out of the lower ? Or are sex characteristics about the same in their significance at all stages of animal existence? Obviously there is no evolution of sex in plants, though some plants carry both kinds of sex in one flower and others two kinds of flower on one plant, and others, again, two kinds of flowers on separate plants. There is simply more differentiation in one type of plant than in another; and at first sight the same appears to be the fact in regard to animal life. Many male and female insects are widely different in appearance, some parasitic worms look almost as if they belonged to different species of life; birds seem to be very sharply marked off, one sex from the other; while even in one group, such as the lions, some are maned and others maneless. And man, as compared with other animals, is curiously free from these sharp contrasts, so that it *appears* as if sexual differences in animals depended upon no evolutional law, are simply marked in some forms of life and little marked in others.

In plants where male flowers exist on one plant and female on another the leaves and shape of the whole plant are sometimes different; but, taken as a whole, male and female plants differ less in their plant forms than male and female animals do in their animal forms. John Hunter, Thomas Laycock, and after them Charles Darwin, spoke of these bodily differences as secondary sex characters, and those immediately concerned with parentage as primary. In Darwin's work on sexual selection he has collected an immense quantity of these secondary differences of sex, and the variety is such that it seems as if no law could be deduced from man.

If, however, all characteristics are excluded which are confined to one species or two species of related life, and only those bodily sex differences which pervade the whole scale of animal life are for the moment considered, it will be found that there are some characters which are constant in being always present, and that these constant characters do undergo a very definite change, becoming increasingly marked as we pass from the lowest forms of life up to man. We have thus three groups of characters in relation to sex: primary, those essential to parentage; secondary, those present in all sex states; tertiary, those present in one or more related species, but not present elsewhere in the animal kingdom. Thus spurs are present in many male birds, horns in some cattle in both sexes, in only the male sex in others, and where they are only present in the male sex they are tertiary characters. In like manner the male salmon has the lower jaw, in some varieties only during the breeding season, turned upward, and in the permanent varieties of this feature it is armed with teeth. This is not a characteristic of all fishes, but only of the salmon species, hence it is a tertiary feature, not a secondary one.

The most constant secondary feature is the development of the hip region of the body in the female and the chest region in the male, and whether we turn to man or lower animals, this broad generalisation holds true.

Sexual Evolution in the Race

1st stage. The fixation and specialisation of sex tissue. The lowest form of animal multiplication is by division of a single-celled organism into two parts, and certain lower forms of many-celled organisms can do the same, and, of course, this is quite a common form of multiplication in plants, runners, or elongated stems, developing roots where they touch the earth, and leaves and flowers where they are exposed to the air, and thus a new plant is produced from a simple shoot. Animals early lose this power, and germinal tissue becomes specialised and localised at one spot, probably, quite early in animal evolution, as the formation of a new individual is a more complex problem than in plants.

2nd stage. The hermaphrodite condition. In several invertebrate organisms the two sexes are united in one body, just as in some plants, and it is not until this condition of sex life has become highly specialised that one of these sets of structures becomes subordinate.

3rd stage, a unisexual one, is reached, and throughout the vertebrata, up to its highest mammalian order, the bodily forms of the two sexes, always retaining traces or rudiments of the complementary sex, are increasingly defined, and in man the greatest differences of bodily form are to be found. In several important features it can easily be demonstrated that the diflFerences in man are greater than in any living creature.

1. The contrast between shoulder and hip development is more than in any other animal.

2. There is a marked difference in the blood of woman as compared with man, it containing one-ninth fewer red blood corpuscles, and therefore a proportionately smaller quantity of oxygen. This almost certainly means a less rapid tissue-exchange, which in adolescence in girls, and later in women, may be associated with a seriously impoverished condition of the blood, chlorosis or anaemia. This state is only very exceptionally known in men, and there is probably nowhere else such sharp contrast between males and females of the same species.

3. The woman is mentally much more "affectable" than the man, and in extreme cases hysteria or an exaggeration of this affectability takes place. There is no recognised mental state corresponding to this in animals.

4. The change from immaturity to maturity runs a more widely contrasted course in boys and girls than in any other known forms of animal life.

These four points are sufficient to prove that, in essential secondary bodily and mental characteristics, man is the most sexed of all creatures, and were it necessary to demonstrate the evolution, it could be shown that mammals are more so than birds, and birds than amphibia and reptiles, and these more than fishes; but these points will become clearer and their meaning more certain when we consider the physiological significance of sexual evolution. It ought here to be pointed out that each of these four characteristics that separate man from the animal group also separate civilised from savage man, and that, in face, form, and mind characteristics, barbaric women and men are more alike than members of either Eastern or Western civilisations, though in this respect, as in some others, both the Eastern and the Hellenic Greek and ancient worlds are midway between barbaric tribes to-day and the Western life in which we live.

Sexual Evolution in the Individual

The three stages, of fixation of germ tissue, hermaphroditism, and unisexual development, are all passed through by the child before birth, and after birth childhood, pubescence, and adolescence mark three further stages of immaturity; the asexual feelings and capacity of the child, the bodily and at last the mental consciousness of sex following in order.

The history of the race and of the child alike point to the conclusion that mental and bodily sex individuality is of progressive importance in human evolution, and therefore, after the childhood period is passed, biology cannot favour co-educational or co-occupational systems of social life.

Physiological Significance of Sex

To understand the physiological significance of sex one must see it clearly in two distinct and correlative lights: *(a)* one must see that sexual evolution has developed in the animal kingdom, and that it must remain a great force in man; *(b)* also that this accentuation of sex has made possible for us individual value in life, and in addition added to our individualities ranges of feeling and incentives to action that otherwise would have been absent from life.

Why Sexual Evolution has Developed in the Animal Kingdom

The significance of the various manifestations of sex in the plant world is a problem that awaits solution, but the main reasons for its development in animal life are known and easily comprehensible, because there is a continuous thread which widens and thickens in importance as higher forms of animal life are reached, whereas among plants the changes are so indefinite at times, and so unexpectedly sudden and emphatic under other conditions, that one principle seems very difficult to establish.

In the higher animals the development of the immature organism needs increasingly delicate and protected nurture from exposed external surroundings, and it is probable, if one fully grasped the whole significance of the process, that one could predict with unerring certainty from the pre-natal demands of the organism, in its life before birth, its high or low stage in evolutional life that it was to rise to afterwards.

The exact reason for the early specialisations of sex in two individuals is a little obscure. It has beep assumed that in the interests of hereditary variability two lines of heredity, male and female lines, will favour a wider range of adaptability than could be obtained from an hermaphrodite condition. Whether this is so or not, it is more probable that the main cause was the strain exerted on any organism that carried forward two separate tissue specialisations of sex at the same or closely alternating periods of time. Whatever the reason, far back in the history of animal development, millions of years ago, the sexes for all higher forms of animal life became distinct, manifested in two separate organisms, and from that time the process has increased in its tendency towards more and more specialised masculine and feminine bodily forms.

In all cold-blooded animals the egg-cell, which may be fertilised inside or outside of the feminine body, develops outside, and in a large number of instances the spawn is left to take care of itself, to grow and develop if conditions allow of it and it is not eaten by foes of the species, for its male and female bearers of its germ tissue leave it uncared for, to take its chances in existence. Many parent insects are dead before their progeny are hatched, and though there are the widest differences in the kind of provision made for larvae and other forms of early life, yet they have been too little studied for one to assert that the uncared-for cell that is to begin a new life is really to give rise to an animal form on a lower plane of mental capacity than one more cared for. Thus the spawn of a frog is deposited in an open ditch, exposed to changes of temperature, rain, and movement, and attacks of other life around it, the eggs of a bee are carefully housed and protected from the weather, and guarded from intrusion, but it cannot be asserted on present knowledge that a bee is higher in its organisation than the frog, though it can that the bee is one of the highest of the insects while the frog is one of the lowest of the vertebrates. In these lower forms, whether of insect or lower vertebrate life, the number of offspring possible is what primarily determines the persistence of the species; as we ascend the scale, with many exceptions it is true, fewer lives are created and more care is taken to preserve them, and the individual counts more and more in the survival of the type. Thus no bird, no mammal bears progeny in such prodigality as almost all life forms do beneath them. In birds and in egg-laying mammals, the latter nearly extinct, a rise has taken place from the cold-blooded to the warm-blooded type, and there can be little doubt that this rise of bodily temperature allows of more complex chemical changes going on in the body, makes possible a higher type of organism, but the egg now has to be more carefully provided for, it must have a larger supply of food for its incubation, as it is longer or more rapid or both in its development ; the egg has to be protected by a hard shell, and the heat necessary for the development of warm-blooded life has to be supplied externally by the heat of the parent bird "sitting" upon the egg. When the young are hatched their immaturity is so great that the parent birds are needed to feed and care for them until they are mature or fledged. In the egg-laying mammal the female parent feeds the young after they are hatched from its own body by its milk, a carefully prepared food. In the pouch mammals the external incubation period is dispensed with, the young develop in the mother's body, thus secure of an even temperature, of a completely protected life, and of a food supply, in part at least, so perfectly ready for assimilation, that it has been completely digested and passed into the mother's blood to be transferred to the offspring. There has been a steady rise in the call and meaning of motherhood. In the full mammal all the early stages of development, up to the infant form of its type, take place before birth, the little life developing in a soft muscular organ, filled with fluid in which it floats, so placed that no shock can easily reach it, so environed that one fixed temperature is secured, so nourished by an exchange of food supply from the mother organism that it takes up fully prepared food, gives off to its parent poisonous waste products, and develops its life free from the vicissitudes of external existence, in surroundings that are normally germ-free and free from disease. Nature takes every care to favour a quiescent growth of the complex new life, and it is evident that no other interpretation is broadly possible than that this provision is necessary, otherwise it would not have been provided, and the differentiation of sex have advanced to the degree which it has obtained in the mammalian type. It does not end when man is reached; the barbaric type of woman takes her part, though this varies among different primitive peoples, in the life of the tribe until near the birth-time of the child, in some tribes almost up to the hour of birth, whereas the civilised woman would in the large majority of instances be quite unable to bear the exposure and roughness of life thus involved, and the act of childbirth is itself more painful for her, because the child that is born is larger-headed and being more frail needs greater after-care.

We see, if we look at the history of our own European Continent, this increasing need for the care of woman reflected in her occupational life. Man under primitive conditions is concerned with fighting, hunting, fishing, a maker of war and chase implements, a builder of huts and a reader of cattle.

Woman fetches wood and water, prepares the food, dresses the skins, makes clothes, takes care of the children, cultivates the ground, and supplies the household with vegetable food, gathering roots, berries, acorns, where agriculture at its dawn has scarcely commenced.

In mediaeval society agriculture had passed into man's hands—except for the care of certain kitchen herbs, and the management of poultry where it existed, and the dairy in later times—and spinning, weaving, knitting, embroidery, sewing, cooking, and gleaning and lighter work in the fields, the care of the children, and at first nursing, doctoring and midwifery, being woman's sphere.

So day-work in the fields has almost gone, and is now universally regarded as unsuitable, even in those lighter field industries, such as strawberry and hop-picking, which, as a fact, draw women of the lowest class ; gleaning has almost gone, spinning and weaving have passed out of the home, and, varying in different districts, it is now true for Great Britain, and in various degrees in other countries, that seven-eighths of the whole employment of women is domestic, in which the rougher work of scrubbing, boot and window-cleaning is already passing to the man. This, with the fact that the immature period of the child is slowly lengthening, demonstrate that the life of the female mammalian up to and including the latest period of the highest mammal man is tending towards a quieter, more protected life, in which rougher employments are taken over by the male, and the domestic field, viewed in its widest and most mental manner, becomes more and more the feminine possession.

Why the Individual Value of Life has become possible through the Creation of Sex Types

At first sight it seems as if woman in this is being sacrificed to the species, or rather, more accurately, that man and woman are being driven into lines of development that consider mainly the requirements of the species, and heed little those of the individual member. This was the mistaken assumption that so troubled Tennyson in his thought. Yet in no real sense is this true. It is broadly true that specialisation of sex has led the way in the thought of peace as Darwin pointed out in his sexual selection, and as Drummond and Kropotkin have popularised in their thought. Males and females of the same species rarely fight, and though in some instances early man did treat woman roughly, it has always to be remembered that the times were rough, and acts seen with their eyes must have looked very different to ours. It is certain that without sex little of the gentler influences of life that have opened the way to civilisation could have originated, and the best and the greatest joys are unquestionably those that centre round the home, the place where the individual man or woman makes an individual atmosphere, becomes really an individual, and directs his life as an individual mind. The home originally would never have been conceived of but for the need of protecting the young. As a fact, the glory of motherhood on its mental side has never been stated, and though it brings its troubles and its difficulties, the opportunity and the desire that is opened out in the care of a child, the awakening influence on the woman's life, the understanding of mind or soul in another human being, could have been reached by no other conceivable means. The mistake is that it is so seldom even faintly realised. Imagine a woman trained to understand and, above all, feel the wonder of existence ; imagine the sudden increase of that wonder that should come to her when she is herself the bearer of a new life, when that new life that she has been expecting is at last born, when it grows in mind and body at her breast, when its little life looks into hers, and when, day by day, during the first years of toddling childhood, the mind unfolds to a mother's love, as a child mind opens to no other influence in the world. And though the father can only distantly share in this, as compared with the true mother, he brings from the world a fresh influence, and it is the reaction of two minds with one common aim, and yet approaching this aim from different points of view, that give charm and beauty to life which could not be obtained by two men or two women living under the same roof. This evolution testifies to when it supersedes the love of man to man in Greek times by the love of man and woman, which from Dante onwards has belonged to our own and has been the great ideal of life.

The Application to Human Life To-day

So far it has been pointed out that sex is among animals a real evolutional character, that differences between men and women will increase rather than decline with advancing civilisation, because this specialisation of sex is necessary, in order that a higher type of life can be originated, nurtured, undergo uninterrupted development, and be born into a world where, in its long immaturity, it can be cared for, and, lastly, that specialisation does not sacrifice the individual to the race.

There is no mistaking the teaching of Nature and her demands. Woman stores, man spends. It is because woman stores that at nearly all periods of life her chances of living are greater than the man's, unless she takes up callings that draw upon her reserve strength; her digestive organs are relatively to her body weight as large, or larger, than the man's, her lungs are smaller, and her blood supply is probably less, and certainly carries less oxygen; she spends less than the man under healthy conditions of life, because oxygen is the great spending agency. If, however, she becomes dyspeptic, so that her food digests badly* she is opening the door to the time of ill-prepared motherhood, because, as her future child will draw its nourishment from her blood, its chances of well-nourished life are smaller; as are her own if that unborn child draws from a faulty blood supply, in which half-digested products circulate to her cells and to the child's. It must be obvious, too, that in the same way the child's natural food will suffer after it is born, when fed, as it is or should be, by its mother's milk, which would thus be formed from an impure blood. Yet no real substitute can be found for this which she can give, that is always blood temperature, that is clean and sweet and pure and free from germs of disease, that is adapted to the child's needs. The mother's life must be quiescent, free from worry, free from competitive struggles, free during the time of her motherhood from work that compels her to labour regardless of Nature's call for frequent rests. This is merely hygienic physiology.

We have seen something of the lesson of the primary functions of motherhood. It is because the child is of so high an order that its demand on its mother and its mother's life is so insistent and lifelong ; we have seen that the secondary characteristics of women and men reveal that in the human species sex is more insistent in its requirements, and has moulded our bodies to its needs. What lesson have tertiary sex characters to teach ? They teach that the male is the fighting, that is the active animal, over nearly the whole field of insects, nearly the whole fields of fishes and reptiles and birds, and over the whole range of mammalian life it is the male that fights, the male that strives, the female that is quiescent. What is it in man ? Man is, and always has been, the fighter, and except for the probably mythical Amazons, no race has bred a permanent fighting female type. Even the Spartans never attained to this; it was the men who fought. In man war has been slowly, and is being slowly, superseded by industrial competition. What part has woman taken in these two processes ? The great struggle for victory in war and in industry turns mainly on invention and originality. The great warriors, from Hannibal to Napoleon, have been men ; the inventors of war weapons have been men ; the inventors of horse and steam ploughs and of agricultural implements were men, not women; spinning and weaving were in the hands of women, but men, inventing spinning and weaving machines, took the spinning and weaving processes out of the home ; medicine was for some centuries in women's hands, but men invented surgical instruments, not women, even those instruments specially designed to help women in their childbirth cares, the new drugs that have been introduced have been by men, even chloroform and anaesthetics, that have so much softened woman's special difficulties, Simpson or American pioneers, it is still men. All the great engineers have been men, even the inventors of sewing machines. All important cooking appliances have been men's work: gas stoves, coal ranges, oil stoves and spirit. Pottery, architecture, hygiene, and sanitary science, men, not women. Furniture is mostly man's design, Chippendale, Sheraton, or some other. It is man always that has done the creative work. It will not do to argue that women have had no opportunities in cooking, in medicine, in household designing, in spinning and weaving, for their opportunity was *originally* greater than men's. It will not do for another reason, because Genius makes its own opportunity. There is a difference, a fundamental difference, of mind, and nothing else that can account for so invariable a law present in all ages and in all dimes.

In music we see the same truth, whether it is in the development of an instrument, a violin, a piano, a bugle, or a flute, or an organ, the inventors are men, not women. And in genius. In music there are no great women geniuses, though there have been women musicians. There have been no great women artists whose genius commands the world, though thousands of artists; no great poets, except one woman, Sappho, and extremely little is known of her, but perhaps millions of women who have written, secretly or openly, verses and poetical thoughts. In science the great names are again exclusively men, and in philosophy the same. Bach, Handel, Beethoven, Mozart; Phidias, Michael Angelo, Raphael, Turner, Watts; Homer, Shakespeare, Goethe, Dante, Milton, Browning, Wordsworth; Aristotle, Roger Bacon, Harvey, Newton, Darwin, Hippocrates, Sydenham, and John Hunter ; Socrates and Plato, Francis Bacon and Descartes, Locke, Berkeley, Kant; Confucius, Buddha, Christ. How foolish to assert that of these names, from the East and the West of the world's life, in all lands and in all climes, under all conditions of civilisation, it is accident that they are men; that, given opportunity for women, there might have been women too. Even in cookery we have a Count Rumford. Was there ever a time when women were suppressed to this extent ? Was there ever a time when genius was not ? If a woman could be a Cleopatra, dogmatic, tyrannical, might she not have been a feminine Marcus Aurelius ? In actual historic fact there never has been a century where woman has not had much liberty, where the opportunity could easily have been made, had women had the capacity and the desire. Here is a comparison far more certain and unchallengeable than that Germany is musical or that England is scientific. *All* the great lines of creative and inventive thought within historic times have been made by men, not by women.

But if a glance is given over these names two great exceptions to the word creative, as distinctive of them, may be rightly and wrongly made in Homer and Shakespeare. It is doubtful if Homer added one original, one creative thought to Greek life, Shakespeare certainly added nothing to English thought or English life. They were *scenic* geniuses, not creative, and from this point of view one ought to exclude them from our list, and yet one knows if one did so a gap would be felt at once. And the reason lies surely in this, that Homer made the Greek speech expressionable, Shakespeare did the same for English, and to a less extent Dante for Italian, Goethe for German. Dante also was creative on the thought of love, Goethe in a far lesser way in science, but one real grandeur of their names is that they gave flexible, free voice to a national tongue, a language that had been halting became free; in this they were creative.

In Homer, Dante, and Shakespeare, a grandeur not less impressive is their scenic power; they depict rather than originate. We see the Greek life glorified, it is true, made to move and act as in a stately pageantry, but still it is Greek life, and not Homer's ideal of it, that we see in Homer. Had Homer been asked, he might have agreed with Socrates and Euripides and other Greeks that his picture of the gods was ungodlike, but his answer would have been, "It is Greece, none the less." Had Shakespeare been asked whether Falstaff was a noble enough character, he would have said, "No, but he is English." Dante was national, but not in this sense, Goethe was national, but in a different, or one might have almost said a more indifferent, cold, contemplative way than either. Dante would have felt, "Italy must be this, I love her"; Homer felt "Greece *is,* that is enough"; and Shakespeare, like Homer, "It is my England."

A woman who loves a man feels as Homer felt, as Shakespeare felt, not in their creative language side, which belongs to manhood and manliness, but in their *scenic,* contemplative side. Greece is, England is, my husband is, it is enough, I see, I know. The gods of Greece were the shadow of Greece, the Parthenon and its joy of life its glory ; Homer knew this, perhaps, better even than Socrates, and he saw that the glory and its shadow are one, Greece, as he knew her, and it sufficed. A real wife knows her husband as the husband does not even know himself, with his littlenesses, with his shadows, but also—for there is this side in all men, if it can be reached—its glory. The glory requires at times much seeing; sometimes because it is great but hidden in the recesses of a silent mind ; sometimes because the glory is small and overlaid with fierce, rough, broken litter, jagged and dangerous, and to the outer world the one man is a dead mass, large but incomprehensible, and the other a creature, scarce a man, to be avoided, to be shunned. Tell the real wife—for a woman's genuine love goes down to the reality that is good and reaches it, much or little as it is there—tell the real wife, as Socrates might have told Homer, that his gods, her husband's, were ungodlike, and she would not say "I know," but she would know. Tell her the like of her son, and she might be angry, because she would be less sure and because she takes her husband as he is, but she wishes for her son, as Dante of his country, "My son must be this, I love him." That is why a noble mother may err sometimes, in spite of her great love and her insight, over her son; but a noble wife almost never over her husband; "My husband is, I see, I know him, rock and cranny, crack and crevice." A husband, even when he is f arseeing and true and loyal, never knows his wife in this perfect way; and the wife, good woman as she may be, does not know herself. A woman's genius is scenic, therefore ; human character is seen by her as the higher artist sees a landscape, as he paints an old-world village, while its evil odours from an old pool near by come to him as he paints. The man wants the odours gone, and sometimes, in destroying the odour he sweeps away the beauty too. This is the same reason why a woman never really quite believes in perfection of character. She admires gold, and can judge it when she sees it, but in a state of nature, here on this earth, she always expects to see it as rough ore, alloyed, not pure. She knows that the ore is richer in some natures than in others, but also that in none is it wholly pure ; if it counterfeits purity it is a sham. This is a wise axiom of a woman that she follows, and a man seldom does, when the woman's being is unspoiled by a barren intellectual training that has taught her to distrust her powers.

There are two fields, consequently, where women might have been expected to succeed, and where, as a fact, they have succeeded: in fiction, the scenic portrayal of life in words; on the stage, the scenic portrayal of life in actions and spoken words; and a Jane Austen or a Charlotte Bronte can compare with a Scott or a Dickens, an Ellen Terry with a Forbes Robertson. It may be asked how it is that man, a creative being, can have this scenic power too, that a Shakespeare or a Homer, men, can have that which belongs above all to women; and the answer consists, I would suggest, in two considerations. One, the scenic power necessary for the drama is less than for life. An absolutely faithful drama is not possible, and if it were, it would be too harrowing to human feelings to witness it. This allows the lower scenic powers of man in this direction to find an outlet. Two, even scenic thought, to be presented to the world, needs some creative skill, the skill of selection and rejection, which, while it presents a picture to the world, makes it by this selection a little false in doing so. For both of these reasons a man has an opportunity in woman's fields, but it is only because the topmost power of womanhood is unrepresentable to any but the woman herself. This is one reason, I am convinced, why the unspoiled woman by her mere presence makes her greatness felt, and why a test of that greatness in action is not demanded.

It might have been thought that in the scenic outlook the woman, taking this whole view of existence, would have been fitted as no man could be to take the whole outlook which leads by an external confirmation or rejection of life to what is called a faith, and it is, of course, a noteworthy fact that to-day it is the women, rather than the men, who support the churches and the chapels, who form far more than half of the attendants at the services; but in this, too, woman's influence is indirect, her mind is rapid, deep-seeing, and intuitional, not slow and reasoning—process-forming—as man's. She does not, therefore, *construct* a view of life, she simply sees the view, and she knows, though she frequently does not know why. In the past, as the friendships of Buddha, of Christ, of Socrates, show, though this is least true of Christ, men drew their inspiration from men; to-day, while they look to other men for a critical acceptance or rejection of their teachings, they look to the woman for a belief in or a rejection of them and their views as men. And I am inclined to think that part of the lack of religious feeling in an age that is permeated by religious thought and questioning is due to woman's dewomanising modern education, which teaches her to value mathematics and reason instead of literature and life. A woman knows her husband by feeling, sight, and insight, not by reason ; and that is also how she really knows the world ; and so long as she can see the sunlight, catch the scent of the morning air, and the beauty of flowers, and feel her life pulsate to the life around her, she knows that the alloy in life is but the incident and the true metal the reality, and she has faith. Rationalise her, and this faith is gone, and man's too, for the influence of the mother's mind, the wife's, the sister's, and women friends create an atmosphere of belief that is true and contagious, from which the man cannot, and as a fact does not wish to, escape. But the modern schoolgirl, with her standards of learning which she must pass, and which at best are superficial, and which she, like the schoolboy, almost completely forgets a few years later, though the pedagogic influence remains, tries to take in the universe as if it were a problem of geometry, despises home life, from which real inspiration would come, and as a lady clerk or an anaemic, tired shop assistant brings home to her family, and afterwards to her husband, a tired mind and a broken spirit, broken not in the higher religious sense of being humbled before the sublime, but because her natural powers have been ruined by a false scheme of life. Whether this is entirely so or not, I am convinced that a return to Nature's thought of woman in education is one aspect by which a revival of religion quite consistent with scientific truth may be brought about.

To return to our main thought: the evolution of animal life, and of man, and of individual man demonstrate the increasing importance of sex; modern physiology demonstrates the paramount need for a quiet, restful, healthy life in the mother ; a restfulness and quiet and a health which is a lifetime's culture, not to be acquired by a fortnight's quiet before the birth of a child. The facts of a study of sex demonstrate that the combative, active side is the male's throughout animal life, and of human life that the active fighting side and the active creative and inventive, mental side are man's, not woman's.

The Venus of Milo, the Sistine Madonna of Raphael, the Beatrice of Dante have not come down to us through the centuries for nothing. A Lucretia Borgia might have come down, not these. The great calm and repose of the Greek Venus, the great quiet and rest of the Madonna's face, the gentle presence of Beatrice are not accidental portrayals of the type of woman who *is* rather than does; they are the ideals that mankind has treasured and still accepts. Dante, Raphael, and the Greeks saw nothing of the law of affectability, which proves that woman reacts and responds to her surroundings, while man tends to override them; but they set up ideals in conformity with it. It is not an accident that all three aesthetic types agree in spirit, and that these agree with the teaching of science, woman a presence, man a force. Nature says, "Two types of body and mind I need," womanly and manly, a state of being for motherhood and for a measure of existence, a state of doing for achievement; and for a moment our age says one, the woman's, is to be lost, but it is Nature that will prevail.

Since animal life began its long upward evolution, since sex appeared, and it appeared very early on this earth, sex has slowly differentiated itself into two types, male and female, whose minds and bodies have grown more masculine and more feminine in this upward path. In the animal world the direction has been male-dominated until man, and man-directed ever since, in the beginning, and it will be so in the end. Man directed in his creative strength; none the less, it is the woman who sees. And what I ask myself as this chapter closes, as I reiterate thoughts that I know are the reader's thoughts as well as mine, keeping before one the ideal of calm and rest for the woman and of energy for the man, ideals based on our natural desires, what I ask myself is, Have we as a people, having gone far astray from the natural healthy ideal of womanhood and manhood, have we the courage to return, on a higher plane, with wider knowledge, to the old thought, that is healthy and sane ? I cannot say, but I know that, whether we do or not, the world will. Rightly understood, the Bible saying stands; "In the beginning .. . male and female created He them," in body, but not less in mind, in the beginning and in the end; but will modern England have the courage to accept it ? I ask myself this question, but I cannot say.

●●

3

Birth and Infancy

"May I, as I increase in this my house nourish a thousand. May fortune never fail in his race with offspring and cattle. Thou strong woman hast borne a strong boy. Be thou blessed with strong children, thou who hast blessed me with a strong child. And they say of such a boy, 'Ah, thou art better than thy father, ah, thou art better than thy grandfather.' Truly he has reached the highest point in happiness, praise, and Vedic glory who is born as the son of abrahmana that knows this." —*Brihadasanyaha Upanishad.*

The Indian child, whether boy or girl, may be said to come into the world amid a cloud of strange superstitions, and for the latter there will be no loving welcome from parents or grandparents. For weeks before the mother and mother-in-law have toilsomely observed every mystic ordinance which should propitiate the divine powers to bestow a little son; they have wreathed flowers at every auspicious shrine, they have lit lamps, they have burned spices, and when after all the tiny girl has come into the world, it seems in the gloom of the zenana, where the doors are jealously closed and the atmosphere is heavy with the stifling fire that must be incessantly burnt, in order to exclude the evil, spirits which might exercise a baleful influence upon the child's future, that the gods are angry, and it is the poor young mother who has offended their majestic wrath.

Still, there is a little progress to be recorded in the native mental attitude even on this point. Time was, and not so very far back either, when it was regarded as quite justifiable to end a baby girl's unwanted life by some such summary process as strangling. Upon that view advancement has assuredly been made, though still even, if the little one die, her little body is often thought not worth the expense of burning, and, with incantations and charms, it is carried out by some of the women folk to the jungle, where it is left to jackals and carrion birds with the words—

> "Thus we drive you forth, O daughter! Come not back, hut send a brother."

That infant mortality is very high, is not on account of evil intent, but is due to the appalling ignorance of the *dhais*, the professional class of midwives or monthly nurses, whose methods of treatment are simply barbarous, and, indeed, viewed in the light of our western scientific knowledge, seem as if they would be enough to kill every unfortunate victim upon whom they were practised.

In an Indian house of any pretensions to being anything more than a mere hovel, the women's quarters, known to us as the zenana, and in colloquial Hindustani as the *bibighar*, are always, architecturally and artistically, its meanest part. In one of its poorest and remotest apartments the poor woman will wait her hours of trial, while outside the door symbolic foliage and flowers will be twined. To these, the Hindus of the north-west add a swinging sickle, the sharp edge outwards, as a barrier against malignant demons, while as night comes down, and the feeble flicker of the rank-smelling cocoanut oil-lamps and the birth-fire kindled inside the close chamber penetrates the outer gloom, the other women move about with quick noiseless tread, and stand chattering to one another in eager curiosity.

"Only a girl, after all!" Prayers, offerings, pilgrimages, have been of no avail; but it seems like a sturdy little life, and there is much talk about the omens with which its birth was surrounded, for these are all-important. If the baby's ears first heard pleasant sounds, if its eyes rested upon white things, or such objects as rice, flowers, fruits or honey, or if crows or pigeons flew over the room from left to right, the signs were propitious, and some of the disappointment would be mitigated. If, on the other hand, a snake or monkey crossed the road, or a vehicle went by carrying a cot or stool with the legs upwards, or flowers associated with funeral observances were brought into the house, then life would seem to promise little worth having for the youthful arrival. An astrologer, too, must be consulted among many tribes and castes, who will foretell from the stars, and there is a fixed rate quite understood among all classes for his fee.

Not only the women of the household, but friends and relations from far and near come to visit the mother, crowding into the close little room which is often kept at such a degree of heat that existence must be well-nigh unendurable. This is not only due to the absence of ventilation, for which, as a rule, scarcely the slightest provision is made, but on account of a belief that whenever the child cries more fuel must be put upon the fire. Observances like this, however, are regarded not merely as sanitary, but as religious obligations, and accordingly many of the *dhais,* who may be classed as true Oriental prototypes of the late Mrs. Sarah Gamp, alike in ignorance, cruelty, and avarice, will often stop in the performance of necessary offices to haggle for higher payment than was bargained for, and will refuse to proceed with their duties until a guarantee has been given them that their exorbitant demands shall be satisfied. These and many more practices, which would be criminal were they not sanctioned by long custom, prevail throughout India, and are common to almost every creed and class. They are the broad outlines of the picture which touched the heart of the Marchioness of Dufferin and Ava, as they go straight to the sympathies and feelings of every other woman, and to recognize them at the outset of any effort to understand the conditions of woman's life in India, gives a degree at least of respect for the gentle fortitude that, in my opinion, is one of the most admirable traits in the native female character.

In minor details birth customs, however, are diverse as the tribes, sects, and septs of the dependency. In North Malabar, where a proportion of the population are Karavas, the woman is taken to a shed at some distance from the house, and is left absolutely unaided for twenty-eight days. Even her medicines are thrown to her, and beyond placing a jar of warm water near her about the expected hours of delivery nothing whatever is done for her. Ideas as to pollution from birth I found very strongly held all -along the Western shores of India, and, in fact, worse uncleanness was supposed to be conveyed by it than from the touch of death itself. To trace the customs of isolation of the mother, and the still more curious one which also obtains of regarding the father as also impure for fourteen days, only to be freed at the end of that time from his defilement by holy water supplied by Brahmins from temples or consecrated tanks, would be a study well worth undertaking; but, for my own part, I think that some of the exceeding severity of convention in the matter here is clearly traceable to Jewish influence. At Cochin, long a great centre of industry, commerce, power, and fighting, are to be found two colonies, side by side, of black and white Jews. The origin of their respective settlements there is lost in dim antiquity, though it is the tradition of the latter that they are descended from those who came out with King Solomon's fleets, that "Navy of Tharshish," which brought "gold, and silver, ivory, and apes, and peacocks." The Jew of to-day makes his personality felt in any community, and even though these Cochinese representatives of the Chosen People have a far more recent birthright in India than the one they claim, there is at least a sufficient community of practice to give one grounds for the belief that modern Malabar systems found their source in ancient Hebraic ordinances.

The participation of the father in the mother's uncleanness is not confined to the West Coast. It is found among the Kols of Eastern Bengal, though the paternal disability with them only lasts for a clear week, during which time the man has to cook for and wait upon his wife. With the Goalas, the great pastoral caste of the dependency, the father for three weeks is not regarded as eligible for his usual vocations. With these people, the expectant mother is put into a separate house, which is heated highly and kept closely shut, while certain symbolic plants and foliage are hung about the door, and the newly born infant is bathed in water in which other leaves and seeds have been boiled. Among the Rautias, whose legendary extraction is from Ceylon, but who are probably a degraded offshoot of the proud Rajput race, the richer a man is the longer is he unclean. While the middle classes can be purified about the twelfth day, a really wealthy man may have to wait for twenty-one days, or even longer, to be pronounced cleansed.

Among the Hindus the most important person in the birth ceremonials, after the *dhai* herself, is the barber. These form a caste to themselves, known in Bengal as the *Napit,* and standing socially in a good position. He is the first male, after her husband, to see a woman after her confinement, and he has to pare her nails on the day that this has taken place, repeating this operation on the ninth and thirtieth days after. Should the baby be troubled by fits or convulsions, he will be consulted, his method of cure being usually by spells and incantations. Tor the nail-paring, his poor neighbours know that he has a fixed charge of two or three pice, but from his richer patrons he looks for a larger fee, often receiving as much as a rupee and a piece of cloth, besides further doles of rice, salt, and spice.

The Muslims have a curious usage, which they call *thikra,* for which all the female relations of the prospective mother come to the house. Should the newly born baby prove to be a girl, it is optional for any one of these relatives, who may chance to have a son of her own, to slip a rupee or more into a small earthen pot called a *thikra,* where it becomes the perquisite of the *dhai* and she who succeeds in doing this first has secured the first right in later life to the little girl as a wife for her own boy. The word itself, I should explain, is scarcely ever heard outside the zenana, and is one that men never employ. *Purdah nashin* ladies have, however, almost a language of their own in the *chota boli* that they talk to their children or to one another. One soon learns the long drawn out " *oui-i-i* " of assent or exclamation, but it is a little puzzling tc the ordinary student of Hindustani, whether this has been studied under a tutor and with books and paper in London or picked up from the everyday talk to be heard around, to find that even the names oi the months have synonyms peculiar to feminine phrase. In women's lips, the eleventh month of the Mahommedan year *(Zikdd)* becomes *Thali,* or "empty," it being the month that comes between the religious fast and feast of *Shawwal* and the rejoicings of *hijja,* and similarly the second month, *Safas,* is changed to *Terah tizi,* from a superstitious belief in the ill luck of its opening fortnight. A child born during those days is believed to be doomed to a life of misfortune, and save upon the direst emergency no wedding or family festivity is ever held upon them.

The first ceremony in the child's life is, so far as I could see and ascertain, common to both Hindus and Mahommedans, and is called *chatthi,* when the mother eats meat for the first time. The child, too, receives its name, though this is often changed or added to in later life. Most, if not all, of the names given have some special meaning, as "Khurshad Begum," "Queen of the Sun," or "Chandebi," "Daughter of the Moon," among the Mahommedans, unless they adopt such designations as Fatma Begum, Khudaeja Bee, or Aesha-Bee, to perpetuate the feminine names in the family of the prophet; Miriam Bee is another favourite name. Popular Hindu names are Motibai, Tanki, Munna, Kumari, and Bamabai, the suffix *hibi* being often added in colloquial use.

Among many Hindu castes the actual birth ceremonies terminate with *Ekaisi,* or the twenty-first day; but with the Mahommedans *Chila* is the fortieth day, when the mother washes and the child has its head shaved. Feasting and amusement often enters into this, but there are several curious rites common to certain castes and sects, such as *Kua Jhanhna,* or peeping into the well of the Mussulman women, which, so far as I could gather, was a kind of consultation of the oracle, while the Hindus daub red lead upon the well itself. The whole house usually undergoes a thorough cleaning or purification, and life then resumes the even tenour of its way.

Thus, with so much of strange custom and profound superstition, it is not a matter for wonder that lying-in hospitals should have been somewhat slow in winning the support of the native women. Still they have made great progress within the last few years, and those of the presidency towns, supported by Government, are generally well filled by women of the working classes. Among the foremost of these the Eden at Calcutta claims a place, not alone for the admirable accommodation it gives to all women in their hours of greatest need, but for its work as a training school for *dhais* or native midwives. Free instruction is given here as well as pecuniary assistance towards maintenance while under tuition, and the work is taken up by Hindu as well as native Christian women. The services of these trained *dhais* are finding satisfactory appreciation by those for whose benefit they are intended, and probably through them the way will be paved for a fuller recognition of the value of qualified medical help. Sister Muriel, of Clewer, is chief hospital directress, and neither in the native nor Eurasian wards does one often find a bed vacant, while the health statistics concerning mothers and infants—always a crucial test of the management of a hospital of this class—are notably good. This point is of especial interest here on account of the high ratio of difficult cases that it receives.

Besides owning a fine State-supported hospital of this class, where Surgeon-Colonel Branfoot has rendered useful encouragement to Eurasians desiring to qualify as monthly nurses, Madras, through the generosity of Sir Savalay Raina-sawmy, K.C.I.E., has been endowed with one of the best institutions of this class to be found in all India. It was opened by the Duke of Buckingham in 1880, and so well were caste scruples and customs respected that, although women of high caste would usually have died rather than enter a public institution, as many as a hundred and fifty resorted to it during its first year of existence. The Hindu women of Southern India, unlike the Mahommedans, do not regard it as a fatal sin to be seen or attended by a man, and the hospital was accordingly placed under the direction of Surgeon-Colonel Cook, whose kindliness and skill rapidly won for him the deepest gratitude of the native women, who, as the repute of the institution spread, came from great distances to benefit by it. By 1887 another ward became necessary, and this Sir Savalay Ramasawmy added as his personal offering in commemoration of the Queen-Empress's Jubilee. Yet another ward was wanted, and this its generous founder gave in honour of the visit paid to, and satisfaction expressed at, the hospital by the late Duke of Clarence and Avondale.

Year by year the numbers who have benefited by its treatment have increased, and up to the day of my visit in November, 718 patients had passed through its wards—an increase of 120 upon the corresponding date of last year. Very homelike and orderly are the wards, which contain accommodation for thirty-two patients, with their comfortable spring beds, pretty chintz-printed coverlets, and distempered walls, while bouquets of beautiful tropical flowers show a greater attention to comfort than is usual in an Indian hospital. The staff of the hospital, under Surgeon-Colonel Cook, comprises his assistant, Mr. Wynn, the matron, Mrs. Kelly, who holds very high certificates of nursing skill, two Eurasian and one native nurses, and six Dufferin nursing scholars, who retain their native form of dress, but have made it smartly uniform by wearing little red jackets over their shoulders, and the white linen sari bordered with dark green. Ample space and perfect ventilation are secured to each patient, while a salutary rule, considering the malnutrition of many Indian working-class mothers, and the extreme youth of others (one or two girl-wives of only fourteen have been in its wards), enjoins that each woman shall spend a fortnight at the hospital before her confinement is expected. In numerous other small details the institution shows evidence of the most thoughtful care, while Lady Ramasawmy herself takes care that every little new arrival shall find a sufficient supply of suitable clothing ready for it, and does much of this work with her own hands. At Bombay, again, there are these notably good institutions of this class, the Motabai, under charge of Sister Gertrude Anna, being the largest. This forms a section of the great aggregate of homes of healing known collectively as the Sir Jamsetjee Jeejeebhoy's Hospital. Then there is the Cama Hospital, to which is allied the Allbless Hospital for obstetrics, the two together providing accommodation for about a hundred patients.

The buildings of the two institutions form a handsome pile, and were both erected through Parsee munificence. Inside the wards are bright, lofty, and airy, with easily cleaned encaustic tile floors and distempered walls. To this Miss Annette Benson, who formerly held a public appointment under the London County Council, has lately been sent by the Secretary of State for India, as this is a Government recognized institution. She is assisted by Miss Cama, a young

Parsee lady, who has lately returned from England after a course of study at home marked by much success. On account partly perhaps of its name and associations, it numbers a rather large percentage of Parsee women among its patients, but its advantages are sought much also by the Hindus, some even of high caste entering its wards, and in rather rarer instances still by Mahommedans.

In these hospitals the training of midwives holds a most important place, and it is very satisfactory to know, in connection with the Allbless department, that really progressive steps are being made. In its first year of work (1887) only two pupils, and those both Europeans, presented themselves for instruction, and at the present moment it has sixteen upon its rolls, of whom two are Brahmins, two Marathis, two of other good Hindu castes, and one of the Rajput race. In 1893 certificates of efficiency were granted to nine nurses, and further gratifying evidences of advance are shown in the facts that although the period of instruction has been recently extended from one year to eighteen months, and with it a higher level of merit in examination has been demanded, the change has not deterred pupils from entering; while formerly the National Association of the Countess of Dufferin's Fund had to bear almost all the cost of feeding, and even clothing, the nurse pupils, the maintenance fees are now almost entirely met and defrayed by the nurses or their friends. These fees amount in the case of native nurses to twenty rupees a month—a high figure for an Indian woman's support—and examinations are held each six months to test the progress made. The three last months are devoted to instruction in midwifery, and it is with the help of a knowledge of this branch of medical science that the truest progress towards wiser methods of treatment in other directions will be made. That the women find good scope after training is shown by the fact that out of the eighty or so who have passed through its school, only some half a dozen have abandoned their career, while the rest who have persevered are to be found practising at distant stations and remote villages, or holding positions in civil or Dufferin hospitals. Among those who passed out certificated last year was a young African woman, one of two rescued from an Arab slave dhow, who is taking the knowledge she acquired to Mombasa. The other saved at the same time entered with her, but unfortunately never recovered fully from the misery and privations she had had to endure, and died ere her course of study was completed.

Besides these, there is a strictly Parsee lying-in hospital, which was founded to combat certain unnecessary superstitions and rites which had grown up concerning birth, and to bring about a more hygienic and common-sense course of treatment. In this it is proving successful, as, however, one would expect as one sees that within the past five and twenty years or so the ladies, as well as the humbler classes of this race, have made progress towards Western ways and customs that is little short of remarkable, especially in comparison with the intensely gradual advances of the people surrounding them.

So much, very briefly sketched, both for native theories and practices in ushering a child into the world, as well as for some of the more important efforts that British influence has provided to ameliorate these trying hours of a woman's life. To bear a son has been, of course, the girl-mother's highest hope, and great indeed is her joy if the new little arrival proves to be a boy. It enhances immeasurably the importance of her position in the eyes of the family, and though she may have been a poor little household drudge before, the Cinderella to her older sisters-in-law, she rises at a bound to a factor of consideration in her circle. If, however, the first-born is only a girl, there is far less satisfaction. Looking into the far future, the family see that she must be endowed with money and jewels, that a husband of her own caste and status will have to be found for her, and that at present the father is not assured of the son whom he regards as essential to the carrying on after him of religious obligations. But it is better to bring daughters into existence than to be childless. That to an Indian woman, whether Hindu or Mahommedan, is the crudest of all curses, and I shall never forget the piteous look of agonized disappointment with which a young Santal woman of about twenty, who had been five years married, turned away to avoid telling me the, to her humiliating, truth, in answer to my inadvertent question, how many children she had.

Certain deities of the Hindu Pantheon are supposed to be susceptible to the prayers of barren women, who, to invoke the desired blessing of fruitfulness, will often make long and painful and costly pilgrimages to special shrines. The Seven Pagodas, between Madras and Masulipatam, are a particularly favoured place for this purpose, and I have heard Southern Indian women aver that auspicious results very frequently follow. But the rites and ceremonies that take place there are, according to all accounts, of a somewhat tantric or phallic character, and it is perhaps best not to inquire too closely into the details of the sacrifices that have to be offered. On the banks of the Ganges, too, at Benares, close to the Nepaul Temple and the Burning Ghat, there is a huge recumbent figure of the god Bhim, which is believed at particular seasons to possess peculiar virtues in this direction. At these times women, young and comparatively middle-aged, will come hundreds of miles to implore the earnestly desired boon, making offerings of oils, spices, and flowers. Very quaint and pretty are the baskets which the women use in all their ceremonials associated with Mother Ganga and her shores. They are of brass-work, made quite round, with the sides charmingly cut or fretted. On either side of the handle there is a tiny cup to contain the more precious gifts of spice and oils to be bestowed. There are many other resorts in different parts of the dependency which are believed to possess this same efficacy, and to them in all faith, and with much preliminary preparation of fasting and devotion, hundreds, even thousands, yearly make journey.

It is not difficult to understand the Hindu or Mahommedan woman's intense desire for motherhood. There is every possible influence directed to foster her innate sentiments, for one of the first of her life's lessons is that child-bearing is her chief purpose in the world. It has religious advantages to her, and removes, according to Brahmanical ideas, some of the disabilities attaching to her in the future state as a mere woman. Strongest, however, of all forces in quickening the passion for maternity is that should she, after a few years of wedded life, prove unfruitful, her husband is considered, even in the most civilized castes, fully justified in taking to himself another wife.

There are many tribes and sub-castes who prohibit polygamy under penalty of loss of caste or caste expulsion, as, for instance, the Agarwals, the Baruis (the growers, by the way, of betel for chewing), the Binds (an agricultural and Hinduized non-Aryan tribe), the Kumhars (the potter caste of Bengal), and the Nagars of Bhagalpur, among many more. Others there are who nominally permit polygamy in theory, but never bring it into practice unless the first wife proves childless ; while with the whole Mussulman race, whose religious prohibitions allow to a man "not more" than four wives at once, it is quite the exception to find any zenanas where there is a plurality save for this reason. In fact, at Calcutta, where one branch of the Church of England Zenana Mission has devoted far more, and more personal, pains than usual to learning the conditions and winning the friendly confidence of the Mahommedan population, I only heard of one case where there were two wives, and these ladies I was taken to visit, under the impression that, like the majority of travellers out from England, I should not be satisfied that I had seen genuine native life unless it was shown me under a polygamous aspect!

The childless woman is, moreover, looked upon with feelings that are, if possible, more painfully humiliating to her than those of her Western prototype, who also, in the humbler orders, endures more than a little of stinging suffering through the not always nice or refined commentaries of her neighbours. In the East there is the added misery of the idea of directly divine wrath visiting itself in this calamity, which may extend itseK further through her to the rest of the household. Then her cup of contumely and sorrow is full, if she finds herself not only dethroned from incontested wifely dignity, but her rival also bears the desired heir, and one hardly wonders if at the end she terminates a life which, according to all she has been taught, is a terrible failure, by charcoal fumes, or hanging, or drowning.

Happily for the individual, sterility in the native women is comparatively much rarer than it is in the more artificially living nations of Europe. To quote an official authority: "There is an abnormally high birth rate, not due to the youth of the married couples, or to their fertility, so much as to the great prevalence of marriage. . . . This rate amounts to between forty-four and fifty per mille, and may be attributed to the encouragement given to marriage first by the religious idea that a son is necessary to the spiritual welfare of the deceased after death, and still more by the fact that in a society organized as is that of India, a wife so far from being an "additional burden on the resources of the household, directly or indirectly adds to them." It may be remembered, too, that a very appreciable ratio of women of the child-bearing age, among the middle and upper classes, as widows, are not adding to the high birth-rate, and certainly, from all that I saw and heard, the numbers who have failed to increase the population by at least one or two is relatively a very small one. Ovarian disease and internal injuries, attributable to unduly early marriage, tend, however, to keep families smaller than might be imagined, when it is remembered that no time is lost, as with ourselves, in beginning the obligations of maternity. This last is an article of the *istri-a-char,* the unwritten but binding woman's code. The men know its existence, and the wiser among them recognize how futile it is to attempt to traverse it. In these traditions of the zenana, however, there is a distinct antipathy to immature union, and in the north-west, indeed, there is a special and an opprobrious term used to denote the weakly fibreless infants that are the results of too youthful a marriage.

Against the large and steadily maintained rate of fruitfulness there is also to be considered a very heavy scale of infant mortality. With parents immature in one, if not on both sides, a high average standard of vitality is not to be expected. The revolting and ignorant practices of the *dhais* may be held responsible for a large number more of deaths that could be avoided, and the mothers who have learnt the comfort to themselves and the greater safety to their offspring of the more scientific Western methods, are certainly showing a willingness to accept them, which they do not accord to other innovations of education or freedom. The multiplication of trained midwives to go out into the villages and districts will certainly mitigate the waste of baby life that goes on, and may in time, and so gradually as to be almost unperceived, effect other salutary changes in the women's condition.

Once out of the *chatthi ghar,* the child of course takes its chance of infantile ailments, as well as of the greater scourges of cholera or small-pox, which at intervals or in unfavourably wet seasons stalk like destroying spectres through the land. But medical skill and amended sanitation, better water supplies, and the daily improving means of food distribution, which every year is making the gaunt image of famine a less terrible vision, are giving yearly a cleaner bill of public health, which is not only reflected in a slowly declining death-rate, but gives promise of sounder stamina and physique for the generations to come. The infant is of course invariably nursed at the breast by the mother when she can possibly fulfil the function, and so soon as it can walk, it enters upon a joyous and untrammelled childhood.

Throughout Western, Southern, and Eastern India the children, boys and girls, disport themselves literally naked until five years of age. In Bengal it is not unusual at about two or three to put upon the boys a piece of cord, sometimes with a key or a small metal charm; and round Madras and in Eastern Ceylon the little girls are generally to be seen with a little zone or circlet of silver or bell metal round their podgy little middles. The girls begin to wear clothing sooner than the boys, and their earliest raiment is usually a comically shapeless sacque of coloured print. Innocent in the sense understood of European children they never are, for reticence or mystery towards them are quite unknown, and one might almost say that they babble artlessly over subjects that elderly matrons at home would discuss under all reservation. The knowledge of, and admission of this fact, is absolutely necessary for the comprehension of much that seems puzzling and suggestive of moral degradation in the Indian character. A knowledge of what one may euphemistically write of as "the facts of life" gives the women a habit of thought which makes them seem perfectly natural and everyday things, and 'as such they discuss them, but not merely from a morbid love of nauseous detail, as those who do-not understand at once define it to be.

I do not know whether those noisy and assertive persons who have lately started the theory that the Western woman's disabilities arise largely from the "ignorance" in which well-brought-up girls are kept, are aware of this. If not, it may give them some difficulty to reconcile their demonstrative sympathy with the Indian woman's "down-trodden" condition, with the knowledge that she sooner and more fully learns the mysteries of existence than any others of her sex in the world. Yet, from their point of view, she is the "awful example" of humiliation! I give them the information, and leave them to argue over it.

The Hindu mother is generally affectionate to weakness, but she possesses very little control over, or direction of, the child after infancy. This is vested in the grandmother—the father's mother—and she has generally become a stern disciplinarian who must be obeyed unquestioningly. Respect to the father and love to the mother—though the prejudiced outsider would discredit this—with of course the elements of religion are the child's first home lessons. The girls are put very young to simple household duties, and the merest children may be seen cleaning the rice and pounding the corn with a dexterity and confidence curiously at variance with their youthful years. In better-class households there is often one at least among the women of the zenana who can read, and should this be the case, she may impart her knowledge to some of the little girls. If it is intended to send a girl to school, she generally begins to go at about six or seven years of age, but it is still far more exceptional for her to do this than to remain at home.

●●

4

Education of Women

Indian social reformers are wont to express the view that when education is generally accepted by parents for their daughters, the complete emancipation of the sex will have come into measurable range. One is reminded a little of a trite old saying as to what pigs would do if they had wings, but those who most glibly speak of the widespread advantages that are to accrue from knowledge fail to see that the women have to be convinced in the first place of the desirability of it at all. And how deeply seated is actual prejudice against it in many quarters still, is one of the last facts that the well-meaning apostle of progress will admit. There are plenty of Mahommedans yet to be found whose educational views are expressed in the idea that women may be taught to read with benefit, since they can improve their minds by the study of the Koran, but it is not wise to allow them to learn to write, lest they should communicate with unadvisable acquaintances, and even be able to make assignations of deceitful purpose.

Over the latter disability, the wit of the zenana has triumphed by attaching meanings that are unmistakable to the initiated to the most innocent of everyday things. It was discussing Rudyard Kipling with an educated Banee, that I learnt first that the "object letter" described in his story "Beyond the Pale," in which a broken glass bangle, a red dhak flower, a pinch of cattle food, and a number of cardamons was intended to be construed into a widow's request for a visit at eleven o'clock, was a perfectly probable missive.

To such and many other objections to female learning *per se,* there is yet to be added a still stronger element of difficulty to be overcome before learning is generally sought for girls. This lies in the fact that Indian woman possesses no practical incentive yet to pursue book learning. She is taught that her calling in life is marriage, and learns to look on that as the end and aim of her existence. Unlike ourselves at home, she is not for ever crying out in newspapers and on platforms for new openings of occupation, nor is she influenced by American examples to endeavour to enter upon vocations vastly better filled by men. In fact, in all my wanderings, I only saw one woman filling a clerk's position, and she was a bright young Tamil who assisted Mrs. Brander, the Chief Inspectress of Female Education to the Government of Madras, in her secretarial department. Even domestic service, save for the inappreciable percentage of ayahs employed, is not fulfilled by women. The woman who fails to marry, and in consequence must earn her daily bread, is far from being regarded as a commendable example to her sex. Rather, she is a social failure, who must explain herself and behave with humility beside mothers who have realized the true mission of womanhood. It is not characteristic of the true Hindu or Mahommedan woman to desire to be independent of man, and education therefore falls to the level of a mere prop, useful only where a better hope has failed.

Moreover, the native temperament measures everything by its utilitarian value. Learning, therefore, for learning's sake, is a merely academic luxury, and one into which elements of changer to accepted traditions may lurk with insidious possibilities.

Still, in spite of the weighty obstacles against which it has had to contend, the educational movement is undoubtedly making way among the sex. Chief among the factors which have tended to break down the barriers of mistrust and objection I should unhesitatingly place the much higher standard of education, which has been gradually raised among the men during the past quarter of a century or so. With the students who have come to England for university or bar studies there has been undoubtedly a regrettable tendency to choose English wives, with results it is to be feared generally very far from satisfactory. For the white girls who go out find themselves in the very awkward position of being better educated and more advanced in thought and freedom than the female part of the family to which they have allied themselves, while, unless they are of singularly adaptable nature, or their husbands have abandoned their own national habits and customs far more than usual, the system of domestic life and the household ways must of necessity present features unpleasant as well as unexpected. European society in India is exceedingly severe upon these mixed marriages, and save in one or two notable instances that might be mentioned, where the lady has had singular force of character and the entire courage of her opinions, it declines to receive either the man or the woman under any circumstances. With the young men who have profited by the splendid schools and colleges open to them now in all parts of India, there has not been the same temptation to which their more travelled and enterprising brothers and cousins have been exposed in this direction; though, in defence of those who have succumbed to it, be it said that English women at home have been very ready to flatter and accept these Oriental suitors. But the home-taught young man, for all the domestic conservatism, which even civil service appointments and national congresses scarcely seem to shake, must gradually come to desire a more even level of companionship on the part of his wife. It is one of the Western misconceptions to regard the wife as of no importance in the family circle. On the contrary, *purdah* though she may be, she is a factor of consideration alike as a dowried girl-bride and later on as sons' mother, as mother-in-law, and grandmother. "While her husband's learning did not carry him into wider interests than the immediate market prices current, or the last bit of litigation upon which his neighbours had embarked, he found in his wife all the sympathy he desired. But now that he is himself a judge it may be, or a deputy-collector on special duty, involving perhaps a really high degree of specialized scientific attainment, he begins to think he would like his wife to know a little more also of the world's broader affairs. I saw several instances in which the ladies of the Church of England or other Zenana Missions had been asked to instruct in English and other branches of knowledge the girl-wives of young men at the universities.

The present position of female education in India may be summed up by saying that it has long left the stage of being actively opposed, and has passed through its phase of passively indifferent neglect to one of toleration. There is no enthusiasm, general or even widespread, for it as yet, and the women who pursue it to its higher walks may be said to bear the same position to the masses of their sex, as those do here, who preach in chapels or wear uncompromising trousers to ride bicycles astride through the city, who are looked upon as unfortunate aberrations by their less go-ahead sisters.

To understand and grasp properly the present aspect of the question a few figures will be useful, and in quoting them I would like to thank the India Office for the ready and ungrudging help it gives to any one in search of information regarding the dependency. Going back to reports of 1877-78, I find that the number of girls at school throughout British India was set down at 66,615. In 1882-83 the numbers had advanced to more than double, and some 3487 schools had then an attendance roll of 162,317. In the mean time an important commission on public instruction, under the presidency of Sir W. W. Hunter, had been appointed, and several valuable recommendations on the subject of female education were made in the report, with the result of very marked increase both in the numbers of. girls' schools and the pupils attending them.

From the latest statistics available, namely those of the years 1891-92, one learns that the total number of girls attending public and recognized private educational institutions was 339,043. Resolved into its factors, this mass gives some interesting details. For instance, only 76 of the sex are yet to be found in the collegiate establishments of first grade, and of these 29 are medical students. Entered, however, in the technical and other schools, are 461 young women, of whom 51 are set down as studying art, a branch of knowledge to which Indian girls are at present curiously indifferent. In fact, except in the high school at Bombay, where one or two Parsee girls had taken it up and showed me a few examples of still life and drawing from the antique, I saw no evidences whatever of a native aptitude or inclination in this direction. Certainly no native woman has so far distinguished herself in it, but an Indian creative female artist, should such ever arise, would be an extremely interesting phenomenon.

In the normal schools for the training of school teachers, 819 are put down as under instruction; and then, coming to the section devoted to private instruction, are two particularly striking entries. The one is that 355 girls are pursuing advanced studies in Arabic, Sanscrit, Persian, and the other Oriental classics which, as these attainments are of no special utilitarian value in the modern system of Anglicized education, shows that even among the women are to be found a few who love learning and literature for its own sake. The other bears silent but eloquent testimony to the Mussulman indifference to female knowledge. Only 8117 girls are to be found attending the private Koran schools, a small proportion indeed to the millions of Mahommedan women.

Put in form perhaps more easily to be comprehended, 99.44. per cent, of the entire female population of India—

enumerated at 113,406,669—is illiterate. Under instruction at the present time is 0.22 of the whole, while of those beyond the school-going age, only 0*34 are able to read and write. Stated thus, it is a startling record enough, even beside the male average of 11 per cent, who are not illiterate.

It is in the Madras and Bombay Presidencies that female education has made its best advances, and in both these the percentage of females over five years of age and not illiterate stands at 1.2. This, however, really gives a better ratio of strictly native educated women to the southernmost tract, as in Bombay, it must be borne in mind, are included the Parsees, who in the past quarter of a century or so have completely emancipated their women from *purdah* traditions, and have accepted for them the advantages of learning quite as unreservedly as for the boys. Madras has, however, been the centre of Indian mission efforts far longer than any other part of the dependency, and indeed we may go back for its commencement to 1542, when St. Francis Xavier's name was first associated with Madura and the Paravas tribes of the Tinnevelly district. The earliest two of the Protestant missionaries, who by the way were Lutherans, began their efforts at Tranquebar, and. to two of them, Ziegenbalg and Schutze by name, is due the credit of having translated the Bible into Tamil and Hindustani.

Even the sternest critics of modern missionary methods are compelled to admit how much the evangelizing agencies have done in the direction of female education. Going back to the year 1850, I find that the Protestant societies then possessed only 285 educational establishments. In 1880, the numbers had risen to 1120, and ten years later to 1507, while the numbers of pupils in the corresponding years were 11,193, 57,893, and 104,159. In the last-issued report of the Department of Public Instruction in Bengal, official recognition of the value of these mission efforts is ungrudgingly given, but whether the British subscriber, who, often self-denyingly, supports these undertakings, grasps how much larger is the work of teaching than that of preaching is another matter. Personally, my own bias was to have admired and defended all missionary labours. Brought up and still an attached member of the Church of England, I would far rather have set it down that the various societies are realizing all that they undertake upon the platform of Exeter Hall. But they are not. Their individual zeal and earnestness is not, as a rule, to be discredited, though I have met instances in which social prestige was ranked as of more moment than the slow winning of native confidence, and servants and horses as things to be appraised rather than a bazaar congregation. It is according to the point of view from which the question is regarded, whether it is advisable to keep Christian dogma discreetly veiled and in the shadowy background or not. There are insidious possibilities in the precept that the reading of a chapter in the Bible and the "force of silent influence" is enough when coupled with prayer, and it is certain that the religious influence exerted in the schools has but the scantiest results.

I was talking one day to a very intelligent Parsee machinist in Delhi, and he mentioned to me that his children attended a certain missionary school there. This somewhat surprised me; and I said, "But you are not Christian converts, surely ?"

> "No," he replied, "I hope we are all as good Zoroastrians as any; but, you see, it is a great advantage to the boys to know English, and *they get no harm if they have to hear a little of your religion.* It' is very little expected of them in return for what they are taught, and they will forget it all in a couple of months."

One point, however, was forcibly borne in" upon me, that the insistence upon religious instruction is invariably slacker where missionary schools are rivalled in the field by

Government ones. In Madras, for example, the Education Department is "exceedingly active, and here there is a" decided tendency to keep the elements of proselytizing in a subordinate position. In Bengal, on the other hand, where the Administration does next to nothing for the advancement of female education, a far bigger pill of Biblical and ecclesiastical learning can be and is given with the jam" of general teaching.

As mere teaching agencies', the mission schools that I saw from Negapatam to Delhi, from Calcutta to Calicut, are deserving of the highest commendation. Modern European methods have been skilfully brought into harmony with native needs, and ideas even of punctuality and truthfulness— virtues in which the average native character is not strong — have been imparted. Yet, ungracious and paradoxical as it seems to allude to the fact, in face of all that has been done for female education, there is an existent drawback to wide development of the movement in its association with evangelization. For there is no denying that even if Hinduism is being imperceptibly weakened, Christianity is not being accepted in its place. On the other hand, the native Christian is viewed with undisguised contempt by his former coreligionists, and we are brought face to face with the undoubted truth that the large proportion of native Christian women who are in the position of school-teachers is the very reverse of a tower of strength in the situation. Till one has moved and lived among the people, it is almost impossible to realize the deep-rooted prejudices' against a woman's doing any work outside her own home sphere. All down the centuries, since the Rig Veda taught that woman had won her right to rise to the world of life when she had fulfilled her duties as a wife to her husband, the traditions have strengthened, till it has come to be regarded as an unnatural and a sinful thing for her to look for other interests. She who has accepted Christianity has in the first place to cut herself away from her own people by her change of faith. Far from being honoured for this, she has become to them as out-caste, and teaching by her, instead of being the commendable work that it is with us, is rather degraded to the aspect of being the one calling into which she could enter.

On the other hand, there is of course to be considered that if converts are made, they must not be placed at any unfair disadvantage to the rest of the community in the struggle for a livelihood. It is not a matter for wonder on any grounds that the missionary agencies have fostered schoolmistress-ship as a female profession, as they have done by means of normal schools and university scholarships. Not only does the adoption of the calling relieve the converting pastorate of the immediately serious questions of maintenance, but it is promising of a possibility of further evangelizing. Moreover, one is asked whether it is not better to have native Christian teachers than none at all. To my mind only one answer presents itself. So long as the vitality of the female education movement is preserved from outside, and European money and energy are forthcoming to fan the precarious little flame, the present system will last, and a certain amount of progress will be recorded. But before we can view the subject with any genuine satisfaction, and feel that from being an artificially fostered production it has become a living reality, we must have created both a genuine desire for learning for its own sake and further provided the means by which it can be naturally and on the spot supplied, according to the inherent prejudices and beliefs of the people.

It is therefore that an experiment, initiated by Eamabai in the Sharada Sadan, at Poona, was of particular interest. Of course Eamabai herself, with her knowledge, her independent views on marriage, and her contentions for women's rights, stands somewhat in the same position towards the luck of her countrywomen as the extremely advanced of the progressive sisterhood bear towards everyday womankind with ourselves, and it may be taken for certain that it will be very long before her pronounced emancipation finds favour with those of whom it has been well said, "Her sway in her own immediate circle is complete, her social aspirations are restricted within immutable limits, while those of her inferiors are similarly kept from encroaching, and she has no conception of any social grievance with which the elders of her caste are not competent to deal." For Eamabai's idea was no less than the training as teachers of children-widows and childless—therefore often unvalued, cruelly treated, and even deserted—wives. Of the caste Hindu widows' lot enough has been written. It is the one point in the domestic system that the sensation-monger feels himself or herself to be upon quite safe ground, since it can always be said it was bad enough to require amended legislation. No doubt, too, with a race which places the sexual pleasures in such paramount estimation, a girl would feel that to live life as thousands of European "old maids" do, her fate was specially hard; while, moreover, in either her own or her dead husband's house she might be viewed as a useless encumbrance, the drudge, the slave, and the despised.

Now for Eamabai to bring such to her home was to do a double good. In the first place, it took the unfortunate girl away from where she was probably not wanted, and placed a useful vocation in her hands; in the second, by only receiving those of caste, she had commenced a band of teachers who can go into the zenanas of their co-religionists on equal social terms. Most unfortunately, I was unable to go to Poona, but my knowledge on the subject is derived from a reliable official source, and it was less value after all, in such an inquiry as I had been commissioned to make, to see the small home details of such an institution than to know in broad outline what were its intentions and purpose. There were some forty inmates till quite recently, ranging in age from twelve to twenty. English was added to the general education given to them in their own vernaculars, and Eamabai herself instructed them in Sanscrit, the language of their own sacred books; but since I left India I have learned that the "Home of Learning" is in a state of collapse. Forgetting, evidently, that there were plenty of evangelizing seminaries in the field, Eamabai was induced to abandon her original plan, which guaranteed that Hindu religious and caste observances should not be interfered with, and to introduce Christian prayer and instruction. The work by this means has been shaken to its foundations, her pupils have left, and what might have been the seed of a valuable indigenous influence has withered away.

There are considerable differences in the general system pursued by the three presidencies, the lieutenant-governorships, and the native states, and it is perhaps not necessary to institute any lengthened comparisons as to their divergencies. It will suffice to say that there are two views from which elementary instruction through the vernaculars is regarded. One is whether it is to be a merely useful scheme of teaching that should assist the masses in their humble and everyday vocations; and the other is, whether it shall be treated as a possible basis leading to higher stages, possibly even the university degree itself.

Under present conditions, I am of opinion that; so far as the girls are concerned, the former is the better fundamental idea. There are few women at this time better competent to speak on such a subject than Mrs. "Wheeler, the native lady who fills the post of Inspectress of Schools to the Government of Bengal. In her own words, she is "but one generation removed from all the narrowness of orthodox Hinduism," but she enjoyed the benefit of a father who felt that his daughters were worthy of being taught. He was an exceptional linguist, holding an important post in connection with the Civil Service examinations, and became a convert to Christianity. Mrs. Wheeler was married to one of the chaplains of the Society for the Propagation of the Gospel. During her brief wedded life she did much in connection with his schoolwork, and on his death, leaving her with two little children to provide for, she was anxious to find occupation which should give her enough to educate them fittingly. Almost by chance she heard Sir Richard Temple express the wish that some suitable lady could be found to fill the post of inspectress of girls' schools, and she offered herself for it, being immediately accepted. When she took up her work she found there were no standards of instruction, no uniformity of books in use, and everything slipshod and haphazard. She had a hard battle to fight in introducing systematic courses, and had to live through much calumny and acrimony; but she triumphed over all, and to-day has the pleasure of seeing all that she has proposed in the code. She has visited England and the Continent twice to see all that she could of European methods, and her inherited knowledge of native character and ways of thought have given her especial advantages for her work.

Under Mrs. Wheeler are the strictly zenana and purdah schools, but for the ordinary day-schools, to which these conventions are not rigidly applied, she has the assistance of the male inspecting staff. As the outcome both of her racial knowledge and her actual experience, she deprecates strongly the tendency to push the girls on to university distinctions. The results are showy, no doubt, and look well in school reports; but in practice the young women become arrogant, are seldom successful as teachers, and very frequently develop hysteria and nervous complaints. It is too great a brain effort without any hereditary preparation, and to exhibit these girls as triumphs of the system is far from advantageous as an object-lesson to thoughtful eyes. Exceptions there are of course, a very notable one being another remarkable native lady, Miss Chandramukhi Bose, M.A., the first of her sex to win this coveted degree, which she did in 1884, before it was even officially opened to women. She is now directress of the Bethune Collegiate School at Calcutta, a well-attended and prosperous establishment, departmentally supported, which may be said to touch the high-water mark of women's education as it exists in India. Its primary school is conducted upon the most, approved of modern ideas; but of more general interest is its collegiate aspect, and the work it does in preparing girls for the First in Arts and B.A. degrees of the Calcutta University. Since these examinations were thrown open to women a steadily increasing number of girls, from eight in 1889 to twenty in 1893, have entered the college, paying only three rupees a month for their tuition. It can claim the credit of having turned out twelve young lady B.A.'s, three of whom passed during 1893." There is a percentage of Christian girls among its collegiate students, but the majority are Brahmos, the most emancipated and advanced of the Hindu community. In consultation with Mrs. Wheeler, Sir Alfred Croft and the Bengal Education Department recently revised the vernacular standards for girls' schools and zenanas, and as a comparison with our English corresponding grades, it will be of interest if I give it in full. That comparatively few go beyond the fifth standard is due to the prevailing custom of child-marriage, which seldom leaves a girl at school after her thirteenth year, though she will probably not be a wife till after she is fourteen. Madras has always prided itself upon keeping well in the van of educational progress, and it is therefore not surprising to find that both for its central and northern circles it has appointed a lady as inspectress of its schools. This post is held by Mrs. Brander, who came into prominent notice both as an advanced exponent of sound knowledge and a sympathetic and accomplished English gentlewoman when she took the control of the Madras Normal Training College for Teachers. Immediately under her supervision are some 590 schools, with an attendance roll of about 28,000 pupils. As showing, however, the occasional energy and ability shown by native - women, it is worth mentioning that during Mrs. Brander's last furlough an acting appointment was given to Miss Govindurajula, a Tamil lady of high qualifications, and she fulfilled the very exacting and responsible duties of the position with full credit.

The higher caste Hindu girls are among the brightest and most satisfactory of native pupils, and they possess certain hereditary advantages in the respect that learning has always maintained among their race. Prom recently compiled figures, furnished to me by Mrs. Brander, I find that out of the total number of 8458 girls receiving public instruction in Madras city, 168 are classified as coming from the "richer" and 2975 from the "middle" classes, and of these by far the larger proportion are Hindus; but perhaps even more interesting is the movement on behalf of the Mahommedan girls.

To reach even the lowest of this race was very hard; to gain the *Gosha* girls seemed well nigh impossible! The first effort made, certainly in this Presidency, and so far as I am able to learn, in any other, dates from about eighteen years ago, when a little band of ladies, at the head of whom was Lady Hobart, conceived the idea of a school where the strictest Mussulman could be as sure of seclusion from male intrusion as behind the purdah itself. Not only should it be a school, but a training college for mistresses also : and under the name of the Hobart Training School it has been one of the most entirely satisfactory features in the educational scheme of Southern India. Such was the fear on the part of Mussulman parents of their daughters being seen in the streets that the school had to provide covered conveyances to fetch and take home the pupils, and even to-day, when there are nine such homes of instruction in Madras city alone, with 498 pupils, this has still to be done. The Church of England Zenana Mission is well to the fore also in this work, and in the schools under Miss Oxley's care the drill and singing are notably good. It must be admitted, however, that Mahommedan girls' education in the northern and central circles of the Presidency showed in 1893 a falling off to the extent of six schools and 179 scholars upon the figures of the previous year.

The code of Madras differs very little from that of Bengal, and it is not necessary for me to repeat it, but over and beyond this I found in the southernmost Presidency three interesting and recent innovations in kindergarten, drill, and needlework. The first has been warmly adopted in the schools, and an admirable little manual on the subject has been written by Mrs. Brander, who, it may be mentioned, has also written a capital little work upon domestic economy for native households, published by order of the Indian Director of Public Instruction, a subject which is also beginning to receive attention in the schools. Miss Rajagopaul has also compiled a collection of kindergarten and action songs, which have been popular, and form a decidedly original line for a native lady teacher to have taken up. As to drill, I cannot do better than quote from the inspectress's last official report, in which she says " a decided change for the better has taken place in girls' schools in the matter of physical exercises. They are practised now in almost every girls' school in the central circle, and in secondary and upper primary schools they are generally well organized and suitable. . . . Many managers are now introducing light dumbbells, rings, and poles into native girls' schools, thereby improving the exercises and rendering them more popular. Grants amounting to Es. 128 have been distributed among four schools during the year for the purchase of calisthenic apparatus."

I think, however, that the most noticeable point in the claims of Madras to be considered a pioneer in matters educational lies in the movement that has been made towards continuing education after school. So long as girls go to live with their husbands at the age of fourteen, no matter how sound a foundation of learning 'may have been laid, the ultimate result can never be more than superficial. It is a matter therefore of importance as well as interest to record that a really earnest effort in the direction of home education classes has been made, and four different sets of teachers are at work in this direction. At the present time about a hundred and twenty women are studying thus, carrying their reading on to English, arithmetic, history, and geography, being visited at home weekly by the native governesses and occasionally attending lectures. I was present at one of these of a series organized by the Hindu Reform Association, given in Tamil, upon the world and its movement, and a fashionable as well as much interested audience of about fifty higher caste Hindu and Brahmin ladies it was. They came in handsome carriages, wore splendid jewels, took copious notes, and showed really intelligent interest in it by frequently asking questions on points they wanted to understand more fully, till one little event proved too much for their and my own gravity. One of the ladies had come attended by an aged widow, who was doubtless an old nurse and attendant, and whose shaven head, flowing white garments, and total absence of jewellery in any form showed that she belonged to the Brahmins, and was respecting all their rigid traditions as to how a woman who has lost her husband ought to appear. An austere and unhumorous person indeed she seemed, but she listened intently to the lecture, while she furtively watched her young mistress, until, in an interval when there was no astronomical diagram upon the screen and it was filled by a round bright circle of light, she made with her thin bony hands, in its exact centre, the shadow of a goose's head! It was one of the best I ever saw done under any circumstances, and she allowed it to rest open-beaked for a few seconds as if amazed at what it was hearing, and then set it wagging as though it were fully endorsing all that the lecturer was saying. Even the quiet Hindu ladies broke into a soft low laugh, and the lecturer, who was a clever young Tamil woman, who had taken a good certificate at one of the Scotch training-colleges, could only pause and smile, till with swift tact she called upon her colleague at the lantern for the next slide of the series. But the old lady was not at all abashed, and at the conclusion of the demonstration, came up to ask of the assistant if she would kindly show her once more "how the moon and the earth ran round the sky!"

Another useful insight into home education was afforded me by being present at the annual inspection by Mrs. Brander of a set arranged under the auspices of the Free Church Mission. Papers were in English, with dictation in Tamil and Telegu, including a certain amount of literature, composition, and poetry, and arithmetic up to fractions, and the *viva voce* work was certainly highly creditable, while the papers were handed in looking remarkably neat. Government assists this work, which costs about six thousand rupees a year, by a grant of over two thousand rupees, and the pupils show great interest in their studies, especially in English, which the greater number of them take up. In this connection may be mentioned the foundation of a women's magazine in Tamil called the *Maharani,* which has been started to meet the difficulty of finding bright and useful reading for girls. It is effectively illustrated, and contains articles on history, natural science, and social topics, as well as a serial story, though the dress, which fills so large a space in English girls' papers, does not form one of its departments. That may come in time!

Bombay treads closely upon the heels of Madras in the encouragement it bestows upon female education, and stands well in advance of Bengal. Curiously enough, Bombay city gives the lowest percentage of girls attending school to the population of girls of the school-going age of all the headquarters of the five educational divisions of the Presidency, with only 8.2 per cent, set down as scholars.

Poona stood highest, with 24 per cent., but there are various reasons for the extremely good proportion of students to girls here. Not only is the place an especially active centre of much and various mission work, but its branch of the National Indian Association is a very vigorous one, and its municipal administration, unlike that of many boards, is thoroughly in earnest in encouraging the movement. It also possesses a very large Parsee community as well as several notably good schools for girls of this race, to which they are sent from all parts of the Presidency. Moreover, when Mr. E. G. Oxenham, Acting Director of Public Instruction, gave me the statistics from which these figures were compiled, Ramabai's school was crowded and thriving.

At the present time, those of administrative influence in Bombay lean rather to the encouragement of primary education. The Government is strongly supported, so far as Bombay city is concerned, in its movements on behalf of education in general by the Joint Schools Committee—a body on which are four members (three of whom are native gentlemen) appointed by the municipal corporation of the town, and four nominated by Government. Twelve schools are devoted exclusively to girls by this committee, and though chiefly attended by Hindus, they include among their pupils Mussulmans, Jews, and aboriginals.

All possible assistance and information concerning these municipal schools was placed at my disposal by the Hon. 1ST. B. Masani, the secretary to the committee, whose views that education among the native women will not be "rushed," agreed with the opinion I had myself formed early, and which was confirmed as I went along. The schools as I saw them are modest in extent and scope, and I was glad to find in most of them that there were either head mistresses or qualified female assistants. I paid a long visit to one of the largest, where the discipline and tone seemed in all respects commendable, and where the informal little examination I was asked to make brought me intelligent and correct answers. That the teaching given in these schools is satisfactory is, however, shown by the fact that one of the valuable Mary Carpenter Scholarships, and another bestowed by the National Indian Association, were won by girls taught in them. Bombay, however, stands behind the other two Presidencies and the North-West Provinces, in not including in its official *personnel* a lady to act as inspectress to girls' schools. To a certain extent this deficiency is met by some of the ladies belonging to the National Indian Association, who have kindly undertaken to visit the schools occasionally; but I found the need of more feminine direction, especially where needlework was concerned. Nothing creditable in this direction was put before me, but some very commonplace embroidery and some absolute horrors of Berlin wool cross-stitch were brought out as the best they could show. The two vernaculars in most general use in Bombay are Marathi and Gujerati, and five of the municipal schools are for pupils of the former and seven of the latter.

As a glimpse of what the people are doing for themselves in the direction of education, I was much interested in a visit that I paid to the Goculdas Tejpal Free School, an institution maintained by the trustees (every one of whom is a Hindu gentleman, not only of high caste, but of considerable official and social status) of the enormous fortune left by the late Mr. Goculdas Tejpal for educational, benevolent, and religious purposes. The school itself occupies a flat in one of the huge many-storied houses one finds in the native quarters of Bombay, and the light and well-ventilated rooms had many pictures, European as well as native, illustrative of scenes from Hindu religious books. It has upon its register 125 girls, most of whom are under twelve years of age, though there are two or three young married women who have reached the sixth standard and who are pursuing their studies at their husbands' desires. The head mistress is a Hindu, and a qualified teacher, as, indeed, the results of the last Government examination, when 78.9 per cent, of the candidates presented passed, are enough to show. Besides the knowledge prescribed for the girls by the Education Department, kindergarten teaching is given to the infants, and greatly enjoyed by them, while needlework of a practical and useful character has a prominent place among the day's lessons. The girls were taught to cut out and make their own *cholis* (little jackets), to darn rents in their saris, and do simple embroideries. I asked what the school was doing in the way of physical education, a point on which one generally finds the most marked backwardness, and found that, so far, very little had been attempted. Still, to prove to me that an effort had been inaugurated, they went through the *gurba*, a curious performance that is more than an action song and less than a drill, a religious exercise and yet a game. In this the girls place a large brazen vessel, with a fire alight, in the centre of their class-room or playground. They join hands and circle round it, stepping sometimes forward, sometimes back, and changing places in an intricate system of movement.

In Bombay, as in all other parts of India, one finds that the Mahommedan girls are the most backward to avail themselves of educational advantages, despite missionary and all other effort. Still, a little progress even here may be recorded, and I learn that a really satisfactory advance has been made in the Presidency in the number attending secondary schools. In the Surat district there are two Hindustani schools for girls, one of which is in charge of a Mahommedan lady teacher, while there is another under similarly qualified management at Karachi. Scattered, however, through the Presidency are a number of small establishments of teaching, under native management, and known as Koran schools. Of these, whose average attendance varies from twelve to fourteen scholars, twenty are for girls, and though the instruction they give may not be of the highest order, still it is an encouraging sign to note any unaided effort on behalf of female learning.

Nothing strikes one more in Bombay than the simply marvellous strides which the Parsees have made towards the complete equality and emancipation of their women. But a quarter of a century ago Parsee ladies were to all intents and purposes *purdah nashin*—not perhaps as rigidly and narrowly as the Mohammedans, but in spirit debarred from any place in social life. To-day one meets them everywhere, from a Government House ball or dinner to a seat on the tramways as they start out, with all the frankness and independence of English women, to do their daily work of teaching, nursing, or study, and I have even heard of one or two who fill bookkeeping or secretarial posts. I have met several of them who drive and even ride fearlessly and well, and as hostesses in their pretty and well-ordered drawing-rooms I have found many who are charming and cultivated to the highest degree. Only in 1893 a young Parsee lady, Miss Cama by name, went over to England to pursue her medical education, and has returned to Bombay with the distinction of a high British diploma, and instances, from Miss Sorabji (though she came of a Christianized family) onwards, of girls who carried off the highest honours in the native universities could be given.

For the most part, the schools are managed without aid or grant from Government, and consequently are exempt from official inspection, but the quality of instruction is maintained by the examinations of the science and art classes and colleges for which the pupils are encouraged to enter. I visited the largest of the three vernacular schools, which have together an attendance roll of something over a thousand scholars. At this particular one there were over four hundred upon the register, and the building, which had been erected by private Parsee munificence in 1885, had cost over a lac of rupees. The class-rooms were excellent, their light and ventilation leaving nothing to be desired. I listened to the lesson in geography which was being given to the fourth standard scholars, and it struck me as being taught with remarkable clearness and ease. The subject was the island and harbour of Bombay, but instead of making her lesson a dry statement of areas and population, the teacher had provided an enormous shallow pan of water, and with modelling clay, tiny houses, trees, and ships, was making one and another of her little charges construct quite an admirable representation of the island. The kindergarten formed a large department, and in no London school or institution have I ever seen one better equipped and supplied than this is. Its completeness is largely due to Mr. Darasha Chichgur, a Parsee gentleman who has visited both England and Germany in -order to-study Western developments most likely to be of use for his own people. Here the needlework was useful as well as artistic, and I saw several charming examples of gold and silver embroideries upon ribbon-velvet as used by the ladies of this faith for the borders of their saris. Another very good institution is the High School, at which the majority of the students are Parsee girls, some of whom are learning drawing and painting.

It would not be fair to conclude this brief summary of educational work in Bombay without passing reference to the useful labours of the various missionary bodies who are in the field, but I have, both in Madras and Calcutta, indicated the scope and character of the efforts usually made by them, and which in broad outlines do not greatly vary. In Bombay the Society for the Propagation of the Gospel, the Free General Assembly, and the American Mission, among others, are doing notably valuable work. If, however, I have not spoken specifically of their schools, it is not from any intention of under-estimating their usefulness, but simply because I have thought it more significant to speak of movements official or indigenous. In the work of training native women as teachers, philanthropic bodies stand conspicuously well to the fore. At Ahmedabad is an excellent training college, and from another in Rajkot some notable examinational successes were obtained. The Karachi municipal female normal class had on its rolls at the close of last year no fewer than eighteen Mohammedans and fourteen Hindus, under supervision of Roman Catholic sisters, and the official comment upon it is that it is "doing admirable work in the way of disseminating knowledge among native women." Commendable institutions exist also in Kolhapur and Hyderabad. So far, indeed, as the supplies of future teachers are concerned, the Bombay Presidency stands very well, as it does also in point of the quality of education and its good intent of encouragement. Where it lags behind is in its ratio of girls attending school to those of the school-going age.

Then, lastly, is to be considered what the native States are doing in the matter of education. Hyderabad, with its preponderant Mussulman population, lags behind; and in Baroda no very striking progress is as yet recorded. Mysore and Bhaunagar lead the way, and though, unfortunately, I had no opportunity of visiting the former vast territory, I enjoyed the pleasure of a chat with its clever and far-seeing Maharajah, and learnt from him that all possible encouragement by means of grants in aid and scholarships are devoted by his assembly to the fostering of female education. The result in practice of this wise policy is, that while Hyderabad can only return three per mille and Baroda five per mille of their female population who can read and write, Mysore stands comparatively high with seven per mille. Mysore, moreover, led the way in another direction, which was the official discouragement of early marriage of both sexes, and while I was staying in Madras, the question how far legislative intervention was to be regarded as justifiable was engaging considerable attention. The example in this direction, or in that of education of the native States, has a more weighty influence than is often admitted, and innovations launched from them are likely to be accepted far more readily and with better grace than anything directly initiated under British prestige.

In Bhaunagar, which is very rarely visited by English tourists, I spent some days, which I rank among the most interesting of my experiences, for the vast Katthiawar district, which is bounded on the south by the Gulf of Cambay, and on the north by the Gulf of Cutch, has played no small part in the making of India, and its rulers earned no small fame in that memorable conflict of 1303, which has given to a good Rajput in the oath "by the sin of the sack of Chitor" the most binding tie he can lay upon his conscience. It was in later days than this that we first hear of Bhaunagar, its premier state, coming forward to help the British. Its ruler, Akherajii, in 1771, lent valuable assistance to our forces in subduing the pirate stronghold of Talaji, as well as in other ways. His son, who died in 1810, also cultivated the friendship of the English, then holding Surat as a chief trading centre, so that hereditary influences and associations have helped, doubtless, the enlightened gentleman upon whom in 1886 the Queen-Empress conferred the honour of Grand Commandership of the Star of India, subsequently bestowing upon him the formal title of Maharajah, while the State itself was. advanced in official recognition to first-class degree. Compared with such kingdoms as those of Baroda or Hyderabad, Bhaunagar may seem but small, with its population of about half a million, and area a little under three thousand square miles; but it is fairer to estimate by prosperity than by mere size, and a revenue of forty-five lacs of rupees is by no means to be despised. It may be safely said that in no State of India are the funds more generously managed or with a more public-spirited consideration for the welfare of the people than in Bhaunagar, and one's first impression on arrival is the extraordinary appearance of well-to-do comfort on all hands. There is one proverbial standard in India for judging of a place's affluence or the reverse, and that is the proportion of earthenware to brass or copper *lotahs*—the water-vessels carried by the women to the wells—metal ones indicating comfortable circumstances.

In all my drives and walks during nearly a week's stay in the capital I did not see one made of clay! The attraction, however, to me to visit the State was the excellent accounts I had heard of the advance that women's education was making there, and these I found had not been in any sense over-coloured. The system pursued showed the best features of progress allied with wise discretion as to the dangers to be feared from undue pressure.

In the State I find that there are sixteen schools for girls, having a total number of 1468 pupils. According to statistics which I have at hand, the proportion of girls attending school throughout India is one to every 343 of the population, so that this number, compared with the 224,803 women of the State, gives the more satisfactory ratio of one girl in each 153. The Maharajah, together with his council, have, however, placed their system, so far as girls are concerned, upon a footing which is, I believe, unique in India, and that is by the appointment of a lady superintendent of female education. This office, which is a State one, is filled by Miss Brooke, who, before its institution, had occupied an important post at the Female Training College at Ahmedabad. The nomination, now of some five years' standing, has proved most fortunate, as Miss Brooke is not only a lady of wide culture, but she has a pleasant sympathy with the ways and workings of native character, while she grasps, as many well-intentioned English ladies fail to do, that the teaching suited to girls at home is not of necessity the best for their sisters out here. Her aim has been to make learning a practical reality. Bather than strive for striking examination effects, she has tried to render knowledge pleasant, and to induce bright, intelligent native girls to come forward as teachers. In this she has succeeded already in a manner which justifies her in hoping for yet better results in the future, and she looks forward to a time when female teachers or assistants will be available for all the schools in the State.

One of the most admirably ordered schools that I saw throughout India was the Mahjiraj School in Bhaunagar city, which has upon its rolls no less a number than 283 scholars, of whom almost all are drawn from the leading and wealthy families of the place. A most public-spirited example has been set by the Maharajah in sending his own daughter, the Kumari Shri (Princess) Kasaba, a pretty and intelligent young lady of about fifteen, to study here, in addition to receiving private tuition from Miss Brooke. The princess takes her place in class with the other girls, earning or losing her marks with complete impartiality, and is a good English scholar already. She showed me some of her exercise books, and her handwriting is extremely good, while she recited some difficult lines of Mrs. Sigourney's in the sweetest of voices and with excellent expression. This school, I learnt from Miss Brooke, was the oldest in the Gujarat province, and had been established as far back as 1857, and in its earlier days had had a hard battle to fight against prejudice and indifference. When she took up her appointment she found about 170 scholars attending, but every year has seen a notable increase up to the present figures. In the last Government examination held, 83 per cent, of the candidates passed. An interesting feature in a recent prize distribution was that ladies only were invited, and the awards were presented by Princess Ramba, an older daughter of the Maharajah's, who was educated in the school, and is now married to the heir-apparent of the Rajah of Brebunder. It is very rarely that such ladies can be induced to take part in anything approaching a public ceremony, and the event therefore is one of sufficient importance to note in any record of woman's progress in India. The singing is made a great feature of this school, and besides an English lady teacher, from whom two or three of the Parsee scholars are taking private lessons upon the piano, two native musicians from the State band attend to give instruction. A song in Gujarati and a simple two-part ditty in English were pleasingly rendered by the girls, who did sums, read English, and altogether went through an informal examination for me. Still I think nothing gave me greater satisfaction after the hideosities I had seen in Madras and Calcutta as specimens of needlework than the altogether delightful embroideries and stitchery laid before me. But I am old-fashioned enough to believe in such teaching as worthy of a place in any code, and its prominence is undoubtedly appreciated by those for whom the school exists, as upon its attendance registers are to be found Brahmins, Rajputs, Jains, Levanas (the wealthy trading caste), Parsees, and Mahommedans, the growing readiness of these to accept education being a source of great gratification to all. Several girls in the school had reached the sixth standard—practically equivalent to our own—and thirty-one were learning English.

The Wadwha school, on the outskirts of the town, which I visited, is more exclusively a working-class school, and numbers about 150. Unlike the experience of many other parts of India, it is less easy in Bhaunagar to secure the attendance of the lower castes than the upper, for, with its docks, public works, and other sources of labour, the people are so prosperous and well-employed that they want their daughters at home. Still, this school, which was opened in 1868, shows a steady increase since its foundation, and is giving a sound and useful education to its scholars, though it does not profess to teach beyond the fifth standard. Among its pupils are children drawn from the gardener and fruit-seller, the artisan, the basket-weaver, and other humble castes, though only two are set down as the children of agricultural labourers. A merry lot of little people were they, to whom a request to show me some of their games was more welcome than questions about the geography of the Bombay Presidency or the history of the Rajputs, and books were adjourned very readily for this purpose.

Bhaunagar, probably, will one day be in the field as a mart of worked silver, an art-industry which is developing there in a satisfactory manner. In conception and execution it is somewhat allied to that associated with Cutch in its palmier days, before European demands lowered its standards of design and craftsmanship. Vigorous and pleasing work is turned out by the Bhaunagar silversmiths in the form of cups, plates, and such accessories for the table as pepper-pots and finger-bowls; but when I was there its best workers were engaged upon the separate pieces to be used for a set of gates for a new temple then in the course of erection. These gates are extremely beautiful and are made of sandal-wood entirely overlaid with silver *repoussee,* chiefly representing scenes from the Hindu mythology.

Thus the movement has been initiated. Patience and tact are wanted for its development; and one little difficulty in the high education of working-class girls, especially when these are Mahommedans, ought not to be overlooked—that is, the danger of teaching them up to a more advanced standard than will probably be their husband's attainment. For again I can only repeat that the *istri-a-char,* the women's code, is opposed to innovation. Let me conclude this chapter with some remarks made before the National Indian Association by Mrs. Flora Annie Steel, who speaks with the knowledge of a quarter of a century of official connection with the Education Department of the North-West, and says—

> "Your village matron is conservative to the backbone, and I doubt if even a revolting daughter would have a chance against a really stalwart Punjabi mother-in-law. I remember an example of this in Muzuffarghar, a district noted for its dislike to education. A boys' school was started in a certain village by the usual bribes to the head men of illuminated certificates, or possibly the still more coveted honour of a cane-bottomed chair to sit in at the district durbar, and a remarkably nice young man a black alpaca coat went out to take charge of it, full

of zeal and high imaginings. He returned to headquarters next day full of bruises. The old women of the village had solemnly beaten him to the boundaries with their slippers. So far as they were concerned the schoolmaster was welcome to be abroad; he certainly should not be at home amongst them."

"Perhaps a beginning might be made by offering prizes at the village fair-time for proficiency in spinning, dairy work, cooking, and the preparation of simples. It is rather an opening of the siege by distant parallels; still I know of several cases in the "West Highlands and Islands where the introduction of a churn thermometer has done more to shake the belief in witchcraft than the board school. For the A B C is not an Abracadabra ; especially when the pupils leave the school long ere they reach words of five syllables."

●●

5

Marriage System in Society

"Enter, thrice happy ! Enter, thrice desired! And let the gates of Hari shut thee in With the soul destined to thee from of old.

"Tremble not! lay thy lovely shame aside— Lay it aside with thine unfastened zone, And love him with the love that knows not fear.

"Because it fears not change; enter thou in, Flower of all sweet and stainless womanhood, For ever to grow bright, for ever new;

"Enter beneath the flowers, O flower fair! Beneath these tendrils, Loveliest, that entwine And clasp and wreathe and cling, with kissing stems;

"Enter with tender blowing airs of heaven, Sift as love's breath, and gentle us the tones Of lover's whispers when the lips come close ;

" Enter the house of Love, O loveliest I Enter the marriage bower, most beautiful! And take and give the joy that Hari grants."

The Indian Song of Songs

Inaccurate sensationalism reaches its climax over the system of child-marriage. The assiduously circulated idea of missionary reports and social grievance seekers is that the wretched girl-infant is married at about five or six years of age, generally to some one vastly older than herself, who takes her away whenever he pleases, and exercises whatever violence of brutal lust he cares for. We are bidden to imagine barbarous results of force too revolting to be set down on paper, too impossibly hideous in suggestion, one would have thought, for any human being to have believed of another. But that the ceremony of infancy is a mere form of betrothal, and that the second series of rites (the *rukhsati,* or bride's home-taking), immediately preceding the consummation of the marriage, is rarely proceeded with until the girl has given unmistakable physical evidence of having reached womanhood, is not explained, and in this fact lies the defence of the whole theory on which Indian matrimonial views are based.

Oriental sex-philosophy goes to primitive and elementary nature, and teaches woman that life without marriage is incomplete. Maternity, it proceeds to impart, is the object for which she was sent into the world, and this obligation, which she has no right to shirk or modify, if fulfilled, brings with it the best of happiness in this life and the best of rewards in the next. Indeed, it is only by the bearing of children that she can rise above her curse of disabilities as a mere woman, bearing in herself the taint of original sin, that demands for its expiation the gift of a son to carry the domestic worship of her husband's family. Mr. H. H. Risley, whose essay on "Caste in Relation to Marriage" is one of the most frank and common-sense contributions that have been made to this subject, scarcely regards the standard Brahmanical explanation that marriage is a sort of sacrament', and the earlier her mystical functions are accomplished in life the better, as a fully adequate one, and thinks rather that enforced competition for husbands—"hypergamy, or the law of superior marriage "—has tended to bring about the present deeply rooted system. His remarks merit quotation, as the opinion of one who has had opportunities altogether exceptional for arriving at sound conclusions.

"Enforced competition for husbands on the part of the higher groups, and the desire to imitate their superiors which animates the lower groups, combine to run up the prices of husbands in the upper classes, while the demand for wives by the men of the lower class, which ought by rights to produce equilibrium, is artificially restricted in its operation by the rule that they can, under no circumstances, marry a woman of the classes above their own. These men, therefore, are left very much out in the cold, and often do not get wives until late in life. An unmarried son does not disgrace the family, but there is no greater reproach than to have a daughter unmarried at the age of puberty. Husbands are bought for the girls, and the family gets its money's worth in social estimation. Bargains, however, must be taken when they are to be had; and no father dares run the risk of waiting till his daughter is physically mature. He is bound to be on the safe side, and therefore he marries her, child as she may be, whenever a good match offers.

> "Many hard things have been said of infant marriage, and the modern tendency is to assume that a population which countenances such a practice must be in a fair way towards great moral degradation, if not to ultimate extinction. Much of this criticism seems to me to be greatly exaggerated, and to be founded on considerable ignorance of the present conditions and future possibilities of Oriental life. In truth, excluding the poetical view that marriages are made in heaven, two working theories of the institution are at present in existence—one which leaves marriages to make themselves by the process of unrestricted courtship, and another which requires them to be made by the parents or guardians of the people who are to be married. The first, which we may perhaps call the system of selection, is accepted, and more or less acted up to, by all Western nations except those who follow the French custom of *manages de*

convenance. The second, a system of avowedly artificial selection, is in force, with few exceptions, throughout the East. For all Hindus, except the handful of *declassees* who have adopted more or less completely European ideas on the subject of marriage, and seem now to be on the high-road to form a new caste, the bare idea that a girl can have any voice in the selection of her husband is excluded by the operation of three inexorable sanctions—by the ordinances of the Hindu religion; by the general structure of the caste system; and by the general tone and condition of social life in India. Religion prescribes that, like the Roman bride of early days, a Hindu girl shall be given *(tradita in manum)* by her father into the power of her husband; caste complications demand that the ceremonial portion of the transfer shall be effected while she is still a child; while the character of society, the moral tone of the men, the seclusion of the women, the immemorial taboos and conventions of family etiquette render it impossible that she should be wooed and won like her European sister. To persons of a romantic turn of mind, the admission that infant marriage in some shape must be accepted as an ultimate fact of the Hindu social system will sound like a final abandonment of all hope of reform. But there is more to be said for the custom than appears at first sight. A moment's dispassionate consideration will show that if any sort of controlling authority is to make people's marriages for them, the earlier it commences and completes its operations the better. Where the choice of a husband must in any case be undertaken by the parents, it is clearly tempting Providence for them to defer it until their daughter has grown up, and may have formed an embarrassing attachment on her own account. As for love, that may come—and, from all one hears of Hindu unions, usually does come—as readily after marriage as before, provided that opportunities for falling in love

> with the wrong man are judiciously withheld. This may seem a cynical way of handling the matter, but it is the only way that accords with the lines of Oriental life as at present ordered, and it were folly to dream of making all things new."

Certainly, so far as my own experience went in my travels, the Indian, women are not dissatisfied with the present system; but the common reply, when one ventures that statement to superior persons who have not been in India, is, "Yes; but if they get a little education they at once want to alter it." On that point, however, I received some enlightenment at Bombay. I was invited, in a very prettily worded and nicely written note, to come with my hostess for the time being to tea with two young Mussulman women. We were received by them and the other women of their family in a beautifully furnished room, with a handsome Axminster carpet on the floors, and well-chosen English engravings on the walls, as well as pretty trifles of china and needlework decoratively employed. The two young ladies were exquisitely dressed in native costume, one being in white satin with a quantity of silver-embroidered gauze over her hair and shoulders, and the other in a cunning blending of pale pink and green. Both spoke English faultlessly, and I learnt that they had only recently been married, one being nearly twenty and the other over twenty-one; while I knew further that they were strictly *purdah* girls. It was too good a chance to lose, and I asked them if, as their husbands were both highly educated men, one holding a position under Government, and the other a barrister of rising practice, whether they would not now "break their *purdah*" .

> "Not at all," they replied together, and the older one continued, "Why should we ? You English ladies don't understand how very little we really lose by it. We see the men of our own families as freely as you can see

yours. Even our cousins of our own age we may meet; but where we differ is that you allow them to take what we should consider liberties, and, I believe, even kiss them. Now, a high-class girl is taught not to touch so much as the hand of a man, and that becomes simply a matter of habit as easy to preserve as any other good manners. European women don't think it hard that they may not sit on a man's knee, do they ? Well, we don't think it hard to keep at a little distance, and that is only a question, I think, of degree. Our husbands would willingly let us go out, but we have been taught all our lives that men other than they are as nothing to us; and you see we have not any inclination or desire to ride or drive or walk in the streets. We go to our family parties, and can see and receive all our women friends. I don't see what there is to be dissatisfied about. And so far," she continued, "I don't think you can call the working results of our system a failure. Take our own family, and we can carry our pedigree back for twenty generations—that means a great many daughters—but never has one of them discredited or dishonoured our women's fair name. Are there many European families who could say as much ?"

Of course, with the aristocracy of the Muslim race, marriages seldom take place outside their own circle, and I fancy it would upset some pet theories as to the results of continued intermarriage to trace the complications of blood-relationship in some of the high-class families of the northwest. If I speak here first of the Mahommedan marriage customs, it is because they vary much less than do those of the Hindus, and can therefore be more quickly dismissed. Where there are more sons than daughters in a family community it becomes necessary to seek an eligible *parti* from outside; but the utmost care is always exercised in this, and the closest scrutiny invariably made concerning the relative social status of both sides. I have already described the advantage that the thikra ceremony gives, and supposing that the child duly lives, it is generally about the age of ten that the mother of the prospective bridegroom makes formal proposal on his behalf. On this point, I may correct an erroneous impression concerning the usual age of the bridegroom. He is generally from five to eight years older than the bride in the ranks of all above the very poorest, so that when she can be taken to his own house he is generally from nineteen to twenty-two, against her thirteen to sixteen. In the case of ruling princes, one often finds them fully married as young as fifteen to seventeen; but the general tendency—doubtless largely influenced by the longer time required for a modern professional education—is, as with us, to raise considerably the average of the male marrying age. As a consequence perhaps of this fact, the young man's consent to his parents pursuing the customary preliminaries is now almost invariably asked by them directly or indirectly.

While she is alive, it is always the mother of the bridegroom who opens the negotiations, and she takes with her as many of her nearest relations as she can. It is seldom that she is not so sufficiently sure of her reception by the bride's family as to render this a merely formal step, but instances arise at times when a pushing or intriguing woman has secured the privileges of the thikra, and the girl's parents had other views as to her disposal. In such case there is often bitter feud, as the prejudices in favour of the old custom are very strong, and at the same time parents may have good reason for not desiring the offered suitor.

Supposing, however, that no opposition has been raised, the mother comes home triumphantly, and the preparations for *mangni,* or actual engagement, are at once begun. An auspicious day is carefully chosen, and one that is equally convenient to both families. It is incumbent on the bridegroom's parents to contribute largely to the feast that will be held at the house of the bride, as their own particular friends, as well as the relatives of their side, will participate in it, and their offerings, which consist generally of the choicest fruits in season and procurable, both fresh and dried, as dates, raisins, almonds, and nuts, are sent in large *bhwans* (trays, with closely fitting covers). The mere public announcement that such a marriage has been arranged suffices to constitute the betrothal, and between the young people themselves no formal ceremony takes place. When this, however, has been made, it is imperative etiquette that the bride and bridegroom shall not see one another. So intensely strong is this curious convention, that the young man's family can insist upon the match being broken off if he has caught a glimpse of his wife that is to be, and as it would be greatly to the disrepute of the contracting family for such a thing to occur, the utmost care is exercised as to the girl's seclusion in the zenana.

There her young mind is fed with ample details of what married life has in store for her. She, and all the older women of the household, watch eagerly for signs of physical development, and hail her attainment of womanhood as an event of great joy, which may be discussed without the slightest reticence. With the. Hindus the chief difference of preliminary detail is only that betrothal has probably taken place at an earlier age. Meantime both prepare their *trousseaux,* to be in readiness immediately that it may be required. Very beautiful indeed are some of the draperies that are put into these bridal outfits; and I recall a *sari* that I saw at Calcutta of *malmal,* the soft silk muslin of the Punjab, in a full rich shade of myrtle, only to be produced with indigo, and the native yellow dyes of *asbarg,* the flower of the Cabul larkspur, and *narsingar,* the sweet-scented blossom of one of the *nyctanthes.* The bordering was a subtle blending of orange and yellow, and the more misty hues of vermilion, into which each of the same dyes entered, and was a harmonious result that could never have been obtained with any mixtures of unallied anilines and chemicals.

During the years that, elapse between *mangni* and *shadi,* as the Mahommedans term the second part of the ceremony, presents of fruit and other things are continually passing between the contracting parties. On festival days the young performed by ladies professionally engaged for the purpose. Both bride and bridegroom wear the *sikra*—a floral garland from which a veil falls over the face—and with this on they are seated opposite to each other.

Thus seated, the *Kutam Majid,* or holy book, is brought before them with respectful reverence, and both their veils are raised. Then it is that the husband beholds his wife for the first time; but it is considered very bold and indecorous for the girl to lift her modestly bent head or to open her closed eyes at this time, and she thus remains, even when he, in survival of old ideas of marriage by capture, lifts her to carry her to the carriage, or *palki,* in which she is to be taken to his house. However' slight he may be, or whatever are her proportions, he is allowed no assistance of any kind in this. The returning procession is made yet more imposing by the addition to it of all the bride's presents, which are usually very numerous. The day after the marriage the bride is brought home to her parents' house for a short time, and the significant rejoicings and games of *chanthi* are held. She goes back, however, with her husband, and enters the zenana of his father's house, where for the first year or so of her married life she has many hard lessons of discipline and forbearance to learn.

The Hindu marriage customs differ in many essential points from those of the Mahommedan race, and great divergencies exist again between those of the various castes. Further variations there are still between the pure Aryans and the aboriginal tribes, even though, as in Orissa or on the Malabar coast, these may have accepted Hinduism either fully or with modifications. It would not be difficult to fill a whole book with these diverse ordinances, or to find reasons and explanations concerning most of them. It will, however, suffice if I describe a few of the most characteristic that came under my personal observation, and particularly interesting are those of the Brahmins, whether in well-known Eastern Bengal or upon the seldom-visited slopes of the Western Ghats.

Among the nine qualities which the Brahmanical statutes-ordain as essentials of right conduct, *avritti,* or the observance of legal marriage, is one. The ceremony has in consequence been hedged round with a vast amount of ritual, but, provided that a girl is wedded before she attains to womanhood, it does not much matter at what age her marriage takes place. After the preliminaries and mutual agreement between the contracting parties have been settled, the first step to be taken is the anointing of both the bride and bridegroom with turmeric. I believe that according to strict custom this should be done to the boy or young man first, and that some of the same preparation as he has used should be sent to the girl, unless he lives at too great a distance for this to reach her the same day. This has always been selected for astrological reasons, and it is essential that both be anointed upon it. Then begins a sequence of entertainments that last, according to the circumstances of the two families and their friends, from three days to a month, the rule being that a great dinner should be given, first by the parents of the young couple, and after that, that kinsfolk and acquaintance should arrange such .a series that neither eats again in their own house till the wedding takes place. The night previous to the wedding as many of the married women friends of both families as possible meet and eat together, and are given betel-leaves and areca-nut, in return for which hospitality they are expected to invoke prosperity and happiness for the pair to be wedded. A *sraddh,* or service of offering, is performed on the morning of the day on which the bridegroom will go in procession to the bride's house, and the favour of the household gods and the departed ancestors for three or four generations back is besought.

The *bar jutri,* or bridegroom's procession, sets out usually in the evening, and he takes with him a "best man," who, as a rule, is his younger brother and a mere boy. The women of the bride's family receive him with noisy shouts of "*Ulu, ulu!*'" (Joy, joy!), but he takes a place upon a raised dais called in Bengal a *masnad,* and waits until the moment arrives at which the ceremony can be proceeded with auspiciously. The first step in this is for the girl's father to take him into one of the inner rooms of the house, where he stands upon a board that has been smeared with rice-flour, symbolic of the plenty that may surround his steps; and water for washing his feet, and a syrup, into the composition of which honey enters largely, are offered to him, both of which he touches as sign of their acceptance.

Meantime, however, the women have their special usages, and the mother of the bride welcomes her future son-in-law by pouring some curds at his feet. The full ritual then gone through is called *satusi,* or, as we might render it, the seven lights of Hymen, and is extremely curious. Seven married women, all in festal attire, one of whom must be the bride's mother, unless she is a widow and so debarred from fulfilling any public function, in which case her place is taken by an aunt, each hold a torch of small twigs and cotton waste. The mother or the aunt leads the way, and bears upon her head a flat basket, round which are twenty-one small lights. Seven times round the bridegroom they walk, all of them assisting to cast the lights in the basket over his head, while water is sprinkled, and one of the number blows a conch-shell, the rest vociferating," *Ulu, ulu!*" This cry is continued by all of them, while the bride's mother (or aunt) touches the bridegroom's brow with an oddly heterogeneous collection of things, which include betel and areca nut, curds, sandal-wood, oil, a bit of clay from the Ganges, a looking-glass, and a cluster of plaintains. This ceremony, I am bound to say, I have not seen, and knowing the Brahmanical caste hatred for Europeans, I imagine that very few not of their own *jat* have done so. My information on this point has been derived from separate and reliable sources, however, and I give it without hesitation. The next step I believe is that the mother places a weaver's shuttle between the young man's hands, and binds him hand and foot to symbolize the fetters he has imposed upon himself, and he then indicates his humility in the situation by bleating like a sheep. There is another and perhaps prettier form, in which future happiness is indicated when she lays upon his lips a padlock and turns the key, so showing that the door of unkind speech has been closed.

A Brahmin bride wears red silk upon her wedding-day, and after these observances concerning the bridegroom have been carried out she is brought in seated upon a board by attendants, who circle seven times round the bridegroom. When she is set down before him, a large cloth is quickly spread over both for a few seconds, and in that moment is supposed to come to them the love that will last them for life. They then exchange garlands, and come out into more public gaze, after which there is little secrecy or mystery even in the highest caste rites.

The next stage is the *sampradan*, or the gift and its acceptance, in which the father of the girl, following the words recited by the priest present, offers her to the bridegroom, and his formula of reception runs, "Who gave her ? Love gave her. To whom did he give her ? To Love he gave her. Love is the giver: Love is the taker. Love pervades the ocean. With love I accept her. Love—may this also be thine." Presents are then exchanged, and the couple are escorted to the bridal chamber, a corner of her *sari* being knotted to his cloth, but it is a part of this item of the ceremony that a number of young women are already in the room, and it is their business to keep the wearied lad from obtaining any sleep for the rest of the night. Lastly comes the *kusandika,* observed among all the higher castes as the final and most binding portion of the whole ceremony. Fire, under priestly manipulation, is kindled from a sacred source, and *ghi* (clarified butter) poured upon it in offering. From it seven points are marked off, upon which the bride must tread, and, treading upon her heel in token of her whole subjection to him, follows the bridegroom reciting certain prescribed forms. Then the newly made wife changes her *gotra,* or family sign, for that of her husband, and the lad with his own hand makes a mark in vermilion upon the parting of her hair.' Three days after marriage the young people are laid upon a bed surrounded with flowers, and afterwards a final feast is given, for which the rice must have been prepared by the girl-bride. If the bridegroom's family eat this, it is a sign that they are satisfied that all ceremonial and caste observance had been properly regarded.

Among the Nambutiris, as the Brahmins of the Malabar coast are called, the early details involve a handsome dowry honestly paid in full by the girl's father. The bridegroom's procession and the feasting and first ceremonies are much the same as in Eastern India, but he carries also a bamboo staff in his right hand and has a thread tied round his right arm, while the bride holds a mirror and an arrow, and wears the sacred *tali,* or string, round her throat. This, with the Brahmins and higher-caste Hindus, and an iron bangle among the lower ones, is the usual equivalent of our wedding-ring, though the right to draw a line of vermilion down the parting of the hair is another outward and visible sign throughout India of marriage.

To proceed, however, with the Nambutiri rites, the father of the bride hands her with her dowry to her husband, the two take seven steps forward together, an offering is made, and as the procession leaves the house for that of the bridegroom he is bidden in set phrase to show her all kindness and consideration. Arrived here, there is further eating and drinking, and the pair are led by a priest to their own room, where a rug is laid on the floor with quantities of rice and paddy round it. The pair seat themselves on this, the priest goes out and locks the door, and then chants in a loud voice passages from the sacred books, which the bridegroom audibly follows. Then the wife has to serve her husband with his first meal, and the union is a completely valid one.

With the Hindus, however, whether of high or low caste, it is only in rare instances that the girl-bride goes to her husband's house until she has attained to full womanhood. Certain sub-sects and particularly devout families perform at this period of her life an office of purification known as *garbhadhan* or *punarbihaha,* or a kind of penance, varying in severity, but, so far as I can learn, usually consisting of seclusion from the rest of the family and a fasting diet of rice and *ghi,* all sweets being forbidden. Even the enlightened Parsees of Bombay have not overcome their racial prejudices as to a woman's occasional pollution and uncleanness, and isolate their girls at certain periods.

So much for high caste ceremonial, and a few words may now be spared for that of the lower orders and working folks, among whom *purdah* is not observed. The first and most important functionary in village or bazaar life is the *hajjam,* or barber, who knows to a nicety the circumstances of all his neighbours. The parents of the girl tell him they are looking for an eligible *parti* for her, and he, in the pride of his knowledge, names to them the two or three he has good reason to think would not be unfavourably inclined. He receives his instructions to negotiate in the matter, and goes to the parents of the bridegrooms in prospective to discuss it, and eventually decides which he considers in every way the most desirable alliance for both sides. Then the question of

Male, or bride's dowry, comes into consideration, though so various are the practices sanctioned by custom upon this point that it is almost impossible to lay down any hard and fast rules concerning them. With many of the non-Aryan but Hinduized tribes, for instance, the system of the bridegroom's paying a bride-price—a survival clearly of marriage by purchase—obtains ; notably among these I may mention the Doms, a large Dravidian caste; the Kols, a hard-working and industrious people, much employed in mining; and the Santals, a really interesting and very large jungle race; and in each of these the bridegroom pays to the girl's parents from three to ten rupees. With the last-named he has in addition, to present to her mother and both her grandmothers, if alive, a new *sari.*

By all, save the very lowest Hindus, it is deemed essential to the validity of the marriage that a Brahmin priest should be present. When the marriage has been brought about through the agency of the *hajjam,* he assists the priest in counting the bride's dowry, and this constitutes a part of the ceremonial. On the west coast, however, with the Kadu-pattars, who are a humble school-teaching caste, the barber is himself allowed to perform certain of the rites, though the *tali,* the symbol of marriage, is always with them tied by a near female relative of the bridegroom's.

On this Malabar coast the Nayars form one of the most interesting studies in racial characteristics to be found in British India, as they, almost alone, preserve in their present day customs evidences of the polyandry they formerly practised. Early history has something to say of them, since the Sheikh Zin-ud-din, somewhere after the middle of the sixteenth century, stated that it was customary for each woman to have from two to four men as husbands, and that these seldom quarrelled, while later, Hamilton, writing in 1727 his "New Account of the East Indies," observed that the husbands, who might not exceed twelve in number at once, "do agree very well, for they cohabit with her in their turns according to their priority of marriage, ten days more or less, according as they fix a term among themselves, and he that cohabits with her maintains her in all things necessary for his time, so that she is plentifully provided for by a constant circulation."

Now, as I saw these Nayars on the coast between Tellichery and on to somewhere beyond Cochin, they are a shy race, the women noticeable for their scanty clothing, and remarkable because even to this day the husband has no legal rights and responsibilities according to the tribal understanding of the law, which is merely undoubted custom, towards his wife or his children. In the early stages of the marriage rites there is little difference to be noted in those that one has seen in other parts of the dependency, neither does there, unless one has been warned of it, seem anything unusual in the tying of the tall round her neck. Yet she is not married to the man who has done this, and the mere fact that he has done it constitutes an insurmountable barrier to his becoming her husband in later life. He is merely an east-coast Brahmin, whose profession in life is to act a part in this pseudo-ceremony, and in return to take a fee for his services.

Still, by the strict technicalities of other castes, the girl is the wife of a plurality of husbands, for later on, and when she is of an age to decide for herself, she chooses a man whom she will wed. In the phrase employed to denote the short office of this comparatively civilized system of marriage she passes the door of good and of bad, and the contract is made by the mutual exchange of two pieces of cloth in the presence of kinsfolk and friends.

It is so common to think of Indian women as deprived of all voice in the choice of their husbands that I may go back again to Central Bengal to mention both the rites and the rights of the Santali and Kol women, whom I saw in the coal-mining district of Girideh.

The former tribe is divided into twelve septs, nearly all of which have passwords of their own, and marriage may not take place between two members of the same sept. The girls, who do not wed at a very early age, are allowed a certain choice of their own in the selection of their husbands. Two whom I saw, who were shortly to be married, were approaching sixteen years of age, and were fine, well-grown girls, who had no shyness in standing for the photograph I wished to make of them. Some of their marriage customs are curiously primitive survivals, and one of these is that while a price, as I have already stated—usually three rupees, with a new sari each to her mother and grandmothers—is paid for the bride, in the case of a widow who is permitted to re-marry only half that sum is asked. The argument on which this is based is that such ladies can only be regarded as borrowed, and each will have to be returned to her first husband in the next world, so that as the second one only enjoys her companionship temporarily, he is only to be expected to pay a reduced price for her. In what is known as a "bazaar-marriage," which, though quite binding, is only resorted to when the girl seems shy and "holding off," the young man dips his fingers into red paint or earth, and watches his opportunity when the young lady is out walking or shopping to make a mark upon her brow. He has, however, to run away at full speed to escape the thrashing that her male relations would administer to him for his audacity. If the girl declines to live with him she has to go through a ceremony of divorce, and I heard of one or two cases in which girls had been thus wedded out of spite in order to compel them to subject themselves to this indignity.

It should never be forgotten that the law nominally protects a girl until she has passed the age of twelve. In the absence, however, of a thorough system of birth registration, and in very many instances the existence of a superstitious unwillingness to state age correctly, it is always exceedingly difficult to ascertain what the true years of any native may be. Nor must the fact be overlooked that, with poor parents especially, it is advantageous to them to hand over their daughters to the custody of their husbands, and thus obtain relief from the cost, small even as it may be, of their maintenance. The Indian girl develops and ages very rapidly, and it is very rare to see a woman over thirty who is not wrinkled, wizened, and unlovely, either in exceeding skinniness or excessive *embonpoint*. The youngest instance of motherhood that I saw was a girl who had just passed her thirteenth birthday, when it happened to be one of the rare cases in which an age could be definitely fixed, and in her arms was a lusty five-months'-old infant. So far, however, from this being an "awful example" of the evils of the system, it was very much the reverse, for the girl-mother was tall, strong, and vigorous, nursing her child adequately, and looking in every sense the picture of robust animal health.

Sentimentality, and that insular habit of thought which decides that what is right in England is of necessity the only right course anywhere else in the world, has launched a big weight of prejudice against the system, which is not at all borne out, viewed in the dispassionate light of working results. If one half of the evils set down as associated with it were true, the Indian race must have been effete, if not extinct, generations ago. He would be regarded, however, as a rash man who ventured any doubts to-day as to the virility, fighting qualities, and capacities for enduring hard strain, of Ghurka or Sikh, Pathan or Rajput, even beside those "raw bhoys that don't know what a bullut manes, and wudn't care as they did," as no less an authority than Private Mulvaney says. In fact, with these fighting races marriage takes place very young, and the tradition concerning the last named is that even, if not now, at least until very recently, premature consummation was the rule and not the exception. Yet to see the stately carriage of the men, and the fine figures and swinging walk of the women, as one traverses Rajputana, as I did, from Jeypore to Ahmedabad and Bombay, gives one no inclinations support the approved paper theories. I hold no brief for child-marriage, and think it would undoubtedly be to the greater happiness of the girl in the long run to let her enjoy two or three years of light-hearted absence from care before she assumed the responsibilities of motherhood. Such, however, is not the view taken of it by Hindu or Muslim religion or custom, and I have tried to view the question as they do, and see the advantages they find in it—for it is idle to suppose that they would have maintained a system down so many of the centuries if it had not possessed certain recommendations in their eyes—rather than to look at it from the strictly European standpoint, and as a peg for all the critical fault-finding to be hung on. Meantime the advocates of Western "reforms" may take note of a tendency to raise the age of marriage among the thoughtful and educated of the two races. It is as it should be that the movement has started in two of the native States, namely, Mysore and Hyderabad. Not only will this have a swifter and deeper influence, coming from such quarters, but with the smouldering ashes of hatred buried darkly, and seldom perceived, as they are against the British rule, any effort in this direction, initiated from our side, would have been undoubtedly met by more than covert hostility. In both these States the age of marriage has been placed at fourteen. In Hyderabad it is true that, by safe-guarding clauses which nullify one another, the act virtually reads: "You shall not marry your girls younger than fourteen, unless your family wants to do so, and then you may." But the point to be noted with satisfaction is that the germ of an idea is there, that excessively early marriage may not be an unmixed good, and that it should be discouraged rather than fostered.

Of, the Parsees and their marriage customs there is not much to be written. Zoroastrian ethics recommends marriage on the ground that wedded life is more likely to be happy than unwedded, and the encouragement of matrimony is a meritorious act. Consequently several rich Parsees have founded endowment funds for the purpose of providing poor but deserving girls with *dots,* and it is unusual to find unmarried women in this community. Fifteen is the lowest age at which a girl may marry; but to find one actually wedded at this period is exceedingly rare, and twenty to twenty-five is the general age. As a result the Parsee women retain their good looks and graceful carriage far longer than those by whom they are surrounded.

The Parsee marriage ceremonial is in itself simple and impressive, though it is usually, even among the humblest, made the occasion of much pretty pageantry. The bridegroom is escorted by a bevy of the bride's girl friends, who wear their most charming saris, and carry flowers from his house to that of the bride, or wherever the rite is to be performed. From him they receive gifts, which also they present, and make certain offerings of rice, rose-water, and other symbolic things, while his own gifts to the bride, of a new sari and articles of household use, are brought in on flower-decked trays and laid down in all due formality before the assembled company. Both bride and bridegroom receive the benedictions and good wishes of their parents, and are then taken to a raised dais, which has been decorated with all the resources of flowers, gold paper, and coloured drapings at command. The service is conducted by two priests, who recite from memory several long chapters and prayers, based upon a verse in the *Gatha,* which runs: "I say these words to you marrying brides and to you bridegrooms. Impress them in your minds. May you twain enjoy the life of good mind by following the laws of religion. Let each of you clothe the other with righteousness, because then assuredly there will be a happy life for you." Between each section of the service rice is cast towards the young couple, to signify plenty and prosperity; but, with the adoption of European ideas, the fashionable tendency of the Parsees is to abbreviate and simplify the service as far as possible. It is followed by a dinner, at which the newly-married couple are present; and they are generally accompanied to their future home by a number of their friends, who continue their merry-making far into the night.

●●

6

Widow-Remarriage and Divorce

"Alone upon the housetops to the north I turn and watch the lightning in the sky; The glamour of thy footsteps in the north ; Come back to me, beloved, or I die.

"Below my feet, the still bazaar is laid, Far, far below, the weary camels lie ; The camels and the captives of thy raid; Come back to me, beloved, or I die.

"My father's wife is old and harsh with years, And drudge of all my father's house and I ; My bread is sorrow and my drink is tears;

Come back to me, beloved, or I idie." *The Love Song of Har Dyal* (Eudyard Kipling's Version).

There is nothing perhaps that gives a thoughtful observer in India a more convincing sign of the utter superficiality of what European influences have effected in regard to native Hindu social customs and habits, than the attitude that they maintain towards the remarriage of widows. Their helpless, hopeless lot has been the theme of more eloquence at Exeter Hall, and upon missionary platforms, than perhaps any other single aspect of the whole evangelizing field. The strong arm of legislation has been evoked upon their behalf, and widow-marriage has been legalized. Schools and educational establishments have been founded for them upon the theory that if they were competent to earn a living, the hardness of their fate would be mitigated, and perhaps as independent and self-respecting members of society they might even be sought in marriage after all. A pen so weighty and unsentimental as that of Professor Max Muller has been enlisted upon behalf of "that strange product of India, and of India only, the child-widows, children who are formally married to elderly men belonging to good families, who often never see their husbands, but who, when their husbands die, are doomed for life to an existence which in the best cases is one of joyless drudgery, excluding all hope of renewed happiness, and fully accounting for the eagerness of Indian widows in former times to die on the same pile with their husbands, or, as the law does no longer allow this, to end their life by slow starvation, or by jumping into a well."

Nothing that public opinion at home or in high official circles in India could do towards modifying the deep-rooted rigours of the system was left unattempted, yet what are the facts to-day ? Simply this, that not only have we failed to amend matters in the slightest degree, but there is to be noted an even growing prejudice against widow-remarriage.

To understand this fact, for fact it is, and borne out by statistics as well as observation, one must know that the prohibition of widow-marriage is a sign of social position and good caste. Among the Brahmins it is completely interdicted, and the Rajputs, with their exceeding jealousy of their women, do not allow it under any circumstances. But under the greater prosperity and the more affluent conditions which settled rule has given to the humbler working orders, these latter can now indulge in the luxury of imitating those above them, instead of as of yore, regarding their examples as impossible of realization. It is this prohibition that evidently appealed to them as a supremely desirable virtue; for it is almost, if not the very first of the aristocratic customs that they adopt, just as I believe they would go back to the practice of suti were they left to themselves. The heartiest burst of approval that I heard in a theatre in India, was when a young woman on the stage, believing her husband to be dead, said, in a fine burst of well-acted grief, that she would follow him through the funeral pyre, a sentiment which her audience evidently thought the most praiseworthy she could have uttered.

As showing, however, how essentially the antipathy to remarriage exists in Hinduism, it is remarkable that it is not only the poor of the orthodox creed who take advantage of bettered circumstances to enforce it, but the aboriginal and semi-aboriginal tribes, as they rise in social status, make it a matter of principle. My inquiries in Bengal brought me a good deal of curious information upon this point. Professor Max Muller has succinctly laid down the theory of the subject, as laid down in the Mahabharata, by saying that "a woman in India always belongs to somebody. She cannot exist by herself. In her youth, it is said, she belongs to her father; if her father dies, to her brother; if she is married, to her husband; if her husband dies, to his family."

Mr. Risley, whom I have already cited as the most outspoken and unconventional authority upon the "true inwardness" of native opinion and custom, points out that the doctrine of spiritual benefit requires her to devote her life to the performance of his sraddh, while the very character of the Brahmanical marriage-rites in themselves constitute a technical barrier. "That ceremony being regarded as a sacrament ordained for the purification of women, and its essential portion being the gift of the woman by her father to her husband, the effect of the gift is to transfer her from her own *gotra,* or exogamous group, into that of her husband's."

Further evidence on this point by an orthodox Hindu gentleman, in the inquiries set on foot by Government as to infant marriage and enforced widowhood, is contained in this argument. "But if her father is out of the question, it may surely be said that she may give herself in marriage. This, though, she cannot do, because she never had anything like disposal of herself. When young she was given away, so the ownership over her, vested then in the father, was transferred by a solemn religious act to the husband, and he being no more, there is no one to give her; and since Hindu marriage must take the form of a religious gift, her marriage becomes impossible."

It becomes, therefore, quite clear by what process of reasoning a tribe, as it emerges from servility and degradation into full-blown Hinduism, raises the importance of this doctrine, even as the Church itself gave to marriage a mystical symbolism to lift it from a mere union of the flesh for the gratification of the passions. Only to mention a few of the instances of sub-castes or tribes who within recent years have assumed this badge of respectability, may be named the Kapalis, who are cultivators of jute and weavers of canvas and matting; the Chandals, of whom one sees much on the cruise along the turbid waters of the Hughli, where they own boats of the strangest variations upon the strict lines of naval architecture that it seems possible to construct.

The name of Chandal has always been associated since the days of Manu with "the vilest of mankind," and it is not surprising, therefore, that they endeavour to ignore their low origin and, when they migrate into new districts, to find fresh titles and callings. They may be found as grass-cutters, potters, carpenters, and pedlars, and as they drift into these vocations, they endeavour to assimilate its more exclusive observances. With them, the prohibition of remarriage has come into practice within the last generation, as it is also doing with the Rajwars who are scattered throughout Chota Nagpur, Western Bengal, and the tributary states, even as far as Darjeeling and Chittagong. These, however, are innovating gently, and began by the interdiction of the marriage of widows with children. The *dhobis,* or washermen, socially almost the lowest of all castes throughout the dependency, in that, as Mr. Lesfield says, "no Hindu, even of the lowest caste, will wash his own clothes, and so the *dhobi* has been formed into a caste which shall bear the impurities of all," are also now forbidding remarriage, and among the Kurmis of Upper India, the custom is gradually coming into effect.

Other tribes also, without placing a stringent veto upon it, are bending to the principle involved by laying down who a widow may marry. This is almost invariably a younger brother of the late husband, wherever it is sanctioned, and it is at least a little curious to find so marked an agreement on the part of the aboriginal and Dravidian peoples, who alone permit it, with ancient Jewish ordinances. With the Santals, Kols, and Oraons, though theoretically perfect freedom of remarriage exists, it is "good form" to make choice of this kinsman, but the first named are among the few tribes of India, like the Nayars of the Malabar coast, whose customs retain any evidences of former polyandric practices. Whether a younger brother of the late husband has already a wife or not, he can, by mutual agreement, wed the widow.

But among the castes which do not absolutely forbid widow-remarriage there exists a form, legal and valid in all respects, known in Bengal as the *Sanga,* and in other parts as the *Sagai* rites. Much of the ceremonial of a girl's wedding is dispensed with, the pacing round the sacred fire being invariably omitted, and the whole observance often resolving itself into no more than the husband's marking the bride's brow with red lead. Even, however, where a greater amount than this enters into the proceedings, it is all on the bridegroom's side, and though he may give feasts and entertain his friends, the bride herself has no part in them, nor does she even appear at the one on the eve of her marriage in her own relations' house. She is sought at dead of night by him in her own room, and before two or three of her closest female relatives he puts the vermilion or some similarly sticky red substance upon the parting of her hair. Among the Santals this is varied by marking a flower and placing that in her hair.

In one very strange form of marriage practised by this non-Aryan people it is the woman who takes the initiative, and if she finds her affections unrequited, she takes a vessel containing rice-beer, enters the man's house, and sits down. The beer shows the object of her visit, and if the women of the house do not favour her intention they may resort to any means short of physical force or personal violence, which are forbidden by custom, to eject her. They may burn red pepper on the fire, drench her with cold water, or apply the most odious names to her; but if she remains passive for two or three hours she has accomplished her purpose—the marriage cannot be set aside. Only a few weeks before my visit to the coal-mining district, the village communities of Girideh were much perturbed over a case in which a widow had thus secured a husband who was very far from reciprocating her attachment. Councils were called, and innumerable palavers held; but no precedent for ignoring such a wedding could be found, till at last an astute young Christian Santal, of rather better education than some, suggested that this form of marriage could only be gone through by a girl, and there was no other known instance of a widow practising it. The loophole of excuse was thankfully accepted, and the designing widow endured her discomfort for nothing.

In the case of a child-bride there is always a certain amount of ceremony connected with the *rukhsati,* or home-taking of the bride, but this, in the case of a widow, is not performed.

There is one respect, and perhaps one only, in which the Hindu widow stands at an advantage to her prototype in

Europe, and that is, that if she has had children, the burden of their support falls upon their father's family. It is only in rare instances that any attempt is made to evade this responsibility, even where the widow marries again, but should they accompany her to her new home, they are debarred from participation as members of the family in the acts of domestic worship.

Lastly, in this connection, is to be considered the attitude taken up by the Hindu community in general upon the question, apart from the technically religious difficulty to which: I have before referred. It is due I think chiefly to the intense competition which exists in the highest castes for eligible husbands, and a fear of increasing that by rendering another and somewhat large class available for marriage. In India, as almost everywhere else, women are numerically preponderant. There are no vocations for them sufficient to make any appreciable difference in the situation, nor are they, like their sisters of the West, able to give their energies to, and find even full happiness in the unmarried state. The education of the men must in due course affect their views upon the subject, but it will be a very gradual work to effect any change in marriage habits, for the superficial reformer, who introduces bills to raise the age of marriage or to legalize widow-remarriage, does not see that these are more than merely social customs to be dealt with by legislation. They are vital elements of religion itself, and to attempt to tamper with them is to lay rough hands upon the heritage of the centuries, and principles that are bound up with all that is most sacred in a Hindu's" faith. If ever there was a system over which the plea that patience might have her perfect work was specially to be urged, it is the social order of India.

Meantime, here and there, a little step forward in improving the status of the widows is made. At present I fear that the training of them to be school-teachers is too closely identified with the missionary movement for it to be regarded as standing upon a satisfactory basis, from the point of view of future native development. One would rather see the humblest indigenous effort of this kind made than the most magnificent of buildings reared by the subscriptions of the generously disposed in England, since the one would indicate a genuine desire, while the other, however nobly intentioned, has all the time an artificial position in the general economy. Some few widows are taking up the work of nursing, though this involves an independence of caste prejudices that at present is very far from general. It is possible, however, that in less wealthy caste families the recommendations of an independent and remunerative livelihood may outweigh these inherent objections, and so far as an effort has been made in this direction, I should be inclined to regard the outlook as certainly promising. A few also, possessing means of their own, have taken up medical studies, and though it may be but a day of small things, such beginnings are not to be despised.

With the Mahommedans there is not the slightest objection to the remarriage of widows, as indeed one would expect, when one remembers that the favourite wife of the prophet himself had been previously wedded. In the case of a young widow, all reasonable effort is made by her family to find her another husband, and this fact should not be forgotten in any attempt to appreciate the degree in which the prohibition of widow-remarriage presses upon the population. Again, with the Parsees, there is a like independence, and in this charitable community there are many institutions and funds for the help of those left without a bread-winner. It is argued, without I believe any reliable statistical information, that an unduly large proportion of Hindu widows are driven to prostitution. This is a statement that in the absence of really convincing inquiries should only, I think, be taken with extreme reservation, for two reasons. The first is the tendency of caste—in some respects quite as much the safeguard as the curse of India. Now, with the long-cultivated habits of thought among the people that a potter's son shall be a potter, and that it would be highly unbecoming for a potter to turn his attention to basket-making, this calling is itself a caste which is greatly against those not of it joining themselves to it. The second is family pride, which would prevent it; and even in the instances where the girl-widow would get more kicks than halfpence as her share, there would be, for the credit of the name, care exercised to prevent her thus dishonouring the reputation of her late husband's kith and kin. To quote Professor Max Muller once more, "Who would deny that there are thousands of well-conducted families in India in which the young widow of any member of the family is treated with respect and kindness—nay, with a mixture of pity and reverence ? No doubt they are made to work, and in many cases the work, which was formerly done by them without demur, appears now, particularly if they have received a better education, irksome and degrading to many of them. To say that all widows, and more particularly all" child-widows, are ill-treated by relatives, or encouraged to lead a disreputable life, is certainly a falsehood, and a falsehood that could find no credence amongst people acquainted with the true Indian character, and with the very strong family feeling that prevails among the better classes."

Speaking broadly upon the subject of divorce, it may be said only to be allowed by those who permit the remarriage of widows. The view commonly obtains that a vast amount of immorality and intrigue is fostered by the zenana system, but I am not at all prepared myself to endorse this hastily-passed verdict as a fair one towards the average standard of native female rectitude. The zenana system *per se* is, I take it, rather a survival in idea of the protection that men gave to their women-folk in days when every man's hand was against his neighbour's, and a woman was quite lawful prey to her captors. Men have inherited a tendency of mind which leads them to mistrust one another's honour and good faith where women are concerned, and this I think is more the basis of the theory of rigorous *purdah nashin* than a fear of infidelity on the part of the women themselves. It is at least a fact, that while a native gentleman will talk freely about the women of his family to English ladies, and admit them gladly enough to the zenana, he would regard it as a personal insult for even an English gentleman to make the slightest inquiry upon the subject. No man, according to strict native idea, has any legitimate right to desire information concerning another man's wife, daughter, or sister, and if he seeks it the inference is that he has unlawful reasons for doing so.

Several causes contribute towards maintaining in practice a very fair level of feminine morality. To say that the lack of opportunity is a factor of leading importance in the result may be taken to imply that, were the conventions of seclusion relaxed, there would be a revolt against chastity; but this is, I think, a very unfounded and unworthy conclusion to draw. I am quite certain that if all present zenana restrictions were withdrawn, the Indian female population would stand woman for woman upon quite as high a platform as ourselves in this direction. What I mean to convey is that women live their lives so closely under one another's ken, that there is not the possibility for anything like a widespread laxity to exist. Where women of varying ages, tempers, and ambitions are living together, whatever they may do in annoying one another over petty spites and jealousies, it becomes a certainty that neither will venture on a course that would give all by whom she was surrounded the most powerful handle of all against her. No punishment is thought too brutal for unfaithfulness, and of this fact the women are well aware. I have myself seen instances, especially in the North-west Provinces, where a husband has cut off the nose of his wife, not even upon actual proof, but upon mere suspicion. Hands are sometimes cut off, and other horrible forms of mutilation are resorted to, while every judge or chief magistrate can tell of cases in which actual torture, ending even in death, has been practised. The woman, robbed of her fair looks, is ruthlessly cast out. A living she may find if she can, for she is branded with a mark more indelible than the Scarlet Letter itself, and alms that would not be withheld from the most impudent of self-asserting "holy men" are denied her.

It follows, therefore, that in the higher castes divorce by law is not much sought. The Rajputs summarily dismiss a woman guilty of adultery from being even a member of the caste, though in cases of incompatibility of temper they allow a couple to separate, each professing to regard the other as a parent. The wife then goes back to her parents, and the husband takes to himself another spouse. A somewhat similar custom exists among the Santals, where the pair, who for any reason of misbehaviour or personal interests desire to separate, upset a jar of water and tear in half three leaves of the Sa'l tree in the presence of their neighbours, saying as they do so, "Now become we to one another even as brother and sister."

Another notable variation is to be noted among the Tharus, a Himalayan hill tribe, who, like almost all the Nepaulese folk, view marriage with extreme laxity, and permit divorce upon almost any pretext. Mr. Nesfield, who has pursued a close investigation into the manners and habits of Upper India, has shown at length that such women with them may marry again by the same rites as widows, and the designation of *urari,* or "selected," is applied to such unions, to distinguish them from the *byalir,* or originally made matches with girls. There is, however, a precedence of respectability about the latter in their favour. A *urari* wife is not accepted in a family unless the chief relations have accorded their consent to the marriage, which they signify by holding a special ceremony called *bhatana;* but if this is withheld, she is simply regarded as the man's mistress, and he cannot take cooked food or water from her hands without lowering himself in social standing.

Most curious of all, however, are the divorce proceedings of the *Nambutiris* or Vedic Brahmins of the Malabar coast. "Western India is now the least-visited part of the great dependency, and of the characteristics of its people perhaps less is known than of any others of the population. But they possess in Mr. W. Logan one of the most sympathetic and erudite historiographers of all India. His account of the whole conduct of a matrimonial cause is so full of detail, and the official report in which it appeared is so inaccessible to the vast majority of English readers that I make no apology for quoting it in full, long as it is.

> "When a woman is suspected by her own kinsmen or by neighbouring Brahmans of having been guilty of light conduct, she is, under pain of excommunication of all her kinsmen, placed under restraint. The maidservant *(dasi,* or *veshali),* who is indispensable to every Nambutiri family, if not to every individual female thereof, is then interrogated, and if she should criminate her mistress, the latter is forthwith separated, and a watch set upon her. When the family can find a suitable house for the purpose, the *sadhanam* (the thing, or article, or subject, as the suspected person is called) is. removed to it; otherwise she is kept in the family house, the other members finding temporary accommodation elsewhere. After further examination of the maidservant, authority is granted in writing to the local *smart/id (e.g.* president of the assembly at which caste offences are tried), who in turn calls together the usual number of *mimamsakas* (persons skilled in the law)."
>
> "They assemble at some convenient spot, generally in a temple not far from the spot where the accused may be. All who are interested in the proceedings are permitted

to be present. Order is preserved by an officer deputed by the chief for the purpose, and he stands near the smartha and members of the tribunal. The only other member is a Nambutiri, called the agakkoyma, whose duties will be described presently."

"When all is ready, the chief's warrant is first read out, and the accused's whereabouts ascertained."

"The smartha, accompanied by the officer on guard and the agakkoyma, next proceeds to the accused's house; the officer on guard remains outside, while the others enter. At the entrance, however, they are met by the maidservant, who up to this time has never lost sight of the accused, and who prevents the men from entering. In feigned ignorance of the cause of being thus stopped, the smartha demands an explanation, and is told that a certain person is in the room. The smartha demands more information, and is told that the person is no other than such and such a lady, the daughter or sister or mother (as the case may be) of such and such a Nambutiri, of such and such an illam. The smartha expresses profound surprise at the idea of the lady being where she is, and again demands an explanation."

"Here begins the trial proper. The accused, who is still strictly *gosha,* is questioned through the medium of the maid, and she is made to admit that there is a charge against her. This is the first point to be gained, for nothing further can be done in the matter until the accused herself has made the admission."

"This point, however, is not very easily gained at times, and the smartha has often to appeal to her own feelings and knowledge of the world, and asks her to recollect how unlikely it would be that a Nambutiri female of her position should be turned out of her parents' house and placed where she then was unless there was some cause for it."

"In the majority of cases, this preliminary stage is got over with little trouble, and is considered a fair day's work for the first day."

"The smartha and his colleagues then return to the assembly, and the former relates in minute detail all that has happened since he left the conclave. The agakkoyma's task is to see that the version is faithful. He is not at liberty to speak; but whenever he thinks the smartha has made a mistake as to what happened, he removes from his shoulders and lays on the ground a piece of cloth as a sign for the smartha to brush up his memory. The latter takes the hint, and tries to correct himself. If he succeeds, the agakkoyma's cloth is replaced upon his shoulders; but if not, the smartha is obliged to go back to the accused, and obtain what information is required."

"When the day's proceedings are finished, the members of the tribunal are sumptuously entertained by the accused's kinsmen, and this continues to be done as long as the inquiry lasts. A trial sometimes lasts several years, the tribunal meeting occasionally, and the accused's kinsmen being obliged to entertain the members and any other Nambutiris present on each occasion, while the kinsmen themselves are temporarily cut off from intercourse with other Brahmans pending the result of the trial, and all *sraddhas* (sacrifices to benefit the souls of deceased ancestors) are stopped. The reason for this is that until the woman is found guilty or not, and until it is ascertained when the sin was committed, they cannot, owing to the probability that they have unwittingly associated with her after her disgrace, be admitted into society until they have performed the expiatory ceremony."

"The tribunal continues its sittings as long as may be necessary; that is, until either the accused confesses and is convicted or her innocence is established. "No verdict of guilty can" be given against her except on her own confession. "No amount of evidence is sufficient."

"In former days, when the servant accused her mistress, and there was other evidence forthcoming, but the accused did not confess, various modes of torture were had recourse to extort a confession, such as rolling her up in a piece of matting and letting the bundle fall from the roof to the courtyard below. This was done by women. At other times live rat-snakes and other vermin were turned into the room beside her, and even, in certain cases, cobras, and it is said that if, after having been with the cobra a certain length of time, and unhurt, the fact was accepted as conclusive evidence of innocence."

"In cases where the accused offers to confess, she is cross-examined and re-examined very minutely as to time, place, person, circumstances, etc., but the name of the adulterer is withheld (though it may be known to all) to the very last. Sometimes a long list of persons is given, and similarly treated."

"Innocent persons are sometimes named, and have to purchase impunity at great expense. In one case a woman, who had indicated several persons, was so annoyed by the continual 'Who else ? Who else ?' of the zealous scribe who was taking down the details, that she at last, to his intense astonishment, pointed to himself as one of them, and backed it up by sundry alleged facts."

"The persons accused by the woman are never permitted to disprove the charges against them, but the woman herself is closely cross-examined, and the probabilities are carefully weighed. And every co-defendant, except the one who, according to the woman's own statement, was the first to lead her astray, has a right to be admitted to the boiling oil, as administered in the temple of Sachindram in Travancore. If his hand is burnt, he is guilty; if it comes out clean, he is innocent. Money goes a long way towards a favourable issue in these ordeals."

"The tribunal meets at the accused's temporary house, after she has admitted that she is where she is because there is a charge against her. She remains in a room or behind a big umbrella, unseen by the members of the tribunal, and the examination is conducted by the smartha. A profound silence is observed by all present except the smartha, and he alone puts such questions as have been arranged beforehand by the members of the tribunal."

"Sometimes the greatest difficulty is experienced in getting her to confess; but this is usually brought about by the novelty of the situation, the scanty food, the protracted and fatiguing examination, and the entreaties of her relatives, who are being ruined, and by the expostulations and promises of the smartha, who tells her it is best to confess and repent, and promises to get the chief to take care of her, and comfortably house her on the bank of some sacred stream, where she may end her days in prayer and repentance. The solemnity of the proceedings, too, has its-effect. And the family often come forward, offering her a large share of the family property if she will only confess and allow the trial to end."

"When by these means the woman has once been induced to make a confession of her weakness, everything becomes easy. Hitherto strictly *goslia,* she is now asked to come out of the room, or lay aside her umbrella, and to be seated before the smartha and the tribunal. She sometimes even takes betel-nut in their presence."

"When the trial is finished, a night (night-time seems to be essential for this part of the trial) is set apart for pronouncing sentence, or, as it is called, 'for declaring the true frame, figure, or aspect of the matter.' It takes place in the presence of the local chieftain who ordered the trial. A" faithful and most minutely detailed account of all the circumstances is given by the smartha, who winds up with the statement that his servant will name the adulterer or adulteress. Thereupon the man comes forward, steps on to a low stool, and proclaims the name or names."

"This duty is invariably performed by a man of the Pattar caste, as it is essential that he should be a Brahman, and as no Canarese Brahman would do it for love or money, a needy Pattar is found, and paid handsomely for doing it. Directly he has performed the duty, he proceeds to the nearest tank to immerse his whole body, and so wash away the sin he has contracted."

"The next proceeding, which formally deprives the accused woman of all her caste privileges, is called the *keik-kottal*, or hand-clapping ceremony. The large Palmyra palm-leaf umbrella, with which all Nambutiri females conceal themselves in their walks abroad, is with them the outward sign of chastity. The sentence of excommunication is passed by the smartha in the woman's presence, and thereupon her umbrella is formally taken from her by a Nayar of a certain pollution-removing" caste. With much clapping of hands from the assembly, she is then instantly driven forth from her temporary quarters, and all her family ties are broken. Her kinsmen perform certain rites, and cut her off from relationship. She becomes to them in future even less than if she had died. Indeed, if she happens to die in the course of the inquiry, the proceedings go on as if she were still alive, and they are formally brought to a conclusion in the usual manner, by a verdict of guilty or of acquittal against the men implicated."

"The woman thus driven out goes where she likes. Some are recognized by their seducers; some become prostitutes ; not a few are taken as wives by the chettis of Calicut. A few find homes in institutions specially endowed to receive them."

"These last-named institutions are of a peculiar character. In one of the best-known of them, the members have baronial powers, and keep up a sort of baronial state, with two hundred Nayar followers. The members of this are recognized as of the Tiyan, or toddy-drawer caste; and the sons of the *machchiyars* (female inmates) become in turn *mannanars* (or barons). The women take husbands from among the Tiyan community. The women who are sent to this one are those convicted of illicit intercourse with men of the Tiyan or of superior castes. If the connection has been with men of lower caste than the Tiyan, the women are sent to another institution called Kutira Mala, deep in the jungles of the western ghats."

"Following on the hand-clapping ceremony comes the feast of purification given by the accused's people, at which, for the first time since the trial commenced, the relatives of the accused woman are permitted to eat in company with their caste fellows, and with this feast, which is partaken of by every Nambutiri who cares to attend, the troubles of the family come to an end."

"Apart altogether from the scandals which are thus dragged into the light, it is a very serious matter for a family to have to incur the expenses of such an inquiry, for the cost rarely comes to less than one thousand rupees, and has been known to amount to as much as

> twelve thousand rupees. Nothing but the dread of being deprived of their caste privileges by the general body of their community would induce a family to incur the odium and expense of such a trial, and this feeling prompts them unhesitatingly to cast out their erring members."

The side lights upon the inner prejudices and rigours of caste conventions thus revealed are instructive, and the severity of punishment meted out to an erring woman is distinctly against the unfair theory that lapses of morality are generally condoned. The procedure of supposing the woman to be guilty until she can prove her innocence, is the reverse of our own basic ideas of justice, but she is at least given opportunities, and is certainly not condemned unheard.

Concerning the Mahommedan practices and customs of divorce, popular knowledge is, I find, singularly scanty, and I have been at some pains to ascertain what these are. I am indebted to Mr. Syed Abdul Majjid Shah, of an old and honourable Mussulman family of Hyderabad, and himself a barrister, for the most reliable information on the subject, which I give as I received it from him.

> "Divorce is allowed in the religion of Islam, but only under stringent conditions."

> "All recorded sayings of the prophet show that he looked upon any system of divorce with extreme disapproval, and considered that any laxity in the binding nature of the marriage oath was calculated to undermine the foundations of society. He has repeatedly declared that nothing could be more displeasing in the sight of God than divorce. He laid down for aggrieved persons the distinct and separate periods at which they ought to make special efforts to become reconciled, and renew their conjugal intercourse; but should all endeavours in

this direction prove unsuccessful, after a third and final attempt, a decree of separation could be pronounced. In cases of conjugal disputes he recommended that arbiters should be chosen on both sides, to endeavour to effect a reconciliation."

"According to the Muslim legists, the wife also is entitled to demand a separation on the grounds of ill-usage, the withholding of due and proper means of maintenance, and certain other causes. The kazi (the Mahommedan judge) is empowered to decree separation if the facts are established. In every case in which the proceedings for divorce are instituted by the husband, he has to give up to the wife everything he settled upon her at her marriage. This deterring influence against mere caprice, the frequency of the admonitions in the Koran against separation, and the reiterated recommendations to heal quarrels by private reconciliation, show how sacred was the marriage tie in the eyes of the Arab legislator, as extracts such as this prove: 'And if ye fear even a breach between them (man and wife), then send ye a judge chosen from his family, and a judge chosen from her family, that peace be maintained,' etc."

"As far as I am aware of divorce in practice, it is exceedingly rare; and the only case indeed that I can remember was one of a Mahommedan servant to a missionary, who, although he was married already, fell in love with a beautiful but low-caste Hindu widow, whom he induced to become a member of his own faith and then married. Some time elapsed before the missionary discovered the affair, and the sahib then told his servant that if he did not separate from the woman, he would at once dismiss him, and this, under pressure of his master, he consented to do."

"This, as my own experience alone, might perhaps be of little worth, but to support my statement I will quote what Mr. Justice Ameer Ali says: 'As regards divorce, speaking from a somewhat extensive experience of this province (Bengal), which alone contains nearly twenty-two millions of Mussulmans, I know of only half a dozen cases occurring within the space of twenty-five years among the respectable classes, one of which, however, emanated from the wife. In all these cases there were faults on both sides.' "

"The language on the subject that I have heard often upon missionary platforms is not even decent enough to refer to. It is sufficient, though, for me to say that there is not the slightest foundation for the slander that I have more than once heard from missionary lips, that a Muslim can divorce his wife by repeating the word 'talag' three times!"

●●

7

Female Life in Field and Factory

" Sing, Gunga! to the millstone
It helps the wheel 1mm, Blithesome heart and willing elbows
Make the fine meal come.
Handfuls three
For you and for me,
Now it falls white,
Good stones bite! Drive it round and round, my Gunga,
Sing soft to the stone Better corn and churrak-working
Than idleness and none."

From the Sanscrit.

The true economic position of woman in India has generally been judged under the dazzling glamour of a cloud of sentiment. The" bare suggestion of working for three half-pence or two pence a day has sent well-meaning enthusiasts into frenzies, they have drawn imaginary pictures of ryots' grievances, they have bidden us think of all capitalists, whether British or native, as so many grinding slave-drivers, against whom no legislation could be too severely aimed, and in short the general idea that has been fostered has been that life among the Indian working classes, and to their women in particular, is simply the hardest work and semi- starvation. All qualifications as to differing standards of comfort and domestic surroundings are ignored, but when these are taken into consideration, and the situation of labour studied dispassionately, I am very far from being prepared to admit that the average Indian woman has any cause to envy her European sister.

Let me take two extreme cases. The Englishwoman in my mind, whom I have actually seen, is a woman aged before her time (for, relatively, child-marriage exists in our own country) and burdened with two or three young children to support. She lived in the East End of London, occupying one small room up a steep and rickety flight of stairs, for which she paid two shillings a week, and considered herself fortunate in being able to earn regularly five shillings and sixpence a week in a cardboard-box factory. And there are thousands of women in London whose weekly wage is not only no more, but often considerably less, as must be the case when matchbox-making is paid at the rate of twopence-halfpenny a gross, the workers finding their own paste, or mantles with elaborate trimming at sixpence each. Out of wages as scanty as these, the Englishwoman in winter must find fuel enough to keep something of the cruelly penetrating fog and frost out of her poor apartment; her food, even in its elementary simplicity of tea and bread, is to be bought; her own and her children's clothes and boots have to be provided, some furniture and bedding are a necessity—yet the slender pittance must suffice to purchase all. Then turn we to the other instance—a poor widow whom I saw at Berhampore. With industrious labour she could earn at reeling the pierced cocoons of silk from half to three quarters of an anna a day, which far more than sufficed for the simple diet of rice, grain, and vegetables which satisfied her. There was a corner for her to sleep in the family hut; she had nothing to provide towards the feeding and clothing of the children; the cost of firing was infinitesimal; except her simple vessels for cooking and eating, her furniture was a negligeable quantity, for among the points in which the balance of advantage distinctly lies on the side of the Indian woman is that of climate. It saves her in house-rent, fuel, and clothes. If she lives outside a town her palm-leaf hut costs her nothing save the labour of her men-folk in building it and keeping it in repair; if she be within the city walls, the mud walls and thatched roofs of the native quarter are far less costly than "two-pair backs" or even garrets or cellars at home. A few sticks or the slowly smouldering cake of dried cow-dung—the preparation of which is among the minor industries of the community—suffices for the cooking of the simple meal, and a pie or two buys a week's supply of this. Thin wheaten cakes in the North-west Provinces, or rice generally elsewhere, form the staple of the food, which becomes an almost luxurious meal if some curry, or a chili, an onion, or a little *ghi* (clarified butter) can be added. The desire for meat, which makes it almost a necessity in our own working people's existence, she knows not, and, indeed, many castes may not touch it at all. Even tea she does not want, while any form of intoxicating drink she never dreams of taking. If her cloth and sari were coarse they were clean, and she could dispose them with folds as graceful as the wealthiest range or begum of the East; and while she draws them round her for her midday rest and ease, she realizes the indefinable pleasure of the *dolce far niente* that the more energetic races rarely attain unto. Yes, for all her three farthings a day, I think that poor old Hindu woman might sometimes have been envied by her who nominally was making twelve times that sum.

To take agriculture first, the greatest of all the "great" industries of the dependency, and in which hundreds of thousands, even millions of the sex are employed, it would perhaps afford a more exact parallel to place the Indian working woman side by side with the women of France, where the system of peasant proprietorship obtains, rather than to institute any comparison with those who toil upon the soil in England, as though occasionally they lend their labour for wages to the wealthier zamindars of their district, they more often assist their fathers and husbands. The Hindu or

Mahommedan woman labourer has at least the interest of the family in her work, and the harder she strives the greater the common advantage. Moreover, there is not the same reason in her case that she should not work in the fields that there is in England. It used to be an accepted article of faith with the Dorsetshire labourers, in whose midst I was brought up, that there was no real gain to the household when the mother went out to labour, since the extra expenditure in "shop bread," and the wear and tear of the children's clothes, which were perforce neglected during her absence, quite swallowed up the apparent gain of her earnings. These drawbacks do not exist in a land where all food is so simple, and where clothes are put on without the necessity for cut, or fit, or stitch, and where the requirements of everyday comfort are so quickly realized.

As to what their simple home-life in the villages or townlets really is, I know no description more charming, and could give none more graphic than that by Sir George Birdwood in his fascinating monograph on the "Industrial Arts of India." "Outside the entrance, on an exposed rise of ground, the hereditary potter sits by his wheel moulding the swift-revolving clay by the natural curves of his hands. At the back of the houses which form the low, irregular street, there are two or three looms at work in blue' and scarlet and gold, the frames hanging between the acacia trees, the yellow flowers of which drop fast on the webs as they are being woven. In the street the brass and copper smiths are hammering away at their pots and pans, and further down in the verandah of the rich man's house is the jeweller working rupees and gold mohrs into fair jewellery. ... At half-past three or four in the afternoon the whole street is lighted up by the moving robes of the women going down to draw water from the tank, and so going and returning in single file, the scene glows like Titian's canvas and moves like the stately procession of the Panathenaic frieze. Later the men drive in the mild grey kine from the moaning jungle, the looms are folded up, the coppersmiths are silent, the elders gather in the gate, the lights begin to glimmer in the fast-falling darkness, the feasting and the music begin, and the songs are sung late into the night from the Rama-Yana or Mahabarata. The next morning with sunrise, after simple ablutions and adorations, performed in the open air before their houses, their same day begins again." A wedding or a death breaks the monotony of an existence which in truth has its interests and its pleasures, even as our own villagers can be happy throughout the recurring round of winter and summer, seed time and harvest. Only in the chill days of the rainy season are the mud huts uncomfortable and the thin cotton cloths insufficient, and then the dread spectres of dysentery and fever claim their own; but even for this, the wide distribution of hospitals and dispensaries into the remotest country districts is bringing much mitigation.

In preparing the ground for the wheat, rice, paddy, millet, pulse, cotton, and sugar, the women take their part, and very curious throughout Bengal is the leading share that is assigned to them in the labour connected with irrigation.

A sufficient water supply is of course highly essential for all these main crops, and for rice, which occupies nearly sixty per cent, of the cropped area of this province, it is all-important. Government provides the main water system, but the tenant often has to bring the supply on to his own land. The canal runs, perhaps, a few hundred yards below the cultivator's rice patch, and he therefore digs for himself a little channel between the two. He knows, however, that the water will never run uphill to him, and he therefore makes a tank or two at convenient stages. A couple of women then stand on either side of the channel on the edge of the canal, with a common palm-leaf basket attached to two stout ropes of twisted fibre. This they sink into the canal, and by a swift, dexterous movement of arm and wrist, throw the basketful of water, with almost inappreciable waste, into the tank of the stage above them, from whence a couple more will probably pass it on in a similar fashion. Tons of water are often thus raised in a day, and it is exceedingly interesting to watch the ease and rapidity which the women have acquired in this work.

The ingathering of the crops, and the subsequent winnowing and grinding, is also largely done by the women, and, with the primitive tools that they have at command, they perform their tasks with a speed and skill that individual practice could hardly have imparted without the help of hereditary instincts. With a palm-leaf tray, not unlike a housemaid's dustpan, and a few shakes to and fro, the chaff or husk is easily separated from the grain, and one may see quite tiny girls in all parts of the dependency thus at work with hardly less speed or neatness than their mothers and grandmothers. The process of grinding varies a little in the different provinces, though I never saw it more strikingly and 'gracefully done than by a group of Tamil women at Kinaya on the shores of eastern Ceylon, up one of the backwaters of Trincomalee harbour. Their mortars were about one foot six inches high, and the pestles were heavy bars of wood between three and four feet long. I regard my own muscular development as fully up to the average of Western and accustomed to work in the fields, besides assisting in the collection of the drug, have been engaged in their special branch of the labour, which is in providing the "leaves" that are required later in putting up the drug in its export form. This is rather an interesting feature of the industry, and is one of the rare instances in which the sex in India has appropriated to itself a little perquisite. A handful of the gently gathered poppy petals are placed upon an earthenware plate set upon a slow fire, and are covered with a moist cloth. With another pad of damp linen they are kneaded until their resinous matter causes them to adhere into a leaf, varying from six to twelve inches in diameter, and from brown-paper up to cardboard in thickness. When well made the sheets have a peculiar haylike scent, which is supposed to give, to Bengal opium something of the delicate aroma its connoisseurs appreciate, and they are a source of real profit to the women. Three qualities are recognized by Government, and are paid for at the rates of ten, seven, and five rupees a maund (82 lbs.). When the cultivator is a Brahman, Rajput, or of certain other high-castes, whose women may not participate in this source of profit, he must employ hired labour, as he is bound to supply a quantity of leaves proportionate to the crude opium collected, and this seriously diminishes the family gains.

To be allowed to visit either of the opium factories at Patna or Ghazipur is a very rarely accorded favour, and in my case was obtained personally for me by Lord Lansdowne. For various reasons I found it more convenient to go to the latter place, which is situated far up the main stream of the sacred Ganges river, about eighty miles above its juncture with the Gogra. To reach it from the main line of the East consistency, rolling and turning the heavy mass for some hours until it is sufficiently kneaded.

The opium is issued from the factory in differing shapes for Indian consumption and for export to China or the Straits. If for the former purpose it is run at a wax-like stiffness into an hydraulic press, which delivers it in square blocks of two pounds each, stamped with the crown of India, and bearing the words, "Benares: Akbari" (Customs). To be packed, each cake is wrapped in folds of a curiously tenacious tissue paper, made only in Nepaul from bamboo fibre. For the Chinese market, which absorbs by far the greater part of the entire output, the drug undergoes no drying process at all, and is made up in the form of balls, suggestive of a heavy artillery projectile in appearance, and weighing about four and a quarter pounds. To make these a brass cup, which constitutes half a perfect sphere, is necessary, and inside it a layer of the leaves of poppy petals before mentioned is neatly fitted in as a lining. This is laid on till a thickness of about one-third of an inch is obtained, and is rendered firm by brushing it with *lewa,* a thinner form of opium. A weighed lump of the drug of standard quality is pressed into the cup, more leaves and lewa are applied to cover any possible fractures between the joins, and the soft yet solid ball is put in the sun, standing in an earthenware cup, and continually turned every three days till dry. These earthen vessels form an important item in the factory economy, and fully 800,000 to 900,000 of them are required in the course of the year, while some 2500 a day are allowed as the average of breakages. When the balls have solidified as far as they ought to do, they are stored in enormous "go-downs," as any big shed is called in India, and in one of these alone—that moreover not being the largest of them —were 83,150 in readiness for immediate issue, while the registered number in store on the day I was there was something over 240,000, that recorded for the year being 823,000 cakes.

According to official definition, "trash," which is a most important adjunct to the packing of the drug, consists of "the pounded leaves and stalks of the poppy plant." The plants are left standing in the fields until quite dry and withered, and all save the hardest stems are then collected and crushed, the nearest sub-agencies of the Ghazipur factory being called upon to supply a quantity rather more than proportionate to their delivery of opium. It is in dealing with this that by far the greater number of the women employed in the factory are concerned. The trash as it is brought in is very dirty, and mixed with sticks, small stones, and such irrelevant matter, and the first item of its preparation is to spread a quantity of it over coarse cotton cloths upon the ground. Nothing that I saw in the factory gave me a better idea of the vastness of its dealings than this scene, for in a long unbroken row from end to end of the enormous enclosure, were a hundred and forty women seated upon their heels in the characteristic Oriental fashion, with several yards behind them of the picked-over material, and moving slowly forward over the wider mass before. There was, of course, a certain amount of fine dust in the air, but as one saw them with their saris of coarse yet clean calico disposed over their heads, and the heavy barbaric ornaments on their wrists and ankles, one's mind irresistibly travelled back to the grimy unloveliness of a walled-in London dustyard, with its noisy sorters, in their tawdry feather hats or battered and rusty crape bonnets, and it was here that I first began to wonder whether the lot of the woman workers in the East is so immeasurably worse than that of her Western sister after all. At least these women, if their wages were only about two pence-halfpenny per day, were under a sunny sky, they could bring their babies with them, and were not disbursing for care of them any portion of their slender earnings to some old "day nurse" who would administer in a noxious form the very drug in whose preparation they were assisting.

A further process of cleaning has to be done with rather a ponderous form of the old-fashioned hand-winnowing machines similar to those formerly used in English homesteads, and all this work, including the carrying of the stuff in its half-sorted and fully cleaned forms, was done by the women, whose graceful carriage with the large baskets upon their heads was very noticeable. I asked Dr. Sedgefield, the superintendent of the factory, whether many of the women were consumers of the drug in any form, and he replied that scarcely one was. Indeed, throughout the factory, he stated that not more than about one per cent, of both sexes employed took it at all. It is about October that the cakes of opium begin to be dry enough to pack for export, and meantime the chests, which are made either of mango or salwood, with a good coating of pitch over any joint, have been seasoning well. The actual work of putting up is a noisy and a bustling scene. At the bottom of each box a layer of thoroughly dried trash is spread, and a frame of twenty compartments upon a larger scale than those used in England for sending eggs by post is laid in. Into each of these a cake of opium is placed, and more trash is shaken well down before a bamboo mat and another precisely similar frame is packed in, so that each case contains forty cakes. The strictest precautions are taken to insure that the opium is not tampered with in any way before it leaves the factory, even to the despatch of a responsible official to Tari Ghat station to see it delivered safely to the railway company.

Another branch of female labour that I explored with exceeding interest were the colliery workers at Girideh. This is the principal coal-mining centre of all India, and, in fact, from these mines come fully three-quarters of the entire coal output (estimated to exceed 2,000,000 tons a year) of the dependency. The mines, which are directly under Government control, lie at the end of a short branch line of the East India Railway, and I arrived at this at the decidedly uncomfortable hour of three in the morning. But I think it was almost worth any small inconvenience to enjoy the crisp, almost frosty feel of a December morning in Bengal, until the spin of a dogcart's wheels and a cheery English voice of welcome rang out in pleasant greeting. Against the sky, as we drove for about a mile and a half, there was a yellowy-white glow of many distant coke furnaces; but, save for these, it was difficult to realize that one had reached the great coal-field of Bengal, for there were fine trees on all hands, and in the fresh night wind there was neither smoke nor black. The superintendent of these collieries is Dr. Walter Saise, a gentleman not only of great scientific attainments, but of unusual kindliness and sympathy in dealing with the curious peoples who go to make up the army of workers under his control, and as we went along he gave in brief summary a few details of the mines themselves. The property covers an area of about five and a half square miles, and its present yearly output, which is almost all absorbed by the railway company, approaches 1,500,000 tons. All told there are 11,560 souls associated with the working of the mines, of whom 8754 live actually upon the estate, forming one of the happiest working communities that one could find in any industrial centre. Schools and an hospital under the charge of a highly qualified native doctor have been established for the people; thrift has been inculcated in them in a fashion to be found but very unusually among natives, improved methods of cultivation have been shown them, and missionary effort among the aboriginal tribes has achieved a much higher degree of success than in many parts. The colliers themselves are especially interesting from the large proportion among them of the Kol and Santali aboriginal tribes, who still preserve most of their primitive customs and characteristics, though they have learnt to appreciate such civilized benefits as sick attendance and elementary education, even for the girls.

My first visit was to the hospital, an airy bungalow, containing three wards for men and one for women, in all of which were good iron bedsteads with mattresses, and due equipments of stretchers and appliances in case of accidents in the mines, which, though fortunately rare, have to be reckoned for in India as at home. Walking through the wards, however, the absence of any nursing staff struck me as curious, and I asked Dr. Saise if all the assistants were off duty. "Not at all," he replied, with a smile; "we have overcome two great difficulties in a very cheap and practical manner. The first is that of caste, where endless trouble would arise by the rigorous conventions which will not allow one to administer or receive food to or from another, and the second is that of home-sickness, which causes the patients to fret terribly to be back with their own kin. Well, when a man, say, is brought in, we send for his wife or daughter, allowing her full working pay, to come and nurse him. She cooks his food, and if he is on any special diet the assistant-surgeon sees that she gives him this, and she keeps him in touch with his own home. Thus he recovers far more quickly than he would under hands to' which he was not accustomed, and we are saved the maintenance of a large nursing staff." This, as I have' explained; is always a costly item in Indian hospital organization, through the prejudices of caste; while one must understand Indian working-class life to realize how easily a woman rolls up a cloth and a couple of cooking vessels and seats herself on the verandah outside to attend to her lord and master or her child under treatment. A benefit club is not a form of economy which commends itself as a rule to the native mind, but it has been adopted here remarkably well, and the small subscriptions are regularly and cheerfully paid up. The women are permitted to participate in its advantages, and receive monetary assistance for their confinements.

Factory legislation in India is likely some day to interfere with female labour underground, and already there are deep murmurs of dissatisfaction in the native community at the prospect. Let me therefore say emphatically and at once that there is nothing like the occasion for hasty steps that there were when the seventh Earl of Shaftesbury stirred British public opinion to its prohibition at home. I went down two of the principal mines, both of which were rather deep sinkings, and quite representative of the others near by. To descend, one stood upon a steel tray and held on to a bar of iron at a level about one's eyes, and as firedamp happily does not exist in these Bengal mines, naked lights could be carried with impunity. With these colliers, the earnings are reckoned rather by the family than by the individual, and the contributions of the women to the aggregate are well worth consideration in a land of low wages, as India is. The men's average earnings are four to five annas a day; the women's one and a half to two, and a little further help to the total is furnished by the boys. The cutting out and breaking away is done by the men, those of the Kol tribe being the strongest and quickest at this work, while the women pile it into the trollies, which they push to the points where they can be dragged on by ponies, to the shaft, or if the distance to this is not very great, they take them all the way themselves. In these Girideh mines, the conditions of work are less irksome for women than they were in many of our own, for the cuttings are, as a rule, broad and high, and only in some of the remoter ones is it impracticable for a tall person to stand fully upright. The unpleasantness of standing in dirty water is very rarely encountered, and save in one or two of the very deepest sinkings the ventilation is remarkably good.

The women, in spite of their marriages at fourteen and fifteen years of age, were strong and well set up. Remembering, as one does, the terrible descriptions of the swearing, drunken, degraded disgraces to their sex that the north-country women workers underground used to be, the most remarkable point about them was their perfect gentleness and modesty. Each was dressed exactly as she would have been for any other occupation, though her cloth and sari were perhaps a little dirtier than they would have been in a less grimy one, and each wore a mass of bangles and anklets, some of them very interesting specimens of barbaric silver and bell-metal work. Save a little pause of curiosity to look at me and my own clothes, they worked steadily on, pushing forward the heavy trollies which, when laden, were a weight of eight hundredweight. One or two had requests to make of the foreman as he went on, in general these being trifling things, such as taking half a day's leave, or some little point about the land they held; but the general quiet, good order, discipline, and respect were all points that impressed me much. The few questions that I put to them about their hours, which only number eight per day at work, their food, and amusements, which seemed largely to centre in the big bazaar of Sunday, were straightforwardly and frankly answered, and as I left them to come up in the same fashion as I had gone down, I felt glad to think that I had the opportunity before me of seeing them, later in the day, in their own homes and domestic surroundings.

The Kols as coal-cutters excel over the other races with whom they work; while their predilection for agriculture gives them an advantage in tilling the plot of land which they can all hold, and which is one of the sources of the pleasant and manly independence one observes throughout the colliery. Their women are among the few native ones who indulge in any vagaries of fashion, and may sometimes be seen all wearing small black bead necklaces, while at another time large coloured ones will have come into vogue. They wear heavy armlets and bracelets of silver and bell-metal, and of the latter substance very large anklets are also made. These are of a very peculiar curved shape, and can only just be forced on with great violence. As wives, the Kol women are well treated, and as I saw them, they were a fine and healthy-looking community, so that I could well endorse Mr. Riseley's remarks upon them in his erudite dictionary of the tribes and castes of Bengal, in which he says, "A Kol makes a regular companion of his wife. She is consulted in all difficulties, and receives the fullest consideration due to her sex. Indeed, it is not uncommon in the Kolhan to see husbands so subject to the influence of their wives that they may be regarded as henpecked. Instances of infidelity in wives are very rare. I never heard of one, but I suppose that such things must occur, as there is a regulated penalty."

The Santali people, who divide the work of the mines with them, resemble them in most racial characteristics, though their women have to suffer one or two disabilities; but, on the other hand, if they are sufficiently Hinduized to venerate the goddess Kali, women may "act as her *chetinis* or priestesses. One of these I saw—an aged creature who lived alone in a tiny hut of palm leaves adjoining the humble little temple in which she, whose name is the "Giver of Fortune," was worshipped. It did not require much persuasion to induce the old woman to show me something of her ceremonial, but the sight and touch of the little board studded closely with sharp upstanding steel points, upon which she sat down (though I fancy that she saved herself from any acute torture by raising herself upon her heels which were drawn under her), and a handful of steel chains with bits of jagged metal loosely attached, which she used as an instrument of flagellation, sent her in a very few minutes into a state of frenzy. During this she lashed herself furiously and foamed at the mouth, chanting the while a weird monotone till she fell back exhausted. Besides Kali, however, *Jair Era,* a kind of sylvan feminine deity, enjoys universal esteem among the Santals, and every village has a grove set apart in her honour, while every family has its *orah bonga,* or household god, and an *abge bonga,* or secret god, the name of which must on no account be divulged to the women of the establishment, but be kept with all care to the men.

Silk, both in its primitive native manufacture, and as one sees it in the Alliance Mills at Bombay—the one silk mill of all India—employs a large percentage of women. To speak first of this latter, which belongs to the Sassoons, one' finds that it possesses machinery not surpassed in Leek or Lyons, and that among its chief out turn are very soft and fine saris in tones of colour delicate and pale, as well as in the stronger, cruder aniline violets, pinks, and greens which "Western methods of dyeing have familiarized, the bright *glace* satins which well-to-do women employ for the skin-tight little choli jackets they admire, and the *masliru* fabrics backed with cotton for Mahommedan wear in obedience to the ordinance of the Prophet which forbade for male wear the use of unmixed silk. There are 224 looms in this mill, and if all are fully at work they can turn out 2200 yards of woven silk a day. Raw silk from Bengal or Japan is used, and it is easy to tell at a glance which is which up to the dyeing process, as the Bengal is a clear canary yellow in colour and the Japan has all been bleached to a snowy whiteness. There are 350 women employed here, their work being, as well as winding the spun threads into hanks, to do what is technically known as folding the short-stapled filaments of silk after they have gone through the top dressing and carding processes. This is a branch of the industry requiring great neatness and dexterity of touch, and in it the women, who were almost unexceptionally Hindus, wearing a great amount of characteristic native jewellery, have developed a very high degree of skill. They are paid by the piece, a capable and industrious hand being able to earn from twelve to fourteen rupees a month.

I was fortunate while in Berhampore in being able to see the whole native series of processes, from the reeling of the silk from the cocoons up to the finished work upon the rough-looking looms. Of the first-named section of work by far the greater part is done by women. The cocoons are softened, and the thread is drawn out very rapidly on to a round frame of light bamboo or cane, which the spinster keeps in quick motion. When a number of skeins are spun they have to be sorted as to their strength and comparative fineness, and in this work delicacy of touch is the only guide.

As the thread passes through the fingers, any variation in thickness is instantly detected; and it is then gathered on to the *latai,* as the whirling cage on which it is being wound is called, of its particular size, and so keenly is this sense of feeling developed that four or five latais are often used when it is desired to make a careful selection in comparative fineness. Like all the subsidiary mechanism employed, these latais are of the most primitive character, and the *polti,* or central reel from which the threads are worked off, is merely turned on its axis in a hole in the floor. For the throwsting or twisting of the silk the whole machinery does not cost more than two rupees to make, though the labour involved brings the price to a rupee per pound of twisted silk. It is difficult to make the process quite clear without a diagram, but four persons are engaged upon the work. A man sits before a rude frame, which supports the strands of silk. These strands have heavy weights on small pieces of stick attached to them, and pass over U-shaped canes, through glass rings (usually the cheap bangles favoured of the working women) set between horizontal pieces of bamboo nailed to poles stuck in the ground. Two more people, often boys or women, guide the strands in their course through the series of rings, and the twisting is due to the adroitness of the turn given by the man with his two hands to the weights attached to the threads of silk, which are wound by a fourth man on to a reel. Simple as this system is, it proves to answer well with the unevenness of native silk, which makes it always very difficult to manage in European throwsting machinery.

The women take a leading share in the several processes of dyeing, although this is performed in the simplest manner possible. Besides white, there are only five colours in general use. To produce a strong blue, pure indigo is employed, and with several successive dippings a black is obtained. For yellow there are three processes, each producing a full and rich tone, the first being with alum and kamela dust, the second with annatto flowers, and the third with lodh wood.

Tumeric and lac give red, and indigo and lac chocolate, while the green, which is the only non-parmanent dye used in the district, is prepared with a decoction of bakosh (*adha toda vasica*) and sawdust of jackwood, the silk, before dipping, being steeped in alum.

Reeling is essentially a home and cottage industry, and one may often find the poorest old grandmother earning a few pice a day by winding the almost worthless silk of defective or pierced cocoons, though their produce can be used to make a coarse garment called a *matka,* which Mahratta women like to put on after morning bath. The women help also in making the pieces known as *haulms,* which are really spotted corahs, and find their chief sale among the women of the North-west Provinces and the Punjab. To produce the spots or rings of white upon a colour, the length of silk is taken, and the woman with a deftly-tied knot raises a series of tight little lumps upon its whole surface. The piece is then dyed, and when the spots are undone, regularly placed white spots are found to have been left. Very little silk printing is now done here, though, if it is executed, it is done in elementary primitiveness, and the parts to be left undyed are merely traced out in clay paste. Three colours are sometimes used in this way on the one piece.

Curiously enough, however, the sex is allowed very little share in the collection of the wild or "tasser" silk. These cocoons are mostly gathered and brought in by the Santals, who have learnt, with that curious habit of close observation which seems to be an heritage of all woodland folk, to note where the insects are spinning, while they are hunting bigger game or cutting fuel. The actual harvesting is attended by many superstitions, and the women may neither assist in the labour, nor even administer to the wants of their lords and masters at the time.

From official and technical information supplied to me, I learn that there are now something over a hundred and thirty cotton spinning and weaving mills, and in nearly all these the greater part of the winding of the yarn into hanks is done by women. They are to be found in all parts of the dependency, from Tinnevelly to the Punjab, from Bengal to Rajputana, though, of course, Bombay is the chief centre of the industry. Cawnpore is, however, making a big bid for commerce in this direction, and with her close-set columns of tall chimneys and heavy smoke-laden atmosphere is winning for herself the name of the "Manchester of India." Here spinning of the rather short-stapled Indian cotton is done by the Cawnpore Mills Company, while the Muir and Elgin Mills weave as well very useful qualities of cotton cloths for European as well as native purposes. From time immemorial cotton spinning has been one of the industries indigenous to the country, but there is a wide difference in the primitive methods one may still see employed by the remoter roadsides, and the huge mills, with their steam power and their thousands of mule, ring, and throstle spindles, and their hundreds of looms. Both here and at. Delhi, where I went through the Delhi Cotton Mills, directed by Messrs. Thornton and Wilson, I had the opportunity of seeing the types of women belonging to the sturdy and handsome races of the North-west Provinces who enter upon factory work. Yet neither in these nor in any others that I saw was there any evidence of the physical deterioration of the workers, out of which a good deal of agitational capital has been made; but I was warned that I would be more likely to note this in Bombay. Here, among others, I visited the huge Colaba Jubilee Mills, and through a sympathetic and reliable interpreter in Guzerati, quietly put a number of questions to the women as to their wages, hours, and wants. But I could hear of no grievance—nothing more than an admission that in the hot season a full day's labour was exhausting enough for an ordinary woman. As a fact, the work is all paid by the piece, and the Indian temperament is not in favour of too great a strain upon its energies. Even in Bombay the general standard of physique, taking into consideration the distinctive racial attributes, was by no means bad, and would have given decidedly better results than one would obtain by placing side by side average North Country mill hands with representatives of other English occupations. Of course, it is said that it is too soon to observe depreciating effects to any marked degree, and that, at present, the higher wages to be earned at factory work are bringing in large reinforcements from the country. The facts are against both these assertions. The first mill started in India was in 1851, and by 1878 there were fifty-eight. The Indian peasant, born upon the soil, is extremely loth to leave it, and moreover, to quote from a high authority, "there is a certain degradation in working in either textiles or leathers, so that, as an outlet for the surplus population now thrown upon the land, the development of these industries cannot be regarded, save in very exceptional circumstances, as likely to benefit more than the lower labouring and menial classes." These, moreover, would find themselves at a disadvantage in labour requiring as much skill as weaving, and it is only to a very limited degree that they are to be found in the mills.

Several modifications concerning women were introduced into the Factory Act of India, in 1892, when the hours of labour were reduced to eleven, and in factories where a system of shifts is not in force, women are prohibited from working before 5 a.m., and after 8 p.m. No girl under fourteen may be employed, and it has strictly laid down how long the hours of labour shall be, stipulating that an hour's rest shall be allowed during the middle of the day. In this interval the women seldom go home, but sit in the nearest shade to the work-yard gates and chew betel or eat the cheap sweetmeats brought round to them by itinerant dealers. Their young children they generally bring with them to the mills, and, indeed, the stranger, going through the departments in which they are employed, has to walk warily between the podgy little brown lumps sleeping or crawling upon the floor.

Another phase of women's work that I noticed with interest was in connection with the preparation of coffee. Coming down the Malabar coast, I gained an insight into the many processes of cleaning and sorting through which the coffee-berry goes ere it appears in the grocers' window, and the most delicate and tedious of these—known to the trade as "garbling"—is all performed by women and girls. There is elaborate machinery to remove the husk of the berry, and a system of sieves of graduated sizes, not unlike those employed for the sizing of gun-shot, can be used to bring the various grades of the bean to the evenness which constitutes an important factor in its commercial value. But when all this has been done there remains an appreciable percentage of discoloured and unsightly berries which would lower much the standard of the samples, and such only can be removed by hand. In an enormous factory which I visited at Mangalore there were nearly two hundred women thus employed. They filled two immense sheds, the floors of which were of hard concrete. Each woman had her little mat of palm fibre, and two baskets before her, as well as a high heap of the grey-green berries. These she spread out before her, seeing instantly the defective grain or grains to be removed and placed in the smaller of the baskets, and gathering up with lightning activity handfuls of the beans, now cleaned and ready for packing. About two annas a day I found to be the usual wage to be earned at the work, though some, particularly expert themselves, and helped a little by one or two of their children, could make more than this.

On this coast also, where fishing forms a staple industry, the women do much of the work of drying and packing for export the enormous quantities of fish that goes inland, up country, to Ceylon, and to the Persian Gulf; and, of course, in the picking and preparation of tea an occupation is found for thousands. Time and great distances unfortunately prevented my going to Darjeeling and Assam, so that I am unable to speak from personal knowledge of this department of work. It is perhaps unnecessary, however, that I should adduce any further specific information, and to those who would turn upon me and say, "Yes, possibly in these material points the lot of the Indian working woman is less hard than it is often made out to be, but see how narrow are her ideas, and how much is sealed to her through her want of education," I would answer, that at home, with all our vaunted codes and standards, I very much doubt if relatively we have added much to the English working woman's range of thought, if one looks at the facts as they are. The London factory girl leaves school so soon as she has crammed enough knowledge to pass her fourth standard, or when she has turned fourteen years at the latest. Though cookery, and very lately laundry-work and housewifery, have been added to her curriculum, she is generally most lamentably ignorant of the domestic arts, while her utter incompetence with her needle is not one of the least factors in contributing to impose what Mr. Walter Besant calls the "inexorable law of eleven-pence halfpenny," and its provision of the cheapest shoddy and sweated labour upon us. Her reading is confined to halfpenny novelettes, save on the rare occasions that she takes up one of those hateful hotch-potches of vulgar jokes and irrelevant snipping which are served out in periodicals of the "bits" order. Of the movements of the world in politics, commerce, art, or literature she knows and cares naught. Her recreations savour more of horseplay than of refinement; the inside of the public-house is not by any means a sealed book to her, and she marries with reckless improvidence. It is not a pretty picture, but it is a true one. Now in India the intense strength of the family tie and the hereditary traditions of woman's self-effacement seem to me to have imparted a kind of compensating mental attribute, that perhaps is not very much less valuable a possession than a power to read without the discriminating faculty what to read. According to modern "emancipated" lights, the answer of a poor Mahommedan woman in Calcutta to my question as to what she regarded as the chief happiness she would desire for herself might seem a contracted one. "To see my husband happy, and to know that what I have cooked and done for him has helped to make him so; to see my sons grow up as men, honest and strong, and to know that my daughters are well married"—is, in my view, a praiseworthy domestic ideal, enough even when set beside the possibilities of a bank holiday on Hampstead Heath. Thought may not be subtle, and talk may not rise much beyond piece and marriage, with these poor women; but relatively it does no more than that with their white sisters.

Moreover, it is to be remembered that the binding laws of caste, which have come down through the centuries, have induced an attitude of submission to things as they are, that it is difficult sometimes for the Western mind to grasp how complete the sentiment of resignation becomes. "That a sweeper woman should always be a sweeper woman, and should marry a sweeper or some equivalently low-caste man, seems to them even as a decree of nature which it were useless to attempt to overthrow. Consequently there is a feeling of content which checks the wild yearnings of ambition, if indeed in the humbler castes this has not been wholly lost from the mental faculties, even as the body in time loses power in muscles or limbs never exercised. Traditions, unimpaired in strength, are handed on from mother to daughter, and thus, with her lack of aspiration and her simple standards of comfort and necessity, I do not think that the working woman of the East is in such bad case when set beside her European sisters.

This perhaps is not an inopportune place to interpolate a few facts as to the legal status of Mahommedan women, on which home views are especially hazy, but which, I venture to consider, are another point over which comparison continues rather in favour of the East. As with ourselves, as long as a girl is under age and remains unmarried under the paternal roof, her father or appointed guardian constitutes a controlling power. Directly, however, that she has attained her majority, the law, as laid down by the Muslim legists, recognizes fully her individual rights. She is entitled to a share in her father's or mother's property, not, it is true, in as large a proportion as her brothers, but still in a strictly defined and well-understood ratio. A woman *sui juris* can under no circumstances be married without her full and expressed consent.

Nor does she on her marriage lose her personal rights, or merge them in those of her husband. An ante-nuptial settlement in favour of the wife by the husband is a necessary condition among all save the very poorest; and, failing this, the law presumes one in accordance with the social position of the woman. A Muslim marriage is a civil act in itself, and all that is binding can be done with neither priest nor ceremonial. After it the man possesses no powers over the wife's person that the law does not define, and none whatever over her goods or property. The rights she possesses as a mother are, moreover, clearly laid down, and are not subject to individual caprice. Her person is protected against ill-treatment or brutality, while any earnings of her own belong strictly to herself, and cannot be touched by an extravagant husband.

In the courts she can sue a debtor or bring any civil action without cover of her husband's name, or the necessity of joining a next friend, and, in short, acts, if *sui juris,* absolutely as an individual. All these ordinances are plainly enjoined by the Muslim authorities on the law, who may be said to recognize no disabilities arising from sex.

I have alluded before to the conditions of divorce or separation; but unless the causes for demanding this were unusually grave, a woman usually has to sacrifice her dowry, or anything she brought into settlement. Should it, however, be the husband who seeks this, he has (except where the ground of complaint was proved infidelity) to make over to her the whole sum of money, with any jewels that he settled upon her at marriage. A woman, therefore, who works (for the Hindu rights are no less clear) does not do so as the mere chattel of her husband. If her earnings go, as they probably do, to swell the family purse, it is not because she has no other lawful method for their disposal, since they are her own to help her to broaden her horizon if she so willed. But instead of doing this, her own natural tendency is to narrow it. Our own example, our own education, has not yet touched the fringe of inner native life, and the first evidence of gratitude that the working-class mother will show for the good wages which the British raj, irrigation, and machinery, have given her, will be, not to send her daughter to school, but to keep her *purdah nashin,* and marry her as a child, as the first evidences of growing social importance. As a journalist, it is perhaps rather my instinct to record things as they are, and not as they should be; and to speak of womanhood in the East as satisfied under present conditions of life is always sufficient to send those of a certain school of thought into something like frenzy. But caste and the zenana system are closely interlocked, and together they are the two keystones of the whole fabric of Indian social life. The former teaches a pride or a humility, as the case may be; but, on either hand, an acceptance of that state of life to which they are called that is marvellously discouraging to restlessness and outside ambition. The latter possesses a prestige and a dignity that I scarcely know how to express adequately, but I think is sometimes, and in a measure, realized by the struggling shopkeeping class when they attain to a competency, or receive an unexpected legacy, which enables them henceforth to "live independent" among their working neighbours, or in a higher circle when knighthood is won. While these two forces are the dominant influences in the life, there can be no appreciable change, even with education and European example. For to abolish them would be to effect a revolution so sweeping and so vast that the India of Hinduism, Buddhism, Islamism, and history would have disappeared, and a new nation would have arisen upon the face of the earth. But the tinkering meddlers who would graft a lot of Europeanized excrescences on to Eastern habits and beliefs seem unable to grasp this as a truth silk or material cut after the English or French patterns, though without any extravagances of exaggerated sleeves or high and stiff collars.

A full-sized sari should be about five and a half yards long, and from thirty-six to forty inches wide. To put it on, a woman makes a few pleats at one end in her hand, which she draws through in front of a band or string already round her waist. The length of the material is then carried round her figure towards the left, and when it has been brought completely round, the end is taken over the shoulder and draped over the head. It is only of course from long practice that the perfect art of disposing it is reached, but one sees tiny girls of three or four emulating the examples of their mothers with pieces of calico about as large as a pocket-handkerchief ; for the Indian girl longs as keenly to leave the shapeless *sacque,* which is the first garment of her baby years, and attain to the dignity of a sari quite as eagerly as her sister of the West desires a long skirt and its attendant privileges.

Certain districts have specially favoured colours, however, and throughout Gujarat this is a very warm, deep crimson, enriched with delightful embroidery. On the West Coast the women of caste generally wear white; while those of the lowest orders have small checks or stripes in various mixtures, a dull yellow and red being much affected. In Calcutta scarlet divides favour with lilac and white, while indigo-dyed blue is more or less general everywhere. *Bandhna,* or "tie and dye" cloth, in cotton as well as silk, is much used in the central provinces and native states. The design, which generally takes the form of flowing lines, squares, and circles, is traced out by a draughtsman. The woman then takes the cloth, and picks up a tiny piece of it, round which she deftly and tightly binds a piece of cotton thread. It is then sent to the dyer, and when the knots are unwound, small white rings appear all over the surface. This method, primitive as it is, is used very successfully throughout Bengal and the north-west, and silks thus ornamented in Berhampore find their way alike to the furthermost frontiers of the Punjab and to the heights of Assam. By means of certain coloured threads for the knotting process, a variety in the colours of the rings is, imparted. These *bandhna* fabrics are also much used for turbans, and in Jeypore, where the work is nearly always done by the wives of the dyers, I was assured that there are no less than a hundred and eight kinds of knot in use.

Very poetic and pretty are the names by which some of the designs and colourings in favourite use for silk are known. These have come down from the sixteenth century at least, for Sir George Birdwood tells how in 1577 three shiploads of Berhampore silks were despatched by way of the Persian Gulf to Russia, and that among them were patterns described as "ripples of silver," "nightingale's eyes," "peacock's neck," and "sunshine and shade." Such names survive still, for fashion alters practically not at all, and a girl desires to include in her trousseau exactly what her mother had before her. In fact, the only instance in the varied inquiries that I made upon the subject in which I found that any whims of fashion existed was among the Kols, who are very capricious about their ornaments, and may sometimes be seen all wearing small necklaces of fine metallic threads, while at another time large beads or lacquered devices will have come into vogue.

A girl of the upper classes takes a long time to gather her wedding outfit together, and this always includes as The chief distinction between Hindu and Mahommedan clothing is that the latter wears much more actually made-up raiment than the former. There are strong Hindu traditions against cut-out and sewn garments, and though these are dying out, especially where the two great races are much thrown together, it is by no means difficult to trace pre" judices undefined yet existent in the prevailing fashions of everyday wear. Indeed, it is believed by Captain Meadows Taylor, and many other high authorities, that, before the Mahommedan invasion of India, anything like a shaped coat or bodice was entirely unknown, and the use of the needle in the making of wearing apparel was entirely a Muslim introduction.

It is not necessary to enter upon a detailed description of the various classes of cotton goods from heavy unbleached calicos to fine and soft muslins, that are produced in all parts of India; but, from an artistic point of view, it is satisfactory to find that there is no very marked deterioration in designs to be noted as a result of European influences. The stripes and checks employed, though commonplace enough, are seldom if ever offensive, while the repeated washings they have to go through soon tone down early crudities of hue. Patterns remain small and unostentatious, and nowhere did I find that large or staring or gaudy ornamentation were favoured. The native taste retains its inherent purity in this direction, and rejects unerringly the vulgar and the ugly. In colour, unfortunately, one cannot speak so reassuringly. Brilliant tones appeal strongly to the Oriental mind, and the vividness of the aniline dyes of the laboratory has proved irresistible. In the great Alliance silk mills of Bombay no pretence whatever is made on the subject, and one is shown the dyeing vats filled with the most dazzling of the coal-tar combinations. It is the gaudiness of rose-pink, of emerald-green, of royal-blue, or amber-yellow which constitutes a leading attraction of our European piece goods, and commends them to native purchasers when they are displayed in the native bazaars. On their mere merits of quality they would be less dangerous rivals to the indigenous manufactures, whose softer, deeper, richer tones, drawn from vegetable sources, are quite eclipsed by the staring, shouting hues of the imported article.

As one wends through the crowded alleys of the great bustling cloth fair of Bombay, with its tons and tons of Manchester—ay, and German also—cotton fabrics, this fact is pressingly borne in. It explains one of the grievances which have led to so much friction and ill-will upon the question of the cotton duties, for the Indian weaver cannot command the resources, even if he wished to do so, of the scientific chemist, and thus indigenous products are handicapped beside the brilliant attractiveness of imported shoddy, to please the manufacturers of which the Home Government has not hesitated to offend alike the native capitalists and workers. It explains too, I think, in a measure that impression of widespread poverty which the superficial traveller dilates upon as evidence of "something wrong" officially, for these wrappings lose their fugitive brilliancy in a very few days under the glare of the sun, and after a washing or two are reduced to a miserably ill-favoured appearance of faded shabbiness. One point that helps to convey the sense of general prosperity in Katthiawar and Bhaunagar is the dark blue and dark red county-woven cloths worn by both men and women down to the very poorest. These keep their warm full colouring to the last, and look therefore always well and fresh. It is perhaps rather deplorable that the merely novel and gay should replace the old and the sober; but when was it not thus ? It is even as when the cheap adulterated silks of foreign looms drove the unsurpassable British brocades and moires, tabinets and damasks, out of the field.

●●

8

Medical Aid and Assistance for Sick

"And those things which have long gone together are, as it were, confederate within themselves, whereas new things piece not so well; but, though they help by their utility, yet they trouble by their inconformity. ... It were good therefore that men in their innovations would follow the example of time itself, which indeed innovateth greatly but quietly, and by degrees scarce to be perceived."—Bacox.

Whenever the history of the social life of India comes to be written, the influences and developments of the movement for supplying medical aid to the women will constitute a factor of weighty consideration. I am not prepared to say that even yet are the problems of the situation all solved, nor that enlightened and scientific methods are everywhere superseding the superstitious and harmful practices of ignorance. Still, an appreciable beginning in the right direction has been made; the Dufferin Fund has laboured long enough to allow of a fair estimate being formed of the results in actual working of its noble intentions.

Zenana medical missions have long realized that the healing of the body seems more apparently, to the native mind, making for righteousness than the healing of the soul; and to-day there exists a sufficiently large body of native female practitioners to demand attention in any discussion of present conditions and future outlook.

Of the inception of the Dufferin Fund it is unnecessary to write much. The scheme, so broad in its scope, so profound in its sympathies, and so high in its ideals, was surely one of the finest ever evolved from woman's brain and heart, and because it has not hurried on to its complete realization with the speed that its generous foundress, in her deep womanly pity for the suffering she had seen around her, would have wished, rather let it not be written of in the bald terms that relate to negative success, but spoken of as only another confirmatory evidence in the long list of experiences that in India, as elsewhere, the best progress is made by gentle steps.

The fund was first started in 1885, under the direct patronage of the Queen-Empress, and a well-considered list of high British officials and native rulers and gentlemen as vice-patrons and central committee was drawn up. No less-a sum than two lakhs (200,000) of rupees were given very readily by the Nizam of Hyderabad, the Maharajah of Jeypore, and the Maharajah of Alwar, and their good example—quite as much, be it fairly stated, from a genuine admiration of the disinterested kindness of their popular vicereine, as from the native characteristic of emulation, which leads the ruler of one petty state to try and outdo his neighbour of another—was promptly and generously followed. Ere long, the committee found itself able to invest five and a half lakhs of rupees, and, thanks to further liberal gifts, its capital now stands at 11,96,300 rupees.

At the risk of criticism to the effect that I am here only stating what is accessible in yearly reports, I think it advisable to dwell a little on the working plan of the fund. Misconception is so pitifully rife as to its purpose and system, and while people are to be found who ask whether it does not train missionaries or provide hospital nurses for the British troops in the East, or send soldiers' wives to homes on the hills, there is at least some occasion to say plainly at the outset both what it does and does not do, to render further remarks properly intelligible. As stated in its own articles of association, the three primary objects of the fund are as follows:—

1. *Medical tuition,* including the teaching and training in India of women as doctors, hospital assistants, nurses, and midwives.
2. *Medical relief,* including—
   (a) the establishment under female superintendence of dispensaries and cottage hospitals for the treatment of women and children;
   (b) the opening of female wards under female superintendence in existing hospitals and dispensaries;
   (c) the provision of female medical officers and attendants for existing female wards; *(d)* the founding of hospitals for women where special funds or endowments are forthcoming.
3. The supply of trained female nurses and midwives for women and children in hospitals and private houses.

It does not pretend to be evangelizing or sectarian, and it frankly faces but does not attempt to crush the grave difficulties with which it is confronted by *purdah* conventions and caste prejudices.

Next, it must be understood that the Indian Government maintains a very efficient state-supported service of medical aid. By this, over eighteen hundred institutions are kept up, in the larger towns in the form of civil hospitals, under the chief medical authority of the district when it is "up country," and under the professors, physicians, and surgeons of the medical colleges of the Presidency towns. During the last few years small dispensaries, generally affording accommodation for a few in-patients and under the control of an assistant-surgeon or a hospital assistant, have multiplied exceedingly. Now, to such institutions as these the poorer and working class women could go, and in the case of the hospitals they could feel assured of special female wards. But—and that "but" covers very much—the doctor would inevitably be a man. To the secluded and low caste women of the community this did not greatly matter, though even such have certain inherited dislikes and what I may call the *purdah* spirit upon the subject. These, therefore, already in a measure provided for, Lady Dufferin could regard as presenting less immediately pressing claims, and the great vital principle underlying her whole splendid effort was to carry help and alleviation into the remote chambers of zenanas and *bibi-ghars,* behind whose jealously closed doors no men, save those of the family, might pass, and to which, if such assistance were to be taken, it must be at the hands of trained women.

It would serve no purpose to trace the growth of the idea along its various stages, for under Lady Dufferin's energetic guidance it took firm root, and spread out branches from Madras to Quetta, from Karachi to Calcutta. Lady Lansdowne took over the work with loving zeal, and though her name may not have come so prominently into English notice in connection with the fund as it deserved, I think none who had seen even a tenth part of what I did of its administration and general working, could fail to be impressed by her whole-souled interest in and wise fostering of the growth of the movement. In fact, in certain ways the task, as Lady Lansdowne undertook it, required quite as much anxious thought as did its initiation and launching, since upon her shoulders fell the details of modification, enlarging, curtailing, or revising according to the knowledge gained by actual experience.

In dealing with the three aspects of the fund, I would take the second one before the first, as it is in that direction that the most tangible results are to be noticed. It is not my purpose, nor would it be specially interesting, to embark upon statistics, inevitable as they are to render the educational position of the dependency clear; but the time has now come when the best friends of the fund are asking whether the building, the equipment, the endowment of the magnificent hospitals of the greater towns has wrought all the benefit that was expected of them. The best answer to the question lies, I think, in a remark made to me by one of the highest medical officials under Government, who said that the Dufferin Fund, alike in scope and practice, was fifty years in advance of its time. So far as patronage of the hospitals goes, it is admitted with all regret that the higher caste and zenana ladies of the East have not availed themselves as freely of the advantages that they offered as Lady Dufferin and her more hopeful advisers expected they would do.

It is not that anything is wanting in the hospitals; for native architects and advisers have directed the building of the *purdah* rooms, and caste traditions are scrupulously regarded in the nursing and cooking arrangements. Stringent regulations have been framed to exclude those not of position or undoubted respectability; while the most jealous husband, father, or brother knows that the patients are absolutely secured against intrusive male eyes. The comparative want of success is due, not to any failure on the part of the promoters to secure it, but to innate ideas and customs which prevent those for whom these benefits were intended from profiting as fully as they might by what is available for them.

Nor, I think, is this surprising, if we look at home. Even with ourselves, and the knowledge that we have of the skill and the kindness and the attention of our hospitals, there are still very few of the middle or upper classes who will voluntarily enter one, even with the privacy of the paying ward. With the native and *purdah* women there is also an intense shyness of strangers even of their own sex and their own race, as well as the sense of home sickness in its most exaggerated form when away from their usual surroundings. Indeed women doctors throughout India told me that it was one of their greatest difficulties to keep their patients after they had been in hospital a few days, on account of the almost irresistible longings of intense nostalgia that came over them. Moreover, the idea is still a new one. The customs and traditions to be overcome are those that have hardened and crystallized through the centuries, and against' those the innovations of a decade are still scarcely realized as existent.

Meantime, while the undiscerning reader in England is looking at the scrappy paragraph which the average reporter culls in a quarter of an hour from the annual Report, and thinking, if the beds are filled all the year, if the numbers in the out-patients' department show an increase, and if there is no specific fault or grievance laid down; there can be no cause for anxiety as to the movement, others there are who are asking, Why is the Dufferin Fund "wasting" money on building hospitals that are not doing what it was reckoned they would accomplish ? For no one doubted for a moment that hospitals could be filled; but those who knew the characteristics of native women feared well lest they should be occupied by the special classes that Lady Dufferin so earnestly desired to benefit. The critics who deprecate the outlay on bricks and mortar do not grasp how very frequently the fund has had large donations from wealthy natives conditionally upon the whole or the greater part being devoted to the erection of an hospital or a dispensary. Only to mention a few specific instances in which this has lately occurred, let me name the gift of the Babu Durga Prosad, who gave ten thousand rupees to the Gaya branch of the fund in order that an hospital should be erected in that town, to be called the "Pavitra," after his mother; while at Baranagore the Babu Benode Lai Ghose, vice-chairman of the municipality, laid down a similar sum, as well as all that was needed to purchase a site, the whole there also to be the memorial to his mother. At Comilla the Nawab Faizunnissa Saheba and three other ladies jointly offered the whole amount required for the building of an hospital. Four thousand rupees were presented to the already existing hospital at Naiserabad by the Srimali Biddaza Charidhrani, that a new ward should be added to it, to be called the Biddaza Morgee Ward ; and at Cawnpore, Pershotam Eao Fantia Sahib, Subadah of Bithoor, has given five thousand rupees towards the building of a better hospital for that place of bitter memories.

The fact is that the erection of fine buildings, with their invariable memorial stones and flourishing inscriptions, is the favourite form for Indian native charity to take. With the Parsees on the Bombay side some few have founded scholarships, and some few have bestowed handsome and even anonymous gifts in other useful directions. But to rear an hospital, to put up a fine hall, to present an institute to a town, are all tangible hereafter as monuments, and thus commend themselves vastly to the Oriental mind. The best answer, however, to any strictures on this point is furnished to me by Lady Dufferin herself, who says that in no instance has the fund put up an hospital that was not urgently needed, nor has it ever sanctioned outlay in this direction disproportionate to its developments on other sides, while it has not encouraged even native gifts of buildings unless there was due prospect of their means of maintenance. Hospitals must necessarily be the schools for the teaching of the future practitioners, and therefore they constitute an integral part of the Dufferin scheme, for, to come back now to the first clause of its intentions, it will be found that women are to be taught and trained *in India,* Lady Dufferin grasped what few Indian social reformers do, in that, if the stream of medical aid was to be an abundant one, spreading its benefits far and wide, the source must be from within, and not one dependent upon the precarious supplies from home charity or Englishwomen's enterprise. One of the most interesting aspects therefore of the whole situation is how far the more emancipated of the educated native women have been worthy of the confidence that Lady Dufferin thus showed in their ability, and have responded to the calls of their suffering sisters.

There are five Indian universities, namely, those of Calcutta, Bombay, Madras, Agra, and Lahore, which give medical degrees to women. At the present time there are close upon three hundred young women under instruction for these degrees, and if it must be admitted that of them a rather large proportion belong to the mixed Eurasian race, I think that that must be accepted as a necessary halfway step. There is a rather unkind legend current in India of a typical street urchin transported to Calcutta who said, "God made white men, and God made coloured men, but English Tommy, he made d—d half-castes," and as a race they seem to possess the faculty of uniting the worse qualities of both sides. Here and there may be found one superior to the usual attributes, and in the case of the women, those who overcome their tendencies to a backboneless, flabby inertia generally have energy and perseverance enough to carry them through the course of study. Provided that they possess these recommendations, there are several distinct advantages in their entering upon the profession. In the first place, it affords them an honourable and useful vocation—a matter of considerable importance when the problem of "what shall we do with our Eurasians ?" is vexing many official minds. In the second, their knowledge of the vernacular most spoken around them, and their innate acquaintance with the habits and prejudices common to half or possibly three-quarters of their ancestry is directly in their favour, even against the more highly skilled woman doctor coming to the East for the first time, and with no more knowledge of Hindustani or Bengali, Tamil or Gujerati than she has picked up from books.

So far as the experiment of training native girls as doctors, assistant-surgeons, and hospital assistants has gone, it is satisfactory. As with school teachers, however, I cannot regard it as an unmixed advantage to the ultimate status and foundation of the movement to allow it to become identified with any propagandist movement, but the same difficulty is encountered as with the other calling. A livelihood must be found for convert girls; must we not at present accept whoever comes forward? Altogether it is a puzzling problem, but I am inclined to think it will be the Parsees who will do the most towards its solution, provided only that they are wise. Of course Hindus and Mahommedans are united in antagonism to this shrewd and far-seeing race, who are amassing money and making themselves almost the rulers of trade, but for all that they are received in every day dealings with an amount of fraternity that is never shown towards the "Western-race. The Parsees have adhered consistently to their religious principles, which are less hateful in Hindu eyes than Christianity, but they have ceased to keep their women *purdah,* and have extended to the sex the same educational privileges as their men enjoy. Meantime, the women have not succumbed to the temptation to travesty European dress, but they have freed themselves from many of the conventional fetters, and several of them have succeeded notably well in the direction of medicine. On the Bombay side at least, therefore, the Parsee girls have it very much in their power not only to mitigate present suffering, but to show the possibilities to other women of a remunerative and honourable career.

There are many who maintain that it would be better to try to make nurses first than hospital assistants, the grade that is at present passed by very few of the native women students. In this I cannot wholly concur. We must face the situation as it is; and so far the idea of trained nursing assistance is not yet borne in upon the native mind, which regards that as one of the intuitive accomplishments of a wife or mother, and would be very much averse to seeking skilled help from outside. No less important as an item to be taken into account are caste prejudices; and even if a woman had overcome her inherent dislike to giving water or performing certain offices for patients of lower caste than her own, it must be remembered that patients of higher religious grade than her own might be unable to accept her ministrations. So rigid are these rules, that in the *purdah* wards of the Victoria Hospital of Calcutta each one has been provided with its own kitchen, in order that no outrage shall be done to these ideas. The hospitals naturally "require nursing staffs; but as long as these customs survive as matters of vital consequence, there are grave difficulties in the way of extending the profession.

My own conclusions in the matter are that the fund has done well in establishing so many fine hospitals, even though these may not have always attracted patients of the ranks it was desired to reach, in that they constitute a magnificent foundation-ground for the training of the women doctors of the future; and that the time has now come when encouragement may be specially and well directed towards inducing more girls to qualify as practitioners. At present I would not demand a very high degree of knowledge ; but whatever is taught should be simple and common-sense, and equal to the everyday ailments of women who are not overwrought with "nerves," nor have ruined their constitutions by unnatural habits. Women of the hospital-assistant class should go out now far and wide. They do not despise fees of two or three pence a visit; their wants are modest, and they can sustain existence on resources that would be starvation to the English lady doctor. And if their skill is but small, be it remembered that what little knowledge they do possess is at least free from superstition and positive danger to life. They will create a demand for something better, and in due time that will be met.

How great this mass of superstition to be combated is perhaps only to be realized after one has seen something of native midwifery. This as a science is supposed to belong to the Chamains, the women of the Chamars, the tanner and leather-working caste of Bengal, Behar, and Upper and Central India. In the North-West Provinces there is a rhymed couplet proverb which says it is unadvisable to cross a river in the same boat with a black Brahmin or a fair Chamar, and by their higher-caste neighbours they are regarded as very lowly folk, who are only fit for the most menial and degrading occupations. There are certain necessary offices connected with childbirth which caste Hindu women are prohibited from performing, but the Chamains have no scruples of this description, or indeed from rendering any "assistance" required. In the absence of a Chamain, a woman of the Chandal or Sudra castes— both servile orders—will be called in; though these latter seldom make a regular profession of the calling, but the orthodox Hindus have a saying to the effect that the household becomes unclean unless a Chamain has been present at one birth at least in its circle.

The Hindu or lower class and Mahommedan non-purdah woman is not affected by any feelings of reserve as to her condition. She pursues her daily and domestic avocations up to the last, so late indeed that all the lying-in hospitals can. record instances in which the child was born before the mother arrived at the doors. It is generally stated that Indian women suffer very little in comparison with Europeans, and possibly, in a perfectly natural and healthy mother, this is the case. In the hospitals, however, the proportion of difficult cases involving the use of instruments is unduly large, and malformations and internal injuries are appallingly frequent. These are often the result of the barbarous treatment resorted to by the ignorant *dhais* or midwives, who, on the first indications of approaching labour, take the poor woman to the *asancha ghar* or *chatthi ghar*, the house or room of confinement, and as a kind of preliminary assistance, roll and rub her regardless of the additional torture inflicted. When the Marchioness of Dufferin and Ava stated, as one of the reasons of her appeal for medical help, that among other atrocities perpetrated by these women was that of placing a heavy beam upon the poor creature, an attendant sitting upon either end, the fact was questioned from the exceeding horror of the idea, but the practice is far from infrequent when parturition is delayed. To stop haemorrhage after birth, there is a dangerous system among them of applying great pressure.

The newly-confined woman is made to stand against the wall, while the *dhai* with her head or bent knees exerts her whole force against the lower part of the stomach. Among their other details of treatment, they employ, to bring about the contraction of the uterus, an embrocation made from the leaves of *Artemisia vulgaris,* and to lessen superabundant How of milk, a plaster made of pea-flour and the dried bark of *Cucurbita* is employed.

Altogether opposed to our ideas of sanitation is the birth-fire kindled with charcoal, which east and south, west and north, with Tamil and Punjabi, with Brahmin and Mussulman women alike, smoulders beneath the *charpai,* or bed, on which the mother lies. In Bengal it is placed at the door of the *chatthi ghar,* while within an oil-lamp is kept brightly burning night and day, as' darkness is supposed to favour the entrance of evil spirits. Among many castes nothing whatever may be removed from the room, and no washing is permitted unless it be that of some of the infant's clothing, and that even must be dried within the stifling chamber. A Mahommedan woman must endure this purgatory for ten days, her more fortunate Hindu neighbour escaping with six. Not until after the "third day since confinement may the mother eat her ordinary pulse and rice, for up to that time turmeric, molasses, spices, and various highly stimulating condiments are given. That fever is not far more frequent than it is, is one of the medical problems of India, as puzzling as the reason of the immunity from typhoid enjoyed by the pilgrims at Benares.

After a premature or still birth, it is a very usual practice on the part of the *dhais* to administer a decoction of bamboo leaves, in which a copper coin has been soaked, the underlying idea of this seemingly risky practice being to correct the internal poison which caused the mischief. Death in childbed is regarded as a curse of wider effect than merely to the woman's own circle, and among the Santals and Kols, it is believed that the spirits of such women, as *kitchni,* are capable of the most diabolic mischief in a district. Among the Oraons any woman dying within a fortnight after a birth becomes a *chorail,* and such are reputed always to walk upon inverted feet, that is to say, with the toes behind. Hardly any tribe or caste, however, could not be named that did not view such a death as a peculiar misfortune.

At present, too, it must be borne in mind that the native girls who come forward to qualify in medicine seldom possess a good preliminary general education. There is no medical school in the world that can make satisfactory doctors out of persons who are ignorant of simple arithmetical calculations or elementary science, and many of the pupils who present themselves are really as untaught as this. The result is that valuable time, which ought to he spent in medical studies, has to be given up to the acquirement of knowledge that should have been attained in the schoolroom.

The requirements of the Indian universities which grant medical degrees to women are high, and as a fair sample of what is demanded by all, I will give the outline course that is followed at Calcutta for the female certificate class.

First Year

Anatomy.

Materia Medica.

Dissections.

Chemistry (thirty elementary lectures).

Compounding (six months).

Test examinations in Anatomy, Materia Medica, and Chemistry.

Second Year

Anatomy.

Physiology (elementary).

Materia Medica.

Chemistry (full course).

Dissections.

Attendance at six *Post mortem* examinations.

Hospital attendance (including out-door departments) twelve months.

Pass examinations in Anatomy, Materia Medica, and Chemistry.

Third Year

Medicine and Clinical Medicine.

Surgery and Clinical Surgery.

Medical Jurisprudence (demonstrations).

Midwifery (with attendance at three labour cases).

Hospital attendance (of which three months in the Ophthalmic Wards).

Pass examinations in Pathology, Physiology, and Medical Jurisprudence,

Pathology (with attendance at six *Post mortems).*

Physiology.

Fourth Year

Medicine and Clinical Medicine.

Surgery and Clinical Surgery.

Midwifery (including six labour cases).

Hospital practice (of which six months in the Medical and Surgical Wards *minus* fifteen attendances at the Dental Dispensary; and six months exclusively in the Midwifery Wards, when the students are to take regular turns of duty, night and day, assisting the regular work of the hospital).

Dentistry (Optional)

Pass examinations in Medicine, Surgery, and Midwifery.

Thirty-three per cent, of marks must be obtained to pass, and there are somewhat stringent rules as to failures. For a lower grade of practitioners, who would be unequal to passing the Entrance Examination of the Calcutta University, or an equivalent test, admission to the Eden Hospital is allowed. Here they receive a year's course of midwifery instruction, and, if found proficient, are entitled to a certificate as fully qualified *dhais* or midwives.

The matriculated female students of the university follow precisely the same course for the final M.B. or L.M.S. examinations as the men, and in this one or two Bengali girls have distinguished themselves. This occupies five years, which are thus filled:—

First Year

Descriptive and Surgical Anatomy.

Chemistry.

Botany.

Dissections.

Second Year

Comparative Anatomy, Comparative Physiology, and Zoology.

Descriptive and Surgical Anatomy.

General Anatomy and Physiology.

Chemistry.

Practical Chemistry.

Materia Medica.

Botany.

Dissections.

Pharmacy, three months.

Preliminary Scientific L.M.S. and M.B. examination.

Third Year

Materia Medica.

Dissections.

Physiology.

Hospital practice, one year.

First M.B. and L.M.S. examination.

Fourth Year

Medicine.

Surgery.

Midwifery.

Medical Jurisprudence with demonstrations.

Hospital practice, twelve months.

Final M.B. or L.M.S. examination.

Fifth Year

Medicine and Clinical Mediciue. Surgery and Clinical Surgery. Midwifery and six labour cases. Medical Jurisprudence with demonstrations. Pathology with demonstrations. Ophthalmic Medicine and Surgery. Hygiene. Dentistry.

Post mortem records. Hospital practice, six months.

Out-door and Eye Infirmary practice, three months each. Final M.B. or L.M.S. examination.

At this juncture, however, I am met by the necessity to allude to the greatest of all India's wants for girl students, and that is an institution upon the lines of our own London School of Medicine for women. The point was first borne in upon me in Madras, where, after some pressure from outside, the university opened its medical classes to women, but—contrary to the strongly expressed opinion of Lady Dufferin and other ladies competent to speak—compelled the male and female students to study together. There are numerous scholarships available for women students; the curriculum is a well-devised one, and the knowledge derived from its training leaves nothing to be desired. Some forty young women, chiefly Eurasians and Hindus, are entered there as students, and some show decided promise. But the point felt by all who have the best interests of the movement at heart is, that until the sexes are permitted to pursue their studies apart, the class of native girl who will take up medicine will not be that most likely to inspire the highest confidence of her co-religionist sisters. They regard it as an extremely "emancipated" thing for her to take up such a calling at all; but when they find that she has prepared herself for it by study side by side with a number of men, they view her conduct as reprehensible; and, rather than advancing the cause of female doctors in India, this course of action (in which, however, Madras stands no worse than the various other universities of the dependency) is decidedly retarding it.

The same I found at Calcutta, where the European and Eurasian far outnumber the native ladies, and I am inclined to think that the better class of these who might be willing to enter upon the medical profession are much deterred from doing so by the knowledge that their studies would have to be pursued side by side with the male students. Certain it is that the district board of Pabna for some months was offering a scholarship of ten rupees a month to any native girl to assist in the medical course, and no one suitable had offered herself for it, while I believe that similar help from the boards of Puri and Mymensingh went a-begging. In the report of the Director of Public Instruction, I observe too that the Superintendent of the Campbell Medical School states with regret that so far it has not been found practicable to raise the standard of female entrance. On the other hand, he is able to mention with satisfaction that in the final Licence Examination only eighteen out of fifty-four male students were successful, while five out of the seven girls who came up were passed with credit. A great and desirable addition to the comfort and well-being of the Calcutta lady students is the Surmo-moyee Hostel or boarding-house for their accommodation, the generous gift of the Maharanee of Cossimbazar, C.I., to advance medical education among the sex. It is situated close to the Eden Hospital, in which, of course, the students have to see much of their practice, and its well-ordered arrangements under Miss Taylor have been keenly valued by its inmates of such varied races and creeds.

I might say the same of the Grant Medical College at Bombay, where, to quote from a *precis* statement, with which I was furnished by official favour, I find that "at the date of the last report the number of female students in attendance was twenty-nine, which was increased to thirty-five by the admission of six new students. Of these thirty-five, six left, one obtained the degree of L.M.S. of the Bombay University, and two have qualified as 'certificated practitioners,' thus leaving twenty-six on the college roll—twenty-two matriculated and four non-matriculated." It is, however, only fair to say that the greater number of these young ladies, whose diligence and conduct are pronounced in every way satisfactory, are Europeans and Eurasians. A few are Parsees, and only one or two are Hindus.

Scattered through the dependency one finds many of the zenana missions maintaining lady doctors, but these are almost invariably Englishwomen who have had their training at home. Here and there, as at Benares or Lucknow, they also support hospitals; and although at one time certain of the evangelizing bodies were rather blamed for their practice of sending out women who did not possess full medical degrees, that objection seems now to have ceased. It may sound inconsistent to advocate the sending out by the Dufferin Rund of women of the hospital assistant class and not commend the missionary societies for acting upon the principle of half a loaf better than no bread, but the cases are hardly analogous. The native practitioners know well that they are responsible to the Civil Surgeon of their district, and that they only treat their female patients under his advice and control. On the other hand, English missionary doctors have been known to attempt cases and even operations of the highest complexity merely upon their own slender knowledge, and the results have not always been wholly satisfactory. However, I visited various zenana hospitals, and generally without any warning of my call, and I certainly saw and heard nothing open to any adverse criticism upon them. Convert women patronize them much, and in this connection may be mentioned a curious little difficulty that the Dufferin Rund had 'to face, and whose solution excited a certain amount of unfavourable comment.

Knowing equally that numerous hospitals supported by mission agencies are available for native Christian women, that the civil hospitals present no obstacles to such that *purdah* or *gosha* women would experience, and that caste Hindu and high-class Mahommedan women regard as something like pariahs those who have accepted Christianity, the Dufferin Fund decided to check the admission to its wards of those who were converts. This of course gave rise to much bitterness in certain circles, but there was no other course open in the matter. The fund had been established to benefit the majority, who would still less have participated in its advantages had they found the hated minority sharing them also. There was consequently no alternative, and it seems unreasonable that there should ever have been any difference of feeling in the matter.

To describe in detail all, or even only the principal hospitals that I inspected while in India would be tedious, and so I will take those only of two of the Presidency towns as representing all that is best and most advanced. I take these in the order that I saw them, and in Madras a place of honour belongs to the Victoria Hospital, which was started in 1885.

Encouragement was given to the movement by the ready and public-spirited action of some of the native princes, including the Prince of Arcot, the Maharajahs of Vizianagram and Travancore, and the Rajah of Pudakota. Very fine buildings were erected, providing all accommodation for general diseases as well as for lying-in, and the medical superintendence was placed in the hands of a staff of highly qualified lady doctors. Gradually the *gosha* women began to appreciate the benefits offered them, and the number of cases treated annually has shown a satisfactory increase.

Intensely and tragically interesting too is the Leper Hospital maintained here, and which by the courtesy of Surgeon-Colonel Cook I was permitted to visit, under his own escort. This magnificently planned group of buildings is controlled by Surgeon-Colonel Cook, and is, I believe, the only hospital of its class officially kept up in British India. Its inmates, several of whom he would not allow me to see on account of the hideous repulsiveness of their appearance, are divided as follows: 22 East Indian (or Eurasian) men, 8 East Indian women, 134 native men, 50 native women, 6 children—doomed, alas! probably to a long life of loathsome disease—and 9 prisoners; the entire number of leper criminals throughout British India. My chiefest interest lay, of course, among the wretched women sufferers, and there was a touch of affectionate pathos in the answer of one soft-voiced Eurasian woman, who had been an inmate of its wards for over twenty-two years, when Surgeon-Colonel Cook asked her if she had "any complaints." She said, "I don't think, sir, we could have a thing more done for us in the world than we get here." All were wonderfully cheerful, and evidently valued the excellent and abundant food and the many comforts provided for them. The men have laid out a pretty garden, and the Eurasian patients occasionally get up little concerts and dramatic entertainments, while kindly hands from outside have helped to fit up modest chapels for the members of every creed within its walls. It is, perhaps, not the least of the testimonies to the breadth and toleration of our Indian Government that in one of the wards a little enclosure should have contained a sanctuary of the Church of England; that another should have had a high altar of the Church of Rome, with jewelled cross and fragrant flowers, while the heavy perfume of the incense just used was still lingering in the air; and a third had concealed behind artfully disposed hangings the signs and symbols of Sivaism; while in yet another were emblems common to all Mohammedan mosques.

At Calcutta the chief female hospital is the Dufferin Victoria, where a great feature is made of its out-patients' department. Here the attendance numbers over twenty thousand yearly. Miss Hamilton, M.D., who was its chief medical officer until she accepted a post as resident physician to the zenana of the Ameer, had a large native private practice, and her great skill and gentleness in dealing with the diseases peculiar to women won widespread confidence in her knowledge. Here, again, arises a difficulty, for though in the wealthier classes large fees are willingly paid for relief from pain or a successful operation, those of middle or humble order seem to imagine that advice should all be gratis.

It is impossible yet to get away from the fact that female life has no very great value in the East, and there are plenty of men still to be found who argue, why should they pay heavy doctors' bills for their wives when, if they die, they can so easily replace them ? It is on this ground that I do not think India offers an unlimited field of work for English lady doctors. So long as these are attached to missions, associations, or hospitals, and are doing philanthropic work, all is well; but it is a matter of greater difficulty than is generally realized for them to build up private practices among the "better-class women in their homes. Some few ladies there are who have done it, and whose gentleness at the sick-bed and skill in surgery have earned for them a far-reaching reputation, but these chiefly have settled and worked in the bigger cities of the dependency, and far more depends upon the individual tact of the lady than many would admit. The movement has passed experiment into permanence, and if it be not going forward as rapidly as we in the vigour of our Western energies think it ought to be, I can only say again, it is only adding one more experience to that long list of trials of patience which tell us that progress in India is only to be made very slowly indeed. By slow steps, however, the women will learn to seek medical help when they want it.

There is only one other aspect of this work upon which I need touch, and that is its indirect educational purpose. On this I will not use my own words, but rather quote a private letter written to me by the editor of one of the leading newspapers of India, in which he says, "The chief value in my eyes of the movement has always lain in the promise and hope it afforded of at last invading the seclusion of the zenana, and thus gradually lifting its inmates out of the appalling depths of ignorance and superstition in which they have for centuries been steeped. For what is it at present that hinders all real progress in the country but the overpowering influence of the zenana. Once break down *that*, or rather shed light into it, and give it a healthy and upward direction, and I believe that progress and enlightenment will make such bounds in this country that the regeneration of India will be a living reality. It is the *educational* influence of the Lady Dufferin movement that I have ever regarded as its chief value (though, curiously enough, I have never seen this idea put forward by any of the professed supporters of the fund, either on the platform or in the press), and I believe that that influence will yet prove to be, when the dark recesses of the zenana shall have been penetrated by reason and light, the most powerful lever to progress, and the greatest stimulus to the spread of Christianity throughout the land that it would be possible to discover. What is it but this influence of the women, moulded in the ignorance and superstition of the women's quarter, that is at present, and will continue to be until it is given a right direction, the great hindrance and drawback that is fatal to all real progress ? Get at the women then; educate them, bring them to a more enlightened frame of mind. Show them the *beauties* of Christianity, appeal to their hearts by wisdom and the personal example of beautiful lives, and you will see such an era of progress set in that the regeneration of India will be a reality, and the conversion of its people an accomplished fact. When *that* is done, England's great mission in India will have been accomplished, and it will be the proudest achievement that was ever entrusted to a great nation to perform in the history of the world."

●●

9

Embroidery and Needlecraft

"Them hath He filled with wisdom *of* heart, to work all manner of work, of the engraver, and of the cunning workman, and of the embroiderer, in blue, and in purple, and in scarlet, and in fine linen, and of the weaver, even of them that do any work, and of those that devise cunning work."

—Exodus xxxv. 35.

Embroidery, in India, is by no means as distinctively a woman's art as it is in the West. In fact, down the picturesque Chandni Chowk of Delhi, where the European sightseer is pressed to buy examples of its famous gold and silver embroideries upon satin, it is the men who are to be seen sitting at large frames and working with infinite patience in glistering metallic thread, it may be one of the immortal designs of the knop and flower, or pomegranate variations. Again, at Bombay, where the wealthy Parsee ladies do not hesitate to pay ten or twelve pounds sterling for a gold and silver worked border for their *saris*, it will be men's fingers that will execute the order. More than probably, too, the cap with its elaborate gold and silver lace, that the Mahommedan gentleman of the north-west wears in the house, will have been adorned by a Hindu man.

Sir George Birdwood, greatest of all authorities on Indian domestic art, wrote in connection with an exhibition of needlework arranged in London, in 1893, by Mrs. David Carmichael and the Society for the Preservation of Indian

Art, "I have myself seen women weaving in India, but never, save for domestic purposes, embroidering. ... I did not know of any needlework being produced by the women of India for sale, excepting the *phul-kari (i.e.* flower-work) of the sub-Alpine Himalayan region of the Tarai." The collection Sir George pronounced of especial interest, and remarked further, that "its public exhibition in this country was not unlikely to mark a distinct step in the advancement of the education of Indian women, in a direction for once happily in complete consonancy with their inherited indigenous culture. Unfortunately the collection, judged by its merits, was very disappointing. It demonstrated, indeed, the presence of widespread accomplishment—in the conventional, not the etymological meaning of the word—but also in the widest absence of that absolute artistic achievement which imparts even to a scrap of needlework a beauty moth and rust cannot corrupt, nor thieves break through and steal, for, once its fair idea, or Divine archetype, as a Platonist would say, is realized, it lives for ever, a heavenly treasure, in the memories of men."

When I saw that display, however, I did not grasp what I have since, and that is, that in no branch of Indian art has British influence been so mischievously detrimental as in needlecraft. The native women are quick to seize upon a small novelty that can be passed on from one to another, and the vulgar showiness and easy accomplishment of our Western woolwork, in all the worst hideousness of Berlin cross-stitch and crewels, seems to have pleased some innate sentiment in them, for, unfortunately, they have adopted and perpetrated these in the vilest form. The mission schools are to be held responsible for most of the evil that has been wrought in this direction. Drawn, as so large a percentage of their teachers are, from the lower middle classes, and imbued with the worst philistinism of their order, these instructors from outside were equally utterly unable to appreciate the wondrous beauties of form and colouring of indigenous embroidery, or to impart a knowledge of anything better than the decorative tastes of the back parlour.

It is bad enough to find a table laid out with such monstrosities on exhibition when one goes to visit a school, but it is a thousand fold worse to find that a wholesale acceptance of their horrors has run like a bad plague into the women's domestic life in the large towns. One may go into a middle-class zenana and find a young wife crocheting an abomination in violet and yellow for her husband, who is employed on night railway duty, which he will wrap about his pate and speak of in the vernacular as a "head comfort." In fact, to take an Indian journey by night in mid-winter suggests nothing so much as that a violent epidemic of acute toothache has broken out, so many are the heads swathed up in these woollen marvels of ugliness. One may go into the women's quarters of a palace, and find an exquisite silver bottle all chased or *repoussee,* and filled with rose-water or some fragrant scent which will be sprinkled over the inevitable bouquet presented on leaving, and standing upon a mat of magenta and sky blue. For under such circumstances one realizes the painful truth that ugliness in these forms has become an everyday fact. Moreover, it is also true that girls come to school purposely to learn how to do crewel-work or how to make "water-lily" mats, an illustration that would be comic, if it were not also very sad, of the perverse instinct of human nature to learn what it had better not know.

I naturally expressed myself with some vigour on this question, alike to educational authorities and school teachers, as well as in one or two of the leading Anglo-Indian newspapers. The excuse invariably put forward was, the official recognition of needlework as a code subject was next to nothing, and that funds for the purchase of good designs and materials were seldom available. But these difficulties are far from insuperable where any sense of artistic purpose exists; for in the Hobart (Mahommedan) girls' school at

Madras I saw a delightful phulkari embroidered in shades of rich orange silk, upon deep red *dungaree* (a native cloth), that was altogether an artistic delight in its rich yet subdued tones and even stitching. Some of the table-cloths here were also quite harmonious and pleasing. Again, at the opposite corner of the "dependency, in the native state of Bhaunagar, where Miss Brooke is to all intents and purposes directress of female education, the needlework was deserving of all commendation. Fashionable young ladies in the Gujerat district affect a lavish amount of embroidery upon the right—the uncovered sleeve of their *cholis,* and have another odd little taste' in placing a tiny square or oval device upon the right breast. Miss Brooke, therefore, set herself to obtain some of the best native designs favoured for these uses, and encourages £he girls to exercise their own wonderful—when not perverted by Western models—taste for colouring, and the results at the Mahjiraj school, both in made-up *cliolis* and decorative work, were nothing short of charming. When I visited this institution, Princess Kesaba, the daughter of the enlightened and cultured gentleman who is the Maharajah of the State, had just completed, according to her own design and taste, one of the daintiest pairs of slippers ever seen outside Cinderella's fairy ball, in pearl white velvet with gold and silver thread, and so delicately pretty were some of the lawn handkerchiefs embroidered in white flax in the well-raised chikan stitch, that I perforce begged one or two to bring home.

From the purely utilitarian point of view even, the folly of fostering the production of so much ugly and useless work should be apparent. Nobody will buy it, for if any appreciable native demand arose for it for "decorative" uses, the machinery of Switzerland and Germany would promptly glut the bazaars with d'oylys and antimacassars of the lowest and cheapest grades of mechanical production. Europe certainly does not want it, as our own "depots for poor ladies' work" can tell; but, on the other hand, Europe will purchase good and characteristically native work to an almost unlimited extent. Since my return to England, however, I learn with great satisfaction that the Society for the Encouragement and Preservation of Indian Art has taken the matter up, for if once there comes a suspension in the sequence of teaching as mother has passed it on to daughter, the beautiful arts of stitchery and taste of colour may be lost, and that would in truth be a loss to India herself as well as art-loving Europe.

It is on the Bombay side, throughout Gujarat and Katthiawar, that one finds the most interesting and uncontaminated indigenous needle-craft. How old, as an art, it is in this district one may judge from Marco Polo, who referred to the "beautiful mats in red and blue leather, exquisitely inlaid with figures of birds and beasts, and skilfully embroidered with gold and silver wire. They are marvellously beautiful things; they are used by the Saracens to sleep upon, and capital are they for that purpose."

Roughly speaking, the embroidery for household uses and personal wear is done by the women of Gujarat, Kutch, and Katthiawar, while that for commercial purposes is mostly wrought by men. It is by no means easy to obtain good pieces of the former character, for the women are loth to part with what has cost them so much and such tedious labour. For general wear they affect cotton cloth of hand-loom native manufacture, and dyed to a rich deep shade of red with, I believe, cochineal and *narsingar,* the honey-scented flower of *Nyctanthes arbor tristis.* The designs are of primitive character, and include rude geometric patterns, squares, stars, cones, pyramids, and sometimes uncouth animal forms. Silk and cotton is often used side by side, and one often finds, as in a petticoat border that I have, green cotton and yellow silk pyramids alternating. The green chosen is usually a warm myrtle, the yellow leans to strong orange, blue is a deep royal shade, and crimson decided though bright. The effect of these embroideries is enhanced by small bits of mirrored glass which are worked in in a curious stitch uniting a little of both button-holing and cross-stitching in itself.

The stitches themselves are all somewhat difficult to classify exactly, as one seldom finds them practised precisely as with ourselves. The chain and feather stitches are employed, however, without much modification, and the satin stitch is also used for careful and ornamental effects. Darning is often very cleverly utilized to produce small and regular patterns upon large surfaces, and cross-stitch both in its primitive simplicity as well as in the greater complexity of its Persian form one meets with frequently. "Couching" or "laid" embroidery is also general, this being the technical term that is used to define all such patterns as are worked by threads, whether of gold, silver, silk, cotton, or crewels stretched flatly upon the ground material, and fastened into position by small stitches brought from the back at intervals. This is employed in many variations, including one very much like the basket stitch, which, in its representation of plaited openwork, is usually reckoned very difficult of deft execution.

Not alone for work upon silk, cotton, or cloth is the Bombay side famous. "With the emancipation from *purdah,* that the Parsee women have secured for themselves, they have also thrown off many of their former conventions concerning dress, though they wisely retain the *sari* in its graceful and becoming drapings as their principal garment. But the style of these has changed enormously during the past thirty years, as I realized when one of the leading Parsee ladies in Bombay showed me what had been her mother's most costly and valued wardrobe, and her own, according to the newer idea prevailing among the more fashionable of her community. The older draperies were generally of native manufacture in heavy silks and in characteristic native or somewhat Persianized design and colouring. Rich and highly decorative as examples of the weaver's craft they undoubtedly were; but somehow, even to me, with all my admiration of the native art, they seemed a trifle heavy and antiquated for personal wear. Nowadays it is Japan and Paris that are supplying the Parsee society women with their materials, the former sending in a very fine and clinging silk, made about thirty-four inches wide, and in the most exquisite shades. Parsee ladies, I should mention, now favour very delicate colouring, and shell-pinks, straw, peach; mauve of the tint of the palest Parma violets, pale sky and twig-green, are among their favourite tints. This the Japanese have learnt, and these silks constitute a very appreciable item in the shipping business that is monthly developing in importance between Bombay and Japan. Paris supplies gauzes and *crepes de chine* in similarly well selected colouring, as well as the rainbow and serpentine effects, lately favoured of European fashion, which are also meeting with approval from Eastern buyers.

But none of these can be regarded as made up saris until a border has been put to them. For everyday and morning wear the girls and women embroider these for themselves upon ribbon, and I noted with great pleasure in the Parsee schools in Bombay, that the students are rather encouraged to do this, to them really useful work, than to waste time over hideous woolwork and mat making. For greater occasions and full dress-wear, at, say, official dinners or dances, these borders are much more elaborate, and are usually worked in gold or silver wire upon the best ribbon velvet. It is obvious that for such a purpose, where the folds must be the softest and most graceful, none but the most flexible metallic thread can be employed, and this, which is known as *kullabatoon,* is thus prepared: "For gold thread, a piece of silver, about the length and thickness of a man's forefinger, is gilded at least three times heavily with the purest gold, all alloy being previously most carefully discharged from the silver. This piece of gilt silver is beaten out to the size of a stout wire, and is then drawn through successive holes in a steel plate until it is literally as fine as a hair. The gilding is not disturbed by this process, and the wire finally appears as if of fine gold. It is then flattened in an extremely delicate and skilful manner. The workman is seated before a small and highly polished steel anvil, about two inches broad, with a steel plate in which there are two or three holes set opposite to him and perpendicular to the anvil, and draws through these holes as many wires—two or three as it may be—by a motion of the finger and thumb of his left hand, striking them rapidly but firmly with a steel hammer, the face of which is also polished like that of the anvil. This flattens the wire perfectly, and such is the skill of manipulation, that no portion of the wire escapes the blow of the hammer, the action of drawing the wire, rapid as it is, being adjusted to the length which will be covered by the face of the hammer in its descent. No system of rollers or other machinery could probably ensure the same effect, whether of extreme thinness of the flattened wire or its softness and ductility.

> "To wind the wire upon silk thread, the silk is very slightly twisted, and is rolled upon a winder. The end is then passed over a polished steel hook fixed to a beam in the ceiling of the workshop, and to it is suspended a spindle with a long bamboo shank, slightly weighted to keep it steady, which nearly touches the floor. The workman gives the shank of the spindle a sharp turn upon his thigh which sets it spinning with rapidity. The gold wire, which has been wound upon a reel as it passes behind the maker, is then applied to the bottom of the silk thread near the spindle, and twists itself upwards, being guided by the workman as high as he can conveniently reach, or nearly his own height upon the thread, but it is impossible to describe in exact terms the curiously dexterous and rapid process of this manipulation. The spindle is then stopped, the thread, now covered with wire, is wound upon it and fastened in a notch of the shank, when the silk thread is drawn

down, and the spindle is again set running with the same result as before.

"On examination of the *kullabatoon,* the extreme thinness and flexibility of the flattened wire, and its delicacy and beauty, will at once be apparent in comparison with attempts made in Europe with rolling machinery. It is remarkable that the gold and silver alike never tarnish, but retain their lustre and colours even though washed. This is the result of the absolute purity both of, the gold - and silver employed. There is, of course, no doubt but that *kullaba-toon,* with considerable alloy in the wire, is also made and used in India, but it never enters into the higher classes of manufactures."

Surat is a great centre for Western India of embroidery work, though it is mostly done by men, of whom it is estimated that about seven hundred are fully occupied by it. The gold or silver thread is supplied to them by native and local merchants, who employ them to do the embroidery at rates varying from 7c?. to Is. 3c?. a day, according to their skill and proficiency, and their average earnings are estimated at from fifteen to twenty-five rupees a month. The designs, which are generally very simple in character, are printed in gum and chalk by means of little wooden blocks, and the ribbon or material to be worked upon" is kept taut over a primitive wooden frame, while ordinary needles are used.

From Delhi, too, comes a great quantity of this gold and silver work, and at Bombay a very large firm of embroiderers from here are settled. In Delhi and Agra, also, considerable skill has been shown in adapting native designs and work to European uses, and that on the whole with a creditable freedom from vulgarization of design. Very charming are satin slippers, unmade up, but suitable for evening wear; and I also saw good work applied to Zouave jackets, and many other accessories of European dress. Here, indeed, it forms one of the staple industries, and in an old report of 1881-82, that I chanced to turn up while at Delhi, it is noted that in the Punjab, with the old Muslim capital and Agra as chief centres, some 50,000 are employed in this craft, and it was then estimated that 328,000 miles of silver and silver gilt wire were produced here for use in the province and export to other places.

More recent official information says the purity of the metals used, which in former times, especially at Lahore, was the subject of stringent regulation and surveillance both on the part of Governments and the guilds of wire-drawers, is now necessarily left to the exigencies of a trade in which cheapness is yearly growing a more essential condition. A sort of assay, however, is consequent on the demand of the municipality for octroi duty. Mr. Stogden, speaking with the authority of official knowledge, thus describes this part of the business: "The Municipal Committee have established an octroi station in Delhi. To this station the dealers bring their raw material to be melted down, and the amount of duty payable by them depends on the quality of the ingot they intend to turn out. The scale is as follows: Gold kandala, Re. 1-8 per ingot of 75 tolas; silver kandala, Re. 1-4 ditto; sham gold, 8 annas per ingot of 75 tolas ; ditto silver, 4 annas; *kandala mel* (half silver, half copper) 12 annas per ingot; silver wire, three pice per tola. The dealer presents his silver and copper to be weighed, and on payment of the duty a receipt is granted to him. He then takes his metal into the station and melts it down in an earthen crucible, called *Jcathdla,* in one of the numerous compartments set aside for the purpose. From the crucible he pours it into an iron mould called *reya.* The bar or ingot of silver and copper when thus melted down is called *gulli.* If it is intended to work gold leaf into it, it is about 8 inches long by *1* inches square. The *gulli* is then made over to the *Jcandala hash,* or wire-drawer."

I was shown an enormous *portiere* at Delhi, worked to give a veritable needle-picture of the Taj, and for the description of the way in which such pieces, are wrought, though few are now undertaken, I may be permitted to borrow a few lines from an article by Mr. Kipling, CLE., on the industries of the Punjab.

"In cases where the whole of the field is to be covered with gold work, a stout cotton cloth is stretched on the frame. On this the design is drawn by the draughtsman, and the parts to be raised are worked over with thick, soft cotton, dyed yellow, passed on the surface from a reel, and stitched down at each passing with ordinary sewing thread. The centre veins of leaves and other forms are marked with stitching, and a kind of modelled surface is thus produced in thick cotton thread. Over these forms the gold and silver thread is laid, their lines following sometimes those of the cotton underlay and sometimes going in opposite directions. For the grounds, varieties of basket-work and herring-bone stitches are adopted; spangles and lines of twisted wire are introduced to mark and relieve the leading lines of the pattern. Several men work at once on these fabrics, and they are not so long in execution as this description may seem to indicate. The sheen of the gold threads, interlaced in different directions as they cross over raised surfaces, produces a brilliant and, in large pieces, a splendid effect. In cases where coloured silk velvet is bordered with raised gold embroidery of this kind, the velvet is sewn on strong cotton cloth, and during the work the parts to be left plain are kept carefully covered up. In the same way caps, cushions, tea-cosies and other trifles are wrought; but as relief is not always necessary, as in large throne cloths, elephant housings, and the like, the forms are not always embossed in cotton."

Another famous centre of embroidery was and still is Dacca, where the 'art is chiefly in the hands of the Fantis, an off-shoot from the weaver caste, which was supposed to possess the secret of making muslins of such filmy fineness, that Sir George Birdwood tells us, in the days of Shah Jehangir a piece fifteen yards long and one yard wide weighed only nine hundred grains, while if such were laid upon damp grass it became almost invisible. Thus it had the name of *shalmam,* or "dew of evening," and another description was known as *ah rawan,* or "the running water," because it was quite indistinguishable in water. Their inherited tastes are therefore towards embroidery upon cotton, and this they do with great skill, varying it often with drawn-thread effects, rivalling those of Sicily and Crete. In India this is known as *chikan kari,* or *chikan dozi,* and for the best classes of it a frame is always used. But although one finds Hindus thus working, in spite of the exceedingly stringent rules of caste which obtain among them, embroidery generally is far more done by poor Muslims. From Dacca still a considerable trade is done with Jedda and Bushire in worked cotton or mixed silk and cotton cloths for Mahommedan wear. Though sketchy in design, and rough in execution, many of these pieces are decoratively effective, but better perhaps is not to be expected for the low rates which are paid for them. It is done almost exclusively by the women of poor though respectable Mahommedan families, and is rather a curious instance of the "pocket-money" wage, as I am assured that only a rupee to a rupee and a half a month is given for it, which is accepted, much as the worker at home, assured of her bread and butter by father or husband, undersells the necessitous wage-earner merely to obtain enough to buy the finery she covets.

I was unable to extend my travels into Cashmere, but in all the towns of the north-west one sees ample example of the splendid boldly designed and coloured work that comes down from its distant hills and plains. As to the embroidered burnouses, caps, and dressing-gowns, upon its exquisitely soft native woollen fabrics, they are familiar enough, but it is a wonder to me that no enterprising dealer in artistic carpets has ever placed upon the London market the worked rugs that the shops of Delhi and Agra display in fascinating temptation. These are of two sorts, one of which is a very thick and soft felt, made usually about six feet long, and three feet six inches wide. They are generally of a beautifully subdued turquoise blue, a natural cedar brown, or bleached white, and are embroidered all over in a running conventionalized floral design, in the most delightfully harmonized colours, both vivid and dull. I have seen them in a dark indigo, and a rich orange ground, but these shades are not so general. For the other description a heavy diagonally woven material, somewhat resembling a rougher form of the European so-called "art" serge, is employed. A stout lining of cotton is given to this, and the stitches of the embroidery are carried right through. These are often made as much as ten feet long, and the shades I have seen most generally used are a rich deep crimson, or a delightful sage green, but it is usual to add to them a black border, which is also worked over.

Wool, very much like crewels in texture, is the medium of embroidery, and a great variety of colours is generally employed, but always with the artist's eye for blending. The stitch used is simply the chain, looped round the needle, with an occasional employment of that known as the stem, but with these, usually so stiff and rigid in Western needlework, these Kashmeri women-workers obtain not only the most gracefully running curves and sweeps, but a very good filled-in effect for impossible flowers and foliage. They are not a luxury that the economical traveller must perforce forego, as in Delhi the prices for such pieces are from five to ten rupees each, while in Bombay they are only very slightly dearer.

In Southern India, where mission effort has been longest at work, and imported ideas have perhaps taken their firmest hold, very creditable copies of Maltese, Torchon, and other laces are made in the schools and homes of the people. Quilon and Alleppy are both well known for their work of this description, which is bought at very low prices of the women makers, and taken round to the European and Eurasian inhabitants of the towns. The average European resident has, however, very little conscience as to fair prices for even hand work, which she expects and bargains to buy for the same price as the products of the Nottingham looms, and really choice work, for which the delicate native fingers would be pre-eminently suited, does not receive the encouragement it deserves. But in this respect lace stands no worse than any other art product of the East. The curse of cheapness has fallen upon all that is popular, degrading design, vulgarizing execution, and I came to the conclusion that the only way to bring back what was covetable and desirable was to look for such things as Guzerati petticoats, the silk, or the brass ware of native use, and the rugs not discovered yet by the "art furnishers," in order to escape the workings of that inexorable law, as it works out in the Calcutta or the Bombay store, "one rupee, fifteen annas, five pice."

●●

10

Jewellery and Ornament

"The bravery of their tinkling ornaments, and the cauls, and the round tires like the moon, the chains, and the bracelets, and the mufflers, the anklets, and the headbands, and the perfume boxes, and the amulets, the earrings and the nose jewels."—Isaiah iii. 18-21. Literal rendering.

From the poorest sweeper woman of the towns, who puts half a dozen glass bangles upon her wrists, or the Kol coalcutter girl who painfully forces heavy curved anklets of bell-metal over her feet, to the wealthy begum of a native state, or the "emancipated" ranee who has broken her *purdah* and goes to the Government House receptions, the love of jewellery is to be found among the entire female population of the East. It forms an appreciable factor in her dowry, it is a fruitful source of troubles in jealousy and quarrels, and it is a perpetual anxiety from the temptations it affords to robbery; but it is a woman's most precious belonging, and nothing, not even fine clothes, affords any compensation for its absence. The taste exists universally, and though forms and patterns differ with almost every province, or even district, it is as characteristic a feature of the sex at Madras as Lahore, in Bhaunagar as at Calcutta.

The very lowest form of all is, of course, the cheap glass bangles. There is a common belief that these are supplied by the continent of Europe, but so far as my own efforts, at tracing them to their source went, I found that a large proportion were Chinese. I bought numbers of them in the original half-dozen sets in blue, green, and amber glass, paying on an average a halfpenny each bracelet for them, and in every instance the cards to which they were fastened bore Chinese characters, and in some cases the words "from China" as well. There is a still lower grade, however, made with waved lines, and in a size so tiny that I could not pass it over my own glove-size and very flexible hand. These, I believe, are manufactured in the north-west; and at Delhi one sees them in great quantities in the native bazaar.

Of only slightly higher importance are the lacquered bracelets, and the process by which these are made gives a good idea of the exceeding cheapness of labour when this allows of their being sold at less than a penny each. A chief centre of their manufacture is in the Panch Mahal district of Gujarat, and the lac used in making them is gathered by the Bhils, a woodland people of Upper Western India. They exchange this for grain with the Banya trading community, who in turn retail it to the actual makers. The lac is softened, and rings of it are formed round the well-oiled top of a rice-pounder, which is about the size of a woman's wrist. Twenty-five of these are thus made, and are just sufficiently heated again to cause them to stick together. They are then rubbed with powdered brick-dust, and polished with blue, red, or yellow-coloured copal varnish. Mr. H. A. Acworth, who has devoted much attention to this industry, states that in the next step, which is to print a pattern upon the bracelet, a whole day is occupied in pounding together two ounces of tin with a small lump of glue, till they form a grey metallic paste, which is afterwards boiled in a copper pot, and then strained. Meanwhile a piece of cotton wool is bound upon a stick, and is wetted and pressed till it is firm enough to retain an impression drawn upon it with an iron point. When this primitive stamp is dipped into the tin solution it brings out a modicum of it, which is pressed on to the ornament in the design. This turns to a bright golden colour on the application of varnish, while specks and points of white or red, produced by the admixture of chalk or vermilion with the tin solution, are dropped on to heighten the effect. These *choories,* as they are called, are immensely popular in feminine estimation, and one may often find a rich lady wearing two or three of them among her gold and silver bracelets, while the poorer woman puts on ten or twelve. The same composition is used in the central provinces and Upper India to make the *sithi* or *bindi,* a head ornament, which has a centre point to fall back upon the hair, and large bosses for the ear.

Until one makes a good deal of direct inquiry, one is unaware that bracelets vary in name according to the position in which they are worn upon the arm. The Hindu women, for instance, have the *guyra,* the *kukna,* and the *punchi,* which are worn next the hand, and which generally have some further descriptive appellation to denote whether they are supposed to represent teeth, seeds, flowers, or beads. Then come the *choories,* but there is a certain *chun,* usually a simple band of silver or metal, which may be put on among them. Beyond these last, and towards the elbow, are the *kuttri, panch-luri, puchna,* and other forms, while above the elbow several forms of armlets may be worn, a favourite one being the *nao megger,* or "nine gems," and occasionally one sees in these a very pretty and uncommon blending of stones. In the marvellous collection of Indian peasant jewellery made by Mrs. Rivett Carnac there is a pair formed of large and pale yellow topaz, surrounded with turquoise, and the delicate charm of this combination is scarcely to be imagined.

The next step up from the cheap glass and lacquer ornaments are those made from bell-metal, this being of various alloys, and often containing, as in the particular manufacture for which Berhampore is celebrated, an appreciable admixture of silver. "Where bell-metal is employed, it is usually in the form of very heavy armlets and anklets, and it is rather a characteristic of the non-Aryan tribes. Many of the Kols of Bengal wear enormous masses of what one may almost call ironmongery, and I have seen them as much as five inches deep and an inch thick, and perfectly solid. From six to eight pounds in weight is by no means unusual, and in exceptional instances they are still heavier. The hammered ornamentation is simple but effective, and they are worn with great pride. Indeed, it is often a matter of severe pain to put these huge things on, and unless it be done while a girl is still very young, it would be impossible to force them over the heel. Even then, as in the case of some that are slightly curved in shape, the process is one of real torture, which would not be borne save at the command of female vanity, and one sees girls with their feet swollen and chafed after it, smiling over the addition made to their beauty. The armlets are generally furnished with some form of clasp. Some of the very low-caste women, as Doms and Dhobies, wear a graduated series of thick brass or bell-metal bangles, almost covering the arm from wrist to elbow.

There is an immense amount of imitation jewellery worn among the poorer classes, and mock pearls and stones abound in the native bazaars. The favourite designs of *jumka,* "the shaking," or pendent for the ear, and the *bala bijli,* or "the lightning" from the flash and shimmer of its light fringe, and many others are freely copied and adapted, and little girls spend their earliest pice in buying gilt and glitter of this sort.

Head-dresses vary greatly in different parts of India. The Mahratta women have the *haituch,* which is composed of three separate pieces, a round boss being worn in the centre of the hair, with leaf-shaped or crescent ornaments extending forward towards the brow. In Madras, however, the side pieces disappear, and a number of smaller circles or brooches are fixed in the hair; and here I may mention the curious fact that no native woman uses hair-pins. The general method of disposing of her tresses, which she is fond of oiling and scenting, is to twist it into a close knot at the back of her head, and I have never seen this "come down" under any exercise or exertion, or look other than neat and smooth. The prettiest and most artistic hair-dressing that I know is among the Nayar and Canarese women of the west coast. They possess this "crowning glory" in abundance, and it is soft and fine. It is all gathered into a mass towards the top of the left side of the head, and with one or two deft twists they throw it round in a perfectly charming coil. Against this, however, the Canarese women are guilty of a hideous practice in wearing the huge earrings with which they distort the lobe of the ear. A small bar of metal is first inserted, and gradually larger pieces are introduced till they can wear a disc of as much as two and a half inches in diameter. With the poorer women this is often only of dark polished wood or bone, but the richer ones have them of gold or silver.

The rings form an important item in the parure, and are worn equally on all fingers of the hand except the second. Indeed, even the thumb is adorned, and in this one often finds a small piece of mirror, or else it has a tiny receptacle to contain a piece of cotton wool steeped in some strong aromatic oil or perfume. There is no special characteristic about native rings, unless they are signets, which though occasionally worn by women, are more particularly a man's ornament. These often bear interesting devices or anagrams, intelligible only to the initiated.

Some of the boxes in which a native woman keeps her betel and areca nut, cardamoms, spices, the soorma to darken her eyelashes and eyebrows, and other cosmetics, are very curious, especially in Southern India. One of these that I brought home was of bell-metal, circular in shape, and divided into nine compartments. Each of these had a separate cover on its own hinge, while to fasten all down in the centre was a screw, finished on the top with a conventionally modelled peacock.

The Mahommedan woman of the north-west and the Punjab does not differ markedly from the Hindu in the ornaments characteristic to her outfit of jewellery. First there is the *tika,* or adornment for the head, which is generally of flexible workmanship, or composed of closely interlocked links. The two parts forming this pass one on either side of the brow and face to the ear, and are generally finished with a pendent but very close-set fringe of tiny devices, which may be balls, stars, lozenges, ovals, circles, or crescents. From the centre, over the parting of the hair, there falls on to the forehead an ornament, round, square, or crescent-shaped, and matching in finish the bordering of the rest of the article. At the lobe of the ear, where the broad strips join it, another large boss appears, but from this further eardrops, which may be quite different in design, are often added. Such an adornment naturally only belongs to the comparatively wealthy, and I have never seen these of anything less valuable than silver. I should add that in the case of such heavy earrings as these usually are, and many more like them, that besides being supported in the pierced lobe, there is generally a wire which passes right round the ear to keep them in position. Except by the Canarese women, just alluded to, it is regarded as a deformity to spoil the natural contour of the organ of sound.

Then comes the nose-ring, which the Muslim women as a rule do not wear so large as the Hindus, and with the former is often no more than a small and inconspicuous jewel.

The necklace has many names and many varieties, as *mala, luchcha, do-lari,* according to design. It is often a broad *collier,* shaped to fit the neck and shoulders, of interlinked rings or cables, and finished, like the *tika,* with a thick but loosely set border of tiny metallic devices. The bracelets usually correspond exactly. Longer necklets, reaching sometimes to below the waist, made of beads, often very beautifully cut or chased, and occasionally of exceedingly quaint oval form, are also worn, and are generally finished with some medallion or pendant. A glance at this will tell one instantly to which of the two great races the wearer belongs, as the Hindu is almost certain to exhibit upon hers one of the many deities of her Pantheon; but the Mahom-medan, forbidden to make any "graven image or the likeness of anything that is in the heaven above or the earth beneath," falls back upon the presentment of conventional figures and geometric patterns. Necklets, like girdles, are also made of squares linked together, and I have seen many really covet-able examples of these in silver, delightfully enamelled in shades of turquoise blue. One of the really prettiest of the Delhi patterns which are most worn in the north-west is the twisted or *babul* setting for large amethysts, turquoises, topaz, or garnets, which are often employed for costly necklets. Each stone is set in a separate little square, and surrounded by fine gold work, based in treatment upon the suggestion of the soft yellow filaments of the flower of *Acacia Arabica,* and the separate pieces are fastened together with small chains. A woman's possessions may begin with quite a short necklet, but as time and prosperity goes on another and another square will be added, until it reaches at last a handsome length.

It is considered right that the bridegroom, wherever practicable, should present the bride with a gold ornament, but a ring is not used to denote the wedded state as with ourselves. A small iron bangle, with no visible juncture, is one of the most usual symbols of marriage, as it is supposed to indicate the strength and indissolubleness of the bond. Certain castes also wear a bead necklet, and it is regarded as an extremely inauspicious omen should this accidentally break, though no harm arises from re-stringing it. I found less superstition, however, concerning jewellery than I expected. There are certain talismanic charms accredited to the diamond, and the *nava ratna,* or *nos ratan* of nine gems, is supposed to bring good fortune. The jewels composing this are the coral, topaz, sapphire, ruby, a flat diamond and a cut diamond, emerald, jacinth, and carbuncle. Another form substitutes for some of these the pearl, ruby, and lapis lazuli. There is nothing, however, as greatly prized for its direct influence with the gods as the salagram, which is a kind of ammonite found in one or two of the tributaries of the Ganges. The most precious are perfectly black, and they then belong to the symbolism of Vishnu and Krishna. If they are violet they are associated with one of the more angry incarnations, but are nevertheless of great value. In the Yishnuite temples, where one is generally kept, they are washed and oiled with exceeding care; but almost every true Brahman endeavours to possess at least one in the house.

Of indigenous gold ornaments, the most interesting specimens perhaps are furnished from Southern India. From Bangalore come large raised discs with crescents attached, worn as earrings, and often remarkable for beautiful beaten work; and Mysore, Vizianagram, and Tanjore all send out the large but very light ornaments for the head that are worn on festal occasions throughout the Madras Presidency, and very widely also in the native States. The Swami ornaments of this district, with their representations of Vishnu and his ten incarnations or *avataras,* in one of which he is found, besides his consort Lakshmi; Rambha, the type of womanly loveliness and amiability; Siva, "the omnipresent, but especially in twelve forms and places," and others in which Krishna appear, are universally popular; while in the Bombay Presidency, and throughout Gujarat, one finds very pretty bracelets and necklets of gold beads threaded on string. They are marvellously thin and light, yet they are beaten into beautiful and always appropriate designs. Some of the fine gold wire jewellery is also exceedingly charming, and bracelets so soft and flexible are made of it as to be almost crushable in the hand.

To European eyes the gemmed ornaments of the women are wont to seem rather gaudy and tawdry, besides rough in setting. The heterogeneous mixtures of stones, which will place a turquoise, an emerald, and a garnet in close juxtaposition, seems strange after the reserve shown in the West as to jewel combinations, and undoubtedly our own styles of cutting show precious stones to greater advantage than the native methods. Mr. Kipling, whose knowledge of the inner workings of the jewellery trade of Delhi is not to be gainsaid, points out that European forms are, however, growing in favour, and that articles made for wealthy natives, even where indigenous designs are retained, are growing noticeably neater. Moreover, many of the richer native ladies of the large towns are beginning to wear genuine Bond Street ornaments. Two very strictly *purdah* brides, with whom I had tea at Bombay, showed me their presents, and among these were dainty watch bracelets of a well-known London house, safety-pin brooches with quaint little sporting devices, and other things which seemed characteristic rather of a fashionable wedding in town. As to the trade in jewels, Mr. Kipling remarks, in the official Punjab Gazetteer—

> "The telegraph and the modern facilities for travel have brought the precious-stone trade of the world together in a way that is surprising to those unfamiliar with its workings. It is now, as always, a somewhat secret branch of commerce. German Jews, trained in Paris, are perhaps the most prominent and leading dealers. There is scarcely a wedding or an accession affording an opportunity for the sale of precious stones that is not telegraphed to Paris, London, St. Petersburg, Amsterdam, Berlin and Vienna. Delhi and the rest of India are now included in

this secret syndicate, and are periodically visited by dealers who come and go unnoticed; so that Tavernier was but the forerunner of a succession of jewel merchants. For pearls, Bombay is a great market; but even there, one of the leaders of the trade, the late Panniah Lall, was a Delhi man. In coloured stones this city has still a considerable trade, and the greater part of the valuable find of sapphires in the Cashmere territory has been absorbed by the Delhi jewellers. Most of these men are in the hands of bankers, or, perhaps more correctly, they are the agents of bankers."

Especially noticeable, too, is the Europeanization of design and purpose that has come over the filagree work of Trichinopoly and Cuttack. It is exceedingly fine still in execution, but all that was primitive and simple has gone out of it. The most horrible degradation, however, that I saw was at Cochin, which possessed once a very good little school of silver filagree workers, who produced stronger and bolder work than that of the two other seats of the industry. I wanted an example or two to bring home, and eventually secured one or two that did not offend me, but I was offered —take note, O Society for the Encouragement and Preservation of Indian Art—brooches in the form of banjoes, tennis-racquets, and parasols! Even so far have the horrors of Birmingham designs wrought their mischievous effects !

●●

11

Amusements and Pleasures

" Therefore the ways were swept, Rose odours sprinkled in the streets, the streets Were hung with lamps and flags, while merry crowds Gaped on the sword-players and posturers, The jugglers, charmers, swingers, rope-walkers, The Nautch girls in their spangled skirts and bells, That chime light laughter round their restless feet; The masquers wrapped in skins of bear and deer, The tiger-tamers, wrestlers, quail-fighters, Beaters of drum and twanglers of the wire, Who make the people happy by command."

"The Light of Asia" (Sir Edwin Arnold, K.C.S.I.).

Indian girls have a few games that are peculiar to themselves, and very pretty and graceful some of these are. As mere children they join of course with their little brothers and cousins in various pastimes, and generally find their first toys in tiny clay models. There are also rude musical instruments which are given to them, and, save in form, the contents of the *bibi ghar* nursery are not so very widely removed from our own. The *jhuta-jhulna,* or swing, is invariably a part of its fittings, and a taste for this exercise survives when the girls are grown up. Indeed, I have seen a portly grandmamma sitting in the seat, which resembled a small cot, and realizing apparently a beatific sense of restfulness with the regular backward and forward sway.

The doll, however, is the delight of all others of a little Indian girl's life. It matters to her very little whether it has been dressed by her mother or aunts—a mere rude rag presentment—or is a waxen triumph from France or Germany, brought by a kindly father from some big European stores in the nearest town, it is a treasured possession, valued with a personal affection that I think her little Western prototype in these days of high schools does not attain unto. The dramatic sense, so strong in the natural child, comes uppermost in these little Hindu and Mahommedan maidens, and the "marriage" of their dolls with those of cousins or playmates is celebrated with pretty travesties of *mangni* and *shadi* rites, of which they hear so much talk from the women by whom they are surrounded. Up to the age of twelve or fourteen years the boys can play with the girls, but whenever these marriage games are gone through, the lads have to act their parts with the same submissiveness which they will have to affect in seeking their own brides later on. These action games are played in all seriousness, the elder girls enacting the parts of mothers and aunts, and finishing up with the cooking of imitations, as nearly as they can manage, of the special wedding dishes.

And the taste for playing with dolls does not end with childhood. Big girls, who have done well in the school examinations, are more pleased with a doll as a prize than almost anything that can be given to them, and I have seen those whom I may fairly call young women show real disappointment at a distribution to find that their first prize was a new sari, while a third or fourth received some showily attired *guryen,* as they will call them, and I am assured that even after they have children of their own the dolls remain a joy. Perhaps the wife of Ibsen's "Master Builder" had hereditary Oriental tastes in the affection that she lavished upon the much-discussed "nine beauties."

In Madras the girls have two extremely pretty and graceful games, which have been systematized for use as physical exercises in the schools. One of these is called *kollatum,* and in idea resembles an English maypole dance, with the substitution of gaily-coloured strings or flower garlands for the ribbons. Each girl, however, carries two short rods in her hands, and goes through the plaiting of the streamers to a soft chant, to which accentuation is given at intervals by short strokes from the sticks, and as certain points in the plaited design are reached, each one slowly sinks to her knees. *Kummi,* the other game, is almost a figure-dance, performed by groups of four, and this I found in almost precisely similar detail to be a favourite pastime in Bhaunagar, where it goes by the name of *ardogardo.* It was beautifully rendered for me here in the Wadwha working-class school, the little exponents assuming the most picturesque poses with an ease that the London pantomime child would find a positive fortune. Here, too, they showed me *phesphedhodi,* in which the little performers cross hands, and whirl round in a giddy crescendo of speed till one expects to see them drop. Not so; when it is finished, each couple is eager to begin again.

Another game which I saw here for the first time was *rhasado.* In this one girl stands in the centre of a circle of her companions, and chants a rhythmic poem on what good girls ought to know, the others taking it up and accentuating each period as they glide around her by a whole turn of the body performed with exceeding grace.

Subsequently I saw this at Bombay, played both by middle-class Parsees and poor Hindus, but in a somewhat different form. Here the girls placed a stool in the middle of the room, and in honour of my visit were allowed to add to the effect by obtaining a brazier full of burning coals. Round this they circled, invoking, in curiously airless strains, Saraswati, the consort of Brahma, who is the goddess of speech, song, and music, as well as of all covetable learning. The words they repeated were curious, and ran thus: "Sisters, let us in the beginning remember Saraswati for the sake of blessings. She will take from us all unhappiness. Sisters, she who has inherited of the spirit of Saraswati alone knows true joy. An educated lady need not be at a loss for pleasure. In knowledge she will find happiness. An educated wife is the greatest pride of her husband."

As a bride in the zenana of her husband, a girl-wife in her new dignity must to some extent forego her games, and the worst feature in the life to an outsider seems its unvarying monotony. I have visited dozens of houses, literally of all sorts and conditions, from slums in Madras and Calcutta up to the palatial houses where ranees and begums live, and the want of broadening interest in the day's continual routine constitutes to European minds at least a terrible blank. There is not even the pleasant fuss of pretty surroundings or artistic furniture to gratify the eye, and I well remember how this deficiency struck me, calling on the wife of a wealthy *zamindar* at Berhampore. I was shown into an apartment absolutely void save for a common *charpoy,* or bed, and judging from the delay in its arrival the whole house must have been searched to find a rickety three-legged stool for me to sit upon. Conversation seemed rather halting, till one of the ladies began to examine the gold bangles I was wearing, and I asked her whether she would show me her own jewellery. This she was quite ready to do, and must have spread out over a thousand pounds' worth of really lovely gold work and gems for me to admire, but the contrast between her costly possessions and the bare chamber in which she set them out seemed curiously sharp.

Of course the ordinary visitor who goes to a well-to-do native house, or a ruler's palace, is received in the public reception rooms, which are generally furnished according to the "regardless of expense" style of Tottenham Court Road, and susceptibly artistic eyes are grieved over flower-patterned carpets, rosewood chairs and tables *en suite,* and rep curtains, such as obtained in the earlier decades of the reign. Only one bright exception do I know to this, and that is the palace of the Nawabs of Murshedabad, where there is an authentic Rembrandt of great price, and a Cuyp, a Teniers, and other pictures worth going to see, with a fascinating collection of early native arms, and a library in which are Korans of untold value, which the non-believer may not touch even with a gloved hand.

But a lady's visit to the ladies of a family shows a very different sight of the home life. One that I paid in Calcutta to a titular ranee, whose state, though by no means as imposing as before family feuds had weakened the heritage, is still upheld with great dignity, was characteristic of many others. In visiting ladies of this rank, it is thought a mark of courtesy to give notice of one's intention to call some hours at least before, and all, therefore, was in readiness for my reception. The house in which this lady lived was enormous.

As seen from outside it would be little exaggeration to call it a palace, for indeed within its walls were lodged the whole eighty (besides servants) who make up the total—brothers, their wives and children—which at present constitutes the chief branch of the family. I entered under a massive stone gateway, surmounted by lions carved in stone, and at the door stood the ranee's little daughter of about eight, clad in much festal bravery of yellow satin underdress and a sari of soft olive silk embroidered in yellow, and wearing some handsome gold ornaments. The child, who was accompanied by several of her cousins, gave us a pretty salaam, and took me by the hand to escort me to her mother. This was evidently a point of etiquette to which she attached much importance. She never let go her hold, though she had sometimes to move from one side to the other, for never have I gone along such a winding intricacy of small chambers, passages, and stairs as that which we had to pass to reach the zenana from the entrance hall.

In this instance the ranee paid me the honour of receiving me in the best room of the zenana, and I took particular notice of its equipment. On the right on entering, through a door which was guiltless of new paint for many years, was a large double bed, at the head and foot of which was some bold wood carving. On this was a flock mattress and sheet, several bolsters, large and small, and a wool-stuffed coverlet of printed modern. There was a large press, something like an old-fashioned dresser, and another one with glass doors, in which were the oddest jumble of "curios" imaginable, from penny china dogs to dainty little cups in damascened silver, from indiarubber dolls in knitted raiment to the engraved talc handscreens of Madras. On the walls were a portrait of her father-in-law (by a native artist, who had given due prominence to the jewelled aigrette of his turban and handle of his scimitar), a German oleograph of the Repentant Magdalene, a photogravure of Lord Ripon, and a "Christmas number" presentation coloured plate. Chairs were put for us round a small table, on which, in the centre of a beaded mat, was the inevitable scent to be sprinkled on one on leaving. The ranee, followed in a minute or so by her sisters-in-law, entered.

She was not one who would be classed as "educated," for I do not think she could read a word, but she possessed intelligence, as well as good breeding, and as a hostess was certainly successful. She was simply dressed, and was not wearing much of her jewellery, for, as she subsequently explained, there was great anxiety in the house as to the illness of one of her brothers-in-law—which she described very much as an English lady would—mentioning that the high temperature, of 102 degrees, at which he remained caused them much uneasiness. Several questions about the Queen and the Royal Family were put to me by all the ladies, who spoke in a vein of respectful loyalty most pleasant to hear; and they asked, also with intelligent interest, about my voyage and what I had seen in Madras, especially what native ladies I had called on there. We remained about a quarter of an hour, and before we left a plate of fruit and sweets—these latter mainly made of cocoa-nut paste, and cloyingly sweet—were put before us, and we duly tasted them. Salaams over, I came to the conclusion that, so far as talk was concerned, I had paid many far less interesting visits in London.

As a rule in a native house one has to traverse a stone passage, opening upon a tiny bricked court, where two or three servants will be cooking, amid a litter of vegetable refuse; some stairs to climb, a balcony with small and dark rooms, in which the only furniture is a bed; and when the lady is reached she will be found in a chamber similarly poverty stricken in appearance.

Mahommedan houses are wont to be, in Calcutta, less alluring, if possible, to European tastes even than Hindu ones, and in one instance that I saw the narrow passage which we crossed was dirty in the extreme, and littered with orange-peel, while in the yard were the female attendants slicing vegetables on a large blade set in a block of wood, and crushing the curry spices upon a stone with a heavy roller. We had to climb some steep and broken brick and cement steps to reach our hostess, whose young daughter, being strictly purdah, was taught reading and writing by ladies of the Church of England Zenana Mission at her own house; and both, who were not expecting any call of the kind, received us in morning *deshabille* of no jewellery and simple cotton saris.

In this case the girl was the wife of a young man coming over to one of the English universities, and her education was being continued at his desire. She showed me her exercise-books and promising English handwriting, and evidently felt some interest in her studies; but when 1 asked her if she would like to accompany her husband to England, she smiled rather hopelessly at the idea, and gently said that native women did not take long journeys, and she thought she would be afraid to go on the sea.

Flowers of course play an important part in the daily life of the people, but the pleasure of their arrangement does not belong to the women of the household. Caste here gives a monopoly to the Malakars, who make up the bouquets and chaplets required for wedding festivities. For a bride the aggrieved at the "insult" to his daughter-in-law. Accordingly the father-in-law resolves to seek redress from the father of the boys, who enjoys the reputation of being an unflinchingly just and wise ruler—a reputation which he maintains in this instance by ordering the lads, despite all their mother's tears and prayers, into exile.

These incidents, told in several scenes, with a gorgeous stage picture of the king receiving his subjects and pronouncing his decision, formed the first act, and in the second the young princes, habited now in sober sable and stripped of nearly all their rich jewels, were seen halting for the night in a dreary jungle. Both are very tired and lie down to rest, but though an angry tiger (which was very cleverly worked, by the way) comes snarling across the stage, one of the deities of the Hindu Pantheon accords a protection to them. Against a wriggling serpent, however, this beneficent protection does not extend, and the younger boy is stung. From the effects of this he dies, bestowing his little bundle of possessions on his brother, and bidding him not trouble about his dead body. This injunction Mansing obeys, and goes on his journey; but presently come on to the scene a party of wealthy travellers apparently making a pilgrimage. The daughter of one of these, seeing the dead body of the beautiful young prince, declares that no other lover will ever satisfy her, and she is quite ready to sacrifice herself in suti for him. Such devotion, however, brings its own reward, for the opportune appearance of a holy Brahmin upon the scene results in a miracle of healing, and on the restoration of the youth to life, the couple are united in marriage on the spot.

Meantime the older boy had found his way to some hospitable kingdom, where his grace and good looks secured him the hand of its heiress-apparent, and in time the younger one, in the guise of a poor messenger, arrives there after having endured great hardships. The story of his resuscitation becomes known, and a wealthy *bunnia*— a term which I should explain is used equally to express a merchant or money-lender, a shopkeeper or a Shylock —has him shipped by crafty means on a vessel bound for

Java, on account of the superstition, that one like him, who has been restored from the dead, can secure safety to the boat and its cargo. Here he and the princess of the place, who possesses boundless riches, become enamoured of one another and marry, and the *bunnia* induces him to take a passage with his wife and her waiting-maid back to their native country. The *bunnia,* however, looks with envious eyes upon the wealth that the princess has brought to her husband, and resolves to possess himself of it by poisoning the young man. This design is frustrated by the waiting-maid, who learns the plot and conceals her master safely. The princess is led to imagine herself a widow, and on reaching the kingdom of her brother-in-law is offered to him in marriage. Again the faithful servant comes to the rescue, and at the wedding ceremony saves her mistress from dishonour by substituting herself, and meantime the father and mother of the two princes, Mansing and Abhazasing, have arrived with a great retinue of relations and retainers. The chambermaid tells her secret, the younger son is brought forward, and there is a general family reconciliation and joy all round, even the wicked *hunnia* and his myrmidons sharing in the universal good will.

Such is the story which occupied some half-dozen acts and hours to unfold. As I have said before, all the female parts were taken by young men, who occasionally acted with a degree of feeling and vigour that one would hardly have expected from them. Notably well played, for instance, was the scene between the queen-mother and her husband, when she was trying to induce him to modify the sentence of banishment passed upon the two boys; and very touching, even to ears like my own, which could not follow the sense of the Gujarati words, was her subsequent farewell and parting advice to them, while in her dark sari and handsome jewels she quite realized the picture of what the senior ranee often is. The parts of the princesses as brides were merely such as at home we should classify as *ingenues,* and required very little subtlety of acting, and all that was demanded of their exponents was to look pretty, according to native canons, be modest and retiring as a Hindu maiden ought to be, and wear rich clothes and showy ornaments with matter-of-fact ease. The lads entrusted with these parts fulfilled these requirements remarkably well, carrying their chatties on their heads with the same erect grace that the girls acquire, and indicating cleverly the half-shy reserve with which young women in the East listen to the conversation or move about in the presence of their elders. Very much in earnest were the two actors representing the two princes, and the one who took the part of the older and less tried exile worked hard to convey the proper sense of Oriental regal repose, while the other bore his manifold troubles with curiously characteristic quiet and even stoicism.

Proportionately the dresses would have borne comparison with those of the average theatre at home. The kings and princes wore kinkhabs of splendidly hued violet, orange, or crimson silks, stiff with golden brocading, and turbans with stripes of metallic threads. Ministers, *bunnias,* and Brahmins were all correctly habited, servants had liveries, and even the supernumeraries were very well dressed. For the female characters some of the cloths and saris were very rich and costly, and the colouring had been chosen with a remarkably good sense of stage effect. There was a constant change of scenery, and the transformations were effected rapidly and smoothly. Many of the "sets" were, indeed, very pretty, and notably among these might be mentioned the jungle scene by moonlight, with the two sleeping boys; and the revels and dances that are held when the older prince arrives in the palace of the princess whom he subsequently marries. From a strictly realistic point of view, however, much of the effect is marred by the custom which obtains of allowing the orchestra—composed, as it is, of weird and shrill wind and stringed instruments and tom-toms, which are played with monotonously vigorous rhythm—to have their places on the sides of the stage within the proscenium.

The managerial room was not unlike that of a London theatre manager. It was simply furnished with a desk, table, and stools, and over all lay a business-like confusion of papers and correspondence. Several "books of the words," in Gujarati, a luxury cheaply supplied to the theatre-goers, representing the present and previous productions, were there, as well as cuttings from vernacular papers, not merely, I was told, of "notices," but of new poems and dramas of whose existence it was well to be aware, and of writers whose names might possibly be worth bearing in mind. The bookshelves contained various volumes of reference, as well as of plays, among which were the renderings of Shakespeare's dramas which have been made into Gujarati; and on the wall were several photographs of former stars and present members of the company. It was, perhaps, more curious than discreet, taking into consideration the sex of the "actresses," to accept Mr. Kussonji's next offer of a sight of the dressing-rooms. Here I was initiated into several of the secrets of the men's successful make-up as women. The little *cholis*, or bodices of bright satin or embroidered net, had a little padding discreetly introduced, which imparted to them the due effect of exceeding tightness which the conditions of Oriental good fit demand. For the hair there were wigs or false tresses, which could be easily fastened on under the heavy jewelled head ornaments so dear to Hindu women; and paints and powders there were in abundance that would not look mean beside those of a Western actor or actress. For raising and lowering the curtain, and shifting the scenery, the manager had availed himself of the best machinery he could get; and the crowd of native carpenters and shifters had been admirably drilled to their work. I remained in the wings during a scene or two, watching the' guardian deity of the wandering boys—a sufficiently awesome presentment, with gilded face and much weaponed in half a dozen hands, riding upon a lion—taken by invisible wires across the stage; and I noticed that the trees and a small bank were remarkably solidly constructed. Then I was taken below the stage that I might judge of the property resources that were stored there, and had pointed out to me with great pride the mahogany counter, with gilded rail and network, which had figured in a previous drama in which was a great bank robbery scene. Thus has realism and modernity reached even the drama in Gujarati.

Of course the wonderful in juggling and acrobatics are always popular, and when an entertainment of these is given, the purdah ladies generally manage to witness it from some gallery or behind a screen. The ordinary tricks, which begin from Port Said, when a clever conjurer comes on board the steamer and wears eggs as eye-glasses, while he produces kittens from his spectators' hair, or' finds live chickens on the arms of a deck-chair, follow one more or less round the whole way, and the oft-described basket and mango tree tricks seem to be known to all "who make the people happy by command." These, moreover, are generally performed with dexterity, and even the closest attention fails to reveal "how it's done." Though in each case the performers were Indian, the newest (to European eyes) and neatest feats I witnessed were in

Ceylon. Sitting in the verandah of the Queen's Hotel, Kandy, I saw a scantily clad and attenuated individual, who laconically said, "Good show, *ek* rupee." I had read all the newspapers of comparatively recent date, and a rupee for at least half an hour's amusement, till it should be cool enough to drive out, did not seem exorbitant. So I ordered the performance, and saw yards of coloured paper produced from his angular elbow, and after realistic contortions as of great internal pain, a heterogeneous collection of stones, knives, pieces of cloth, and small bottles were taken from his mouth and laid at my feet. Presently he brought out a snake-skin, which he offered me to handle and examine, and though I must admit that I possess all the antipathy of my sex to touching anything snake-like, I took this, and it undoubtedly was what it purported to be. As I returned it to him, he apparently laid it on the ground, and touched the gaping mouth with some liquid. Almost instantly it appeared to come to life, and in a few seconds a hissing cobra with hood erect was in its place. It was a most clever bit of sleight of hand, for the live snake was substituted in the same position as that in which the dead skin had lain, and again when, after a few passes, he had brought back the empty skin, the illusion was extremely well performed.

It was at Trincomalee that I witnessed the most brilliant feats of balancing and acrobatics of my tour on the part of a travelling troupe. One item was almost gruesome, and was certainly startling. A man stood upon his head, and gradually lowered his body, keeping it quite rigid till it was only twelve or fifteen inches off the ground. He then moved it round, his head being all the while an immovable pivot, till the idea forced itself upon the spectator that he was bound to twist himself off his own neck.

One must plunge far into the native states to see quail or cock-fighting, which are both extremely popular masculine pastimes, and at the fairs held once or twice a year in the big towns of the feudal territories they always flourish prominently.

Music is not, save with the Parsees, a feminine enjoyment, for it is considered, like dancing, to be an exclusive prerogative of low caste or bad women. The Parsees, however, to their credit, have raised it from this degraded view, and many of them are accomplished performers and highly trained vocalists.. By special invitation, while in Bombay, I was able to attend a concert given in honour of Mr. Naoroji, M.P., with a programme of strictly national airs and songs. It had been organized by Mr. Kabraji, a gentleman whose name is honourably known to English musicians by his really scholarly rendering into Gujerati of the words of the National Anthem with musical adaptation. This was sung by one of his daughters, as solo with chorus, and may certainly be pronounced successful. I do not profess to understand the intricacies of the Hindu scale, which recognizes quarter-tones, and of course to European ears there is a certain airless monotony at first. But in due time one begins to detect that it has subtle harmonies, which are far from unpleasant when well performed.

Whenever sympathy is expressed for the want of amusement or outside interest of the Indian woman's life, I think few have any idea how fully her aspirations in these directions are supplied by her religion, which satisfies so well the cravings of the feminine nature towards the romantic and the dramatic. It so happened that I understood this from the first, for soon after I reached Trincomalee, where I first stayed in the East, and where the native population are for the most part devout Sivaites, I found the great festival of Kali—known in Bengal as the Durga Puja, and in Western India as the Dasara, when her victory over the demon Mahihasura vested Siva with a little brief authority—in full celebration. For nearly a week the quaint little temple was decorated outside with pendent chains of the exquisite "temple flower," and the *jasminum undulatum,* with its strong perfume, while night after night a stream of men, women, and children, in considerable bravery of holiday attire and jewels, passed up to witness in material and tangible performance the episodes of the legend. On the last night but one, Kali, in her aspect of the destroyer, was brought out with all her panoply of upraised trident, coloured flags, and red-and-white flowers, seated upon a lion, the demon first appearing with the head of an elephant. Both were carried upon large wooden platforms, the bearers of which were a number of stalwart and bronzed natives; but while the goddess moved forward with slow and dignified advances, Mahihasura's porters were bidden by peremptory words of command to surge hither and thither, to part the crowd, or to career round the temple. The demon was armed first with a bow, but after a sufficient rushing about on the part of his energetic bearers, a slight movement forward on the part of the awesome "propeller of the chief of weapons," caused the diabolic assailant to drop his arms amid the shouts of the crowd. This proceeding was repeated as the demon reappeared with a sword, a trident, and a club, and was gone through again in same order after he had assumed other disguises, for fully two hours, under the glare of torches kindled with cocoa-nut oil. For the concluding scene processions came up from other temples of Kali, and all met upon an expanse of green which lies outside of Fort Frederick, to take part in the final destruction of Mahihasura; when, after fruit and flowers had been offered, the impersonator of the demon, followed by torch-bearers and a noisy crowd, rushed down to the seashore and cast his garments and masks to the waves, and was carried back prostrate and comatose after the excitement and exertion.

Then again at Berhampore I was fortunate enough to arrive just in time for the Ras Lila festival, which, through the generosity of the Maharanee Surnomoyee, is celebrated there with more than usual pomp. Krishna, as is familiar to those" who know the story of the puranic gods, was changed at birth for the female child of a cowherd's wife to rescue him from the wrath of his uncle, Kansa, to whom it had been predicted that a boy would wrest his kingdom from him. Kansa, hearing of the fraud, tried to kill this lad, sending the demons Arishta in the form of a bull, and Resin as a horse, for this purpose, but he evaded them; and at last Kansa invited his nephew to a boxing-match with him, in which Krishna slew his uncle. In this festival this episode was commemorated by a marvellously dramatic presentment in almost life-sized clay figures, modelled by the famous artificers of Krishnagar. Five or six tiers of seats were ranged round three sides of an enormous marquee. In the centre, at the top, sat Badha,

Krishna's favourite wife, while all the rest were filled with nobles and importancies invited to witness the contest. No two—and there were some hundreds of them—were alike in features, expression, position/ or dress, and it was extraordinary how the sense of fear, awe, satisfaction, or contempt was expressed upon their faces as Krishna, having freed him-self of his persecutor, whose corpse lies on the ground, is bending humbly to perform' the meritorious penance of washing a holy Brahman's feet.

Owing to the association of the god's early days with things pastoral, the cow generally finds a prominent place in any observances connected with him. On this occasion, there was a herd of about forty of them, presented with a fidelity and variety no less astonishing than that of the human models. It was just such a herd as one sees daily in Bengal, some comparatively sleek and well-conditioned, others mere skin and skeleton. There were cows with calves beside them; some were snatching a hasty bite of grass; some were pushing to the front; one was licking a leg in realistic fashion. There were draft-weary bullocks, and the ugly water buffaloes, with their immense down-curving horns, and all shown nearly life-size.

Crowds came and went all day, and outside a fair was in full swing. It was a really interesting glimpse to me of the inner enjoyments of the people to whom this mud Madame Tussauds', if I may so speak of it without offence, was not only a wonder and a delight, but was also a religious ceremonial of high importance.

●●

12
Anglo-Indian Society

> "It is silly to imagine it possible to save India, without having anything to do with natives, without native troops, and with contempt for all national prejudices and feelings."—Viscountess Canning.

"Not quite *Truth,* but something Simla," is said to have been a smart Anglo-Indian criticism of certain Plain Tales, and the same might be said of a good many of the efforts that have been made to depict society as it is in India. In its broad outlines, it is after all very much as it is here. Hard work under enervating conditions may make play when it comes a little more exuberant than with ourselves; little social shortcomings are perhaps more leniently dealt with where each has a kind of feeling of fraternity among aliens; a few nice old-fashioned prejudices as to the correct line of demarcation between friendliness and flirtation with the sexes are perhaps ignored, but on the whole, the presidency towns would not come off so very badly in the statistics of comparative morality with London, Edinburgh, or Dublin, nor would hill stations look very bad beside an average season at Brighton or on the moors.

In India one may belong to the official or non-official set, but one is nowhere unless one can visit at Government House. Officially, therefore, society is guided precisely as it is at the Court of St. James's, and the ladies who represent the Queen in the East may be very well trusted to maintain all the traditions and conventions which the majority of well-bred people have no desire to see overthrown.

If I were an old Anglo-Indian I should begin with a lament over the more middle-class wave that has come across society since competitive examination swept aside the privileges of birth or association. But I ,am not this, and I am recording simply a few impressions, chief among which perhaps is that I am certain, in the palmiest and most renowned of John Company's days, India enjoyed no more cultured and sympathetic administrators than those who now fill the highest positions. For the affection and the prestige that the British raj enjoys in the East, far more credit is due to the individual men and women who have carried out the loftiest conceptions of English truth, virtue, and gentleness, than to the collective wisdom of the office in Downing Street. This book professes only to deal with women, so that I am under no obligations to discuss the whys and wherefores of recent policy shown by Lord Lansdowne, Lord Wenlock, and Lord Harris. Lord and Lady Elgin only took up the reins of office a few days before I left Bombay and India altogether, and beyond formal presentation to them at the great evening party given by Lord and Lady Harris in honour of their arrival, I know nothing personally of them. But to follow the Marchioness of Lansdowne as the leader of society in India is a course of difficulty from which the most finished woman of the world might well shrink. The Marchioness of Dufferin and Ava, gracious and gentle and considerate, yet withal so regal and so essentially the *grande dame de la haute politique,* had won every heart by her sweet sympathy, and had maintained a stately dignity impressive alike to natives and English. The example was a splendid one,; but to come worthily after it was what few women could have done. The Marchioness of Lansdowne was, however, one of the very few able not merely to do as well as her predecessor, but to do it in her own individual way.

Like Lady Dufferin, Lady Lansdowne came to her position of vicereine with an already immense previous experience of official life, and a certain knowledge already acquired of Indian affairs from the fact that Lord Lansdowne had held office as Under Secretary of State for India. Lady Elgin does not enjoy the advantages that come from a long and varied association with foreign governments and colonial bureaux, and in dealing with races so diverse as those which go to make up the Indian Empire, this deficiency must be a serious handicap that no amount of good intention can quite overcome.

The hospitality of the government houses of the three Presidency towns is proverbial, and the fortunate stranger who brings out a sufficient personal introduction is assured of a pleasant reception. Invitations to dinners, balls, or receptions, are of course issued by the aides-de-camp in waiting, and the drawing-room cards pass through the hands of the military secretary, who is therefore a kind of minor lord chamberlain. Lord William Beresford had filled this onerous post with tact as well as firmness, and bitter, very bitter were the regrets at his departure. Colonel Durand, of Gilgit and Nilt celebrity, however, succeeded him, and as he comes of a family who have contributed no small part to the making of Indian history, as well as enjoying a great social repute, there was a small crumb of consolation in the matter. The calling hours at Calcutta are peculiar, and are rigidly fixed between twelve and two, during which time the "book" lies upon the hall table, and the names of those entitled to the privilege of placing them there must be set down at the beginning of the season, and after a dinner or dance. The etiquette of a vicereine's drawing-room, which takes place in the throne-room, is precisely similar to that observed for presentation to the Queen, with the exception that court trains are not worn.

For home life, in the narrower sense of the word, a vicereine has but little time, and Lady Lansdowne's great popularity seldom allowed her an afternoon free from bazaar or exhibition opening, prize distribution or hospital inspection.

She tells of a funny experience that she had in this last connection, when she went to visit a large institution for *purdah* women in Southern India. She was a little surprised at first to see every bed occupied, while apparent patients were squatting on mats on the floor. On closer inspection she saw that there did not appear much the matter with any of them, and asked why so many were under treatment. It was then explained that the women had come, hearing of her intended visit, telling the most piteous tales of non-existing maladies and sufferings, simply that they might enjoy a sight of the great lady whose name they held in affection, and perhaps some wondering awe. The authorities of the institution lent themselves to the little fraud to show that any who entered the hospital would be treated well, and a good deal of prejudice was thus met.

It did not fall to Lady Lansdowne's lot to initiate a great movement as Lady Dufferin did, but I am not sure that the task which devolved upon her was a less difficult one. For she took the scheme of medical aid into her hands at a critical moment, and under circumstances at which wreck and disaster would have followed any error of judgment, while she had also to formulate those alterations of detail which only the experience gained in actual working could suggest. The whole question, however, of medical aid for the Indian women occupied close attention on her part, and I have good reason for knowing that her interest in the subject has not ceased with her departure from the East. There was no phase of philanthropic work, whether missionary or educational, with which she was not familiar, and did not know with more than a superficial acquaintance. It was not enough for her to formally "visit" an institution or school, but she would go into the details of its management, and seldom left without making a really useful or practical suggestion.

As a hostess her tact and grace were unbounded, and under her *regime* it was a pleasure as well as an honour to dine at Government House. As a type of the aristocratic society woman she was perfect, but no less decisively could this word be employed concerning the two other great ladies of the dependency in their respective and differing directions. Lady Wenlock at Madras represents the poetic and artistic order in the trio, but it is only very few who are privileged to hear the sweet verse into which she has poured her heart with feeling, made the deeper by the constant ill-health which often precludes her presiding over the stately dinners and dances of Guindy or the banqueting hall—the handsome annexe to Government House, Madras. Of her talent in painting she is less chary in revealing herself, and once or twice she has exhibited her strong and unconventional work at the smaller shows in London. She has caught, as few ever can, the subtle charm of the brief after-glow of an Indian sunset, and has read aright the mystery of the heat-hazy landscape, where perhaps others would only have seen a few straggling palms and a common-place village tank.

Very thoughtful for others, very ready to encourage well-directed charity, Lady Wenlock is popular throughout the southernmost Presidency, though her tastes in the directions of art and literature are hardly those to commend her to the more rollicking ideas of enjoyment which generally obtain upon a hill station. There are not many in India to give this little leavening to it, and perhaps it will not be among the least of her claims to a social remembrance when she returns to England.

Lastly, the perfect embodiment of the blight, cheery, natural, English country gentlewoman is Lady Harris. Native society could not, and even now does not, understand her complete absence of formality, which would stop her carriage in the bazaar to talk to a couple of poor children, could speak kindly to her servants, and show a personal interest in her *menage* and horses. But they have learnt to recognize that she is gifted with a singular depth of sympathy as well as a remarkable fund of downright common sense. She will spend days of real exertion organizing simple theatricals to give pleasure to *purdah* ladies, whom she frequently invites to Government House; but if any ill-advised enthusiast comes to her with a mission to teach the same ladies the elements of biology, or to recommend them to become lady journalists, she has a most beautifully chilling method of throwing critical cold water down. She is one of the best and wisest friends that the cause of female education has ever had in India, though she does not write articles for magazines or make speeches on the subject, for she has seen that it by no means follows that what is the perfect code for the Western girl is of necessity to be slavishly followed for her of the East. Just as Lord Harris has done far more for the Indian boy in introducing him to cricket, as a much more healthy form of amusement than gambling for pice in a sordid back court, than half the noisy agitators who have led him to wear English dress and seek an English wife, so has Lady Harris, by lending her influence to diffusing general and useful knowledge among the girls, rather than encouraging a handful from among them to effect a few showy sensations in the examination rooms, helped to lay a much more solid foundation for future results than those who do not know how quietly she works are ready to believe.

She is a keen sportswoman, a fearless cross-country rider, and one of the best cricketers of her sex to be met. European society in Bombay, though it is surprised sometimes that she is not more fettered by forms and ceremony, is devoted to her; and the girls, who often find themselves in India as of small importance beside the young married women, are never overlooked by her. She is an artist of considerable skill, and has a very neat turn for writing pungent *vers de societe*. Of her thoughtful tact I may mention in this connection one little episode. She was writing a few of these "up to," as they say in illustrated journalism, some clever pictures to be sold in the "post office" of her annual fancy fair, on behalf of one or other of the Bombay charities. A momentary loss for a happy rhyme led one in the group to suggest a line in which the word "nigger" occurred.

> "That will not do," she said decisively. "It is a word we never employ at Government House."

And here I strike off at a tangent to the really interesting aspect of the position of the European community towards the natives by whom it is surrounded. As long as one remain in the uppermost administrative circles, with governors, lieutenant-governors, residents, high-court judges, commanding officers, and district superintendents of police, all is well. The educated native, holding, it may be, some high civil appointment, and able by manners and breeding (for a native gentleman does exist, and not very rarely either) to conform to the usages of society, is made welcome, treated with courtesy, which it does not lower the proud ruling race to show, and there is a kindly consideration evinced towards what we may regard as mere caste prejudices, but which to him are matters of religious life or death. Shopkeepers, servants, lower native officials, are spoken to with civility, and not summoned by some opprobrious nickname of abuse. The natural good manners, in short, of the English gentleman or gentlewoman, which are extended at home to any inoffensive fellow-citizen, whether he be cabman, or costermonger, or shop-assistant, not to mention social equals, are not wholly forgotten, and one owns on seeing it to the little thrill of satisfaction as to the invariable *savoirfaire* of well-bred people.

It is a satisfaction, however, that does not last if one steps down to the average middle-class Briton filling subordinate posts in the departments of the State, and as a rule, though I know many exceptions here, the mercantile order, with the large aggregate who have come out to take posts as machinists, foremen, managers in the vast factories springing up on all hands. Little Mrs. Drye-Goodes, whose heart is yearning for the joys of the Peckham masonic ball, and whose drawing-room is decked with the fourpenny-halfpenny fans and the "art furniture" of Westbourne Grove, to whom the story of India is not of half the interest of a quarrel between two families in the street at home that she left, tells one with a giggle that "she hates these beastly niggers," and thinks it something commendable to add, " we don't let any of them come to our club." She cuts her servants' wages down to the last anna piece, and if she ascertains that they have not let her benefit to the uttermost pice of their bazaar bargainings, storms at them as pickpockets, and launches forth on the thievish propensities of the dependency Early and late they must be at the beck and call of her sharp tongue, and if she dares she will call her cane into requisition.

To try to learn something of the inner mysteries of the life around them, to collect the queer artistic trifles that every district has of its own, to ascertain the conditions of labour around them—it would seem to such people an evidence of a wholly unaccountable aberration of mind to be interested in such things. It would be regrettable if this detestable insular " side " only had the effect of making them personally disliked in their neighbourhoods, but it has a further effect than that. It tends to discredit the English reputation, and with peoples of the Oriental temperament, to whom flowery courtesy is one of the fine arts of existence, it is bitterly resented at heart. Mrs. Drye-Goodes thinks no doubt that she has effectively admonished her bearer when for some small offence she hisses out the hateful word *sowar* (pig), but he does not forget, and it may be the spark that kindles not his own only, but his tribe's hatred for the overbearing and altogether unnecessarily insulting demeanour adopted concerning them.

It is not a pretty phase of English manners towards inferiors, but I think few grasp how obnoxiously ill-bred such people can and do show themselves to those who are their social equals. In Bombay one may sometimes hear of a "scene" that disturbed its social circles considerably in Lord and Lady Reay's period of office. It was a big dinner at Government House, and a certain English "lady" was introduced by the aide-de-camp to a much-respected Mahommedan high court judge—a gentleman, be it said, of the highest intelligence and learning, and well known throughout India. The English female showed him not the slightest recognition, but turned to the aide-de-camp and said excitedly, "You don't suppose I'm going in to dinner with a native ?" The aide-de-camp quietly said that it had been her Excellency's pleasure thus to assign her, whereat she said, "Then the list must be altered, or I leave." There was some further talk, the irate dame insisting that her grievance should be referred to Lady Reay direct; but she, wise as well as dignified, properly refused to allow ill-breeding to dictate to her, and the insulted one therefore took her offended self away.

The people of whose sympathies this pleasant tale is completely characteristic have a funny little cant excuse which they repeat till one first grows weary of it, and afterwards laughs at. It is always said quite gravely, and as they think is crushingly convincing. "They don't let us know their wives. And until they do that we really must, you know, decline to admit them to society." One softly suggests that their present *purdah* customs are the result of some centuries, and ventures to ask what special effort towards civility the ladies who are volubly assuring one of the "impossibility" of showing courtesy towards native neighbours have ever attempted. "Oh, let them come out and call on us, and let us take our husbands to see them !" say these summary reformers; and it would be comic if it were not sad. For this is the comprehension shown of the characters and peoples over whom our sway is one of moral influence rather than physical force!

No one dared to say it in the recent anxieties concerning the tree-smearing in Behar, but the province contains a more than average proportion of the planting and non-official element, and knowing how objectionable this can be in its dealings with the natives, I have very little doubt that the mysterious marks were a sign of the angry resentment felt towards the alien race. Had the smouldering spark broken out into open flame, British bad manners and want of generous treatment would have been responsible for very much.

The attitude is not a new one. Yiscountess Canning, in those shrewd, sympathetic, far-seeing letters contained in "The Story of Two Noble Lives," makes many references to it, especially deploring the ignorance and prejudice of the Anglo-Indian Press, which then embodied the middle-class sentiments far more than it now does, and when all were demanding mere blind cruel revenge for the atrocities of the mutiny, she was, with her husband, among the few who could show a sane judgment and write, "Strict stern justice, we all agree, is a *necessity*, but I cannot see the wisdom or righteousness of injustice; and these rules were only to prevent very various punishments and cases of injustice. I do not think the objects of 'Canning's Clemency' will very much delight in it; it is not at all in the style of mercy, and very like the hardest and strictest justice. People here would like every Sepoy to be hanged at least, whether for his deeds or for his thoughts. If one mildly observes that the men at Barrackpore, who have never been out of our sight, did not share in the massacres five or six hundred miles off, people say, 'Oh, but in their hearts they approved and would like to do the same by us!' That is the sort of speech one often hears." And, I may add, is precisely the line of defence for dislike that is still adopted!

One is inclined to ask who or what is responsible for the bad form shown in this direction by middle-class and minor society in India. It is certainly not in imitation of their betters, whose conduct in the matter is perfect, but while it exists it is a little inconsistent to hear them blaming caste because this interferes with the bearer undertaking the cook's work. The fact did not escape Mr. Clement Scott, in his rapid scamper across the dependency, who speaks with pardonable sarcasm and warmth about it. "These highly educated, extremely intelligent Parsee ladies and gentlemen constitute the race," he remarks, "whose lavish hospitality is accepted by Europeans, but by some mysterious unsigned order must never be returned. Thus, you may play cricket with a Parsee gentleman, but you must not bring him back to dinner. You may attend the *soiree* of a Parsee lady, but you may not ask her to drink tea at sunset on the terrace of the Bombay Yacht Club. You may beg for subscriptions from a Parsee capitalist to start a gymnasium, but it is etiquette to turn his children from the doors. You may meet the *elite* of Parsee society at the Government House reception on Malabar Hill, but if you asked exactly the same people to your breakfast-table you would be cut by English society." The only qualification to be made concerning this latter sentence is, "English society of sorts." I am glad to be able to say that in the English society it was mostly my good fortune to keep, native ladies and gentlemen associated on equal terms, but the existence of the other aspect is none the less a fact, and is often bitterly commented upon by those whose pedigrees may go back to nobles loyal to the British crown under Olive and Hastings, when the forebears of the insolent and arrogant snobs who snub them were probably sweeping warehouses or packing parcels.

I have tried hard to understand the cause of complaint against the native, for it is always instructive to know how the mental altitude of others has been reached. The conclusion that I have come to is that it largely rests upon the differing standpoint from which the two races view dancing. The native, as we know, fails to see why he should exert himself in this direction, when he can pay others to do it for him, and the professional ladies who accept a wage for their performances are not, as a rule, exponents of the most elevated codes of feminine morality. Being aware that this view obtains, "Western people are secretly a little humiliated in their innermost selves at the ideas that they know that dancing suggests to the native mind. I know instances, indeed, in which tickets have been refused to native gentlemen for charitable entertainments in which skirt dancing has been in the programme, on account of the different light in which it is regarded by performer and spectator. Thereupon Mrs. Drye-Goodes and her class blaze up at the "disgusting tone" of prevailing native opinion round her, quite oblivious of the fact that this with equal warmth feels that the "tone" of women who dance in public leaves something to be desired. This is the most tangible grievance, ludicrous as it is, that I have been able to discover, for the others are merely shadowy abstractions and vague" expressions of dislike.

Incidental reference has been made to the Anglo-Indian Press, and this, from my own journalistic associations, was a source of considerable interest to me. Of the general tone and stamp of the half-dozen or so great papers of the dependency, the *Pioneer,* the *Statesman,* the *Englishman,* the *Indian Daily Hews,* the *Times of India,* the *Bombay Gazette,* the *Madras Mail,* the *Madras Times,* and the *Morning Post* of Allahabad, it is impossible to speak too highly. Their politics differ widely, but each in their several directions loyally supports the crown primarily, though the details of how they do so vary according to conservative or liberal tendencies. I use the word "liberal" advisedly, for rampant radicalism soon tones down in India, and, with the exception of a few publications of small moment and chiefly circulating among "advanced" natives, this phase of politics has very scant journalistic countenance. One finds perfectly fair examination of native views and opinions, and no effort is made to belittle their claims socially or politically. In fact, in the matter of even-handed justice and impartiality, I think the leaders of the Indian press stand very well beside their *confreres* at home. The papers are well edited, well turned out, and are enterprising as to new fields of interest.

Only in one or two cases is the language degraded and our prestige as rulers lowered. In one instance it is through a so-called "comic" weekly publication, which in vulgar impudence and blackguardly obscenity would not be tolerated under Lord Campbell's Act. In the other it is a professedly "religious" organ, which seems to have been called into existence by a desire to show to any natives who may take it up how irreligious all English professing Christians are. Will it be credited that in its columns, the usual courtesy prefix to the names of gentlemen who are members of Council is invariably written in inverted commas, as the

"Honourable" Mr. ———; that such objectionable remarks about Lady Harris were made in it as to compel Lord Harris to demand, and obtain, a public apology; that the occasion of unveiling Sir George Birdwood's statue in Bombay was made the excuse for penning one of the most blasphemous libels ever composed upon a public man; and that if an unfortunate missionary reciprocates much kindly hospitality by asking a few friends to his bungalow, and allows his guests a mild "peg" before leaving, he is held up to obloquy by name and accused of carrying on drunken orgies ? Such mischievous and scandalous prints are not calculated to command respect for ourselves.

Women, who rarely in the East find the same amount of interest and occupation for their lives as their fathers or husbands, are wont to complain of its tedium and monotony. Even the active aspect of housekeeping is lessened by the fact that the hausfrau herself can take so little real part in it, after giving directions and checking accounts. Long custom has decreed that all marketing and almost all ordering and shopping shall be done by the servants, whose assumption of extreme dignity of demeanour makes the youthful mistress feel herself to be lessening her own importance in their eyes if she exercises too close a personal supervision in minor details. Anglo-Indian hostesses often make loud lamentation about the laziness and incompetency of their servants, but I imagine that the majority of them on their return must think regretfully of the deft, obliging, willing, resourceful fellows they have left behind, and must find-marked difference in the attention and quality of the service they can command at home. It is only a really energetic character, in fact, that does not become demoralized into flabbiness and inertia under the combined influences of heat, laziness, and servants at command.

The first sign of deterioration is when a woman omits her corsets from her toilette, and begins lolling about in a sloppy and tumbled tea-gown in the mornings. Then the downward course is rapid, and she soon joins that large army of her sisters in the East, who, save "for company," or in calling hours, or when she goes out, is never to be found trim and neat. If the habit is once permitted to begin, it will develop other forms of laxity, and the slackness and indolence that characterizes so many Anglo-Indian women will become a second nature, requiring all the awakening that busy English folks can give it.

It is not of course those who live in the Presidency or larger cities upon whose hands time hangs heavy. There they have society of their own order, be this middle-class or more exalted; they have theatricals, amateur and professional at intervals, flower-shows, races, balls, and dinners, no less than at home. In the season they go to the hills, and picnics, lawn-tennis, riding, and outdoor amusement they can enjoy to any extent. The less fortunate ones are they who by appointment or necessity must live in up-country stations or the minor towns. Here, where European society is limited perhaps to two or three families, diversion and society is not much varied, and unless a woman can develop some strong interest in art, archaeology, botany, or natural history, the days may seem unutterably long. This is the duller side of Indian life, which fills the homeward-bound steamers with dissatisfied, peevish creatures, who have riot had the courage or the ability to find out how to make it, if not a gay and lively, at least an interesting existence. These, however, form the class that would shriek the loudest at the idea of cultivating the confidence and friendship of their native women neighbours.

It is said by those who remember the India of some four or five decades back, that hospitality is waning, and that the splendid generosity which used to impress English travellers so strongly is rarely met with now. But the diminished rupee accounts for much, and, however sociable instincts may he, it is surely impossible to gratify them when the rate of exchange is at a fraction over a shilling and a penny. Then, too, the cheapness and facility of travel sends out increasing numbers of the "T.G." element, as the *argot* of official Calcutta designates the "travelling gents" of a cold-season trip; and even the most hospitably inclined limits his or her welcome after a long course of experiences of friends' friends. But for all this, the kind, warm-hearted spirit exists still, even if it cannot show itself in some of the extravagantly lavish forms of bygone days, and the moment that it becomes recognized that one has any good reason for being in India, the help and the invitations that one receives claim gratitude that it is difficult to put into words. Even the possibility of entertaining unawares another "Padgett, M.P.," does not seem to act as any deterrent to a gracious reception. As to the friendly lunches and dinners that I used to be invited to at the coast ports, and the pleasant drives to places and people that I used to find arranged for me within a few minutes even of the ship's having dropped anchor, I can only tell those who did so much for me that I shall always remember gratefully their considerate attention.

The strictness of etiquette as to precedence in Anglo-Indian society always excites the cheap derision of those who want to pose on their return as smart observers, who fail to see that this has a perfectly sound reason. In official circles, as we all know, the order is all carefully laid down, and money or display gives no advantage. There is in Indian society so enormous a preponderance of the strictly military and official element, that possibly to the outsider, who at home does not care whether Mr. A. or Mr. B. goes into dinner before him, since neither can claim a social precedence of the other, it may appear that the rigid Eastern code is often a mere affectation. But this it is not, and by making its observance an unswerving law, it not only keeps a continual object lesson as to each one's true position with regard to administrative discipline before his eyes, but is, in the long run, the best safeguard against personal jealousies and piques.

It is the outsider, however, who magnifies any trifling weaknesses and foibles. In itself, Anglo-Indian Society is satisfied with things as they are, and enjoys life in its own fashion with vigour and zest. And in truth, if the generosity and good feeling evinced towards our native fellow-subjects in its upper ranks were displayed in the lower ones, the Englishman or woman out from home would find very little that is unworthy of our jealously maintained British traditions.

●●

13

The Sphere of Woman

This little book draws in this and the next chapter to its close ; in this the practical side, in the next what one may say about the ideal. Our question is partly a more difficult one because our own follies have made it difficult. The excess of women results from one of these. Boy babies are born in greater numbers than girl babies, and were women better mothers and men better fathers, the boy baby, more delicate than the girl baby, would not die to the same extent, and the proportion of the sexes would be equalised at maturity. Still even then there would be single women and single men.

From the beginning of this book I have insisted, and as a biologist I must insist, on the recognition of womanliness as a mental state as well as a bodily one, and have returned again and again to the thought that no system of education, of occupation, and of representation can afford to put this thought on one side.

The problems of sex begin at the beginning of life in the strange fact just mentioned, that the boy baby is more frail, though why he is so we do not know. During childhood, that is for the first eight or nine years, there are few difficulties to face. The boy is a little rougher, needs, perhaps, just a shade more physical exercise, but with care boys and girls can play together, study together, in the home and the school, and are benefited by so doing. This is the relatively asexual period of life, and the kindergarten system of education, with certain modifications, may be accepted, the mother to teach for the first five years of life, and the lady school-teacher for the four that follow for both sexes.

At pubescence, however, the fact of *bodily* change into womanhood begins to appear and develop rapidly in the girl, and commences slowly *two years later* in the boy. Some girls and boys are rapid developers, others are ordinary, others, again, are slow, but it is always true that of the boy and girl *of the same type* the girl is the first by about two years to begin this change, and it proceeds when begun at a more rapid rate, so that between eleven and fourteen years a girl may be actually taller, and is much more mature, than the boy.

There is an undoubted natural tendency for the sexes to separate at this period, as anyone can verify for himself or herself.

And the girl at this period equally certainly is less inclined for severe mental work, and from this time forward throughout her life tends to wish to take, unless encouraged to the contrary, less violent physical exercise.

The boy also is less inclined for mental effort, but his interest in physical, bodily exercise becomes remarkably keen and intense.

There is every reason to believe that these feelings express a natural need in the physical changes of the body.

The girl's hips widen for later maturity, her limbs become rounded and more full of form, and her feet and hands do not grow in the same relation, so that they now begin to appear small. Were there no other facts than these, which are the contrary of the boys, with long limbs and often big hands and feet, they would be enough to demonstrate that muscular exercises of an extreme nature are unnatural. The chief mental fact of this period in girls is its instability, as frequent giggling proves, and of the boy a bodily idealism.

There are no positive facts for or against, but it is probable rather than improbable that much physical, and perhaps mental, exercise at this period would retard womanly development, making it less perfect, drawing off to other quarters nourishment which is needed for womanly changes coming into the young girl's life. This much we do know, that probably at no other time in history has childbirth been so difficult, so unhealthily difficult, as now, and that this has manifested itself chiefly in the last fifty years, a period marked by increasing educational strain for girls and boys, by increased gymnastic and violent exercises, such as hockey, for girls, and by employment for young women outside of the home. It is probable that one or all of these changes are responsible for this childbirth difficulty, and for the nerviness in women. But, of course, on this subject we need painstaking research.

During adolescence, the period up to about sixteen to eighteen in girls, and two years later in boys, the mental side of sex begins to be manifested, and the danger to both sexes alike is a false sentimentalism, which must, none the less, not make us blind to the fact that this period should be marked by a development of real sentiment, of genuine respect for women and men, of love of truth, beauty, and religion. If the minds of the boy and girl were the same, it might be conceivable that their education should be similar, but the girl is unquestionably more affectable than the boy, and ought to be so, is more intuitive, is less combative, and her mind is subtler, more suggestive, and the aesthetic element plays a larger part than in the boy's mind.

The boy is more individual, more rational, more combative, and the ideal of truth and reality plays a larger part with the boy than aesthetic feelings.

It is very difficult to see how these different qualities can each be strengthened so as to form natural sex characters except by distinctive, non-co-educational methods. Each should surely be taught something of the science of life ; but again I doubt if this knowledge could be taught wisely to both sexes at this age.

If the education of either ends at this period there is no more to be said, but if both are to go to college there can be no question that their education should largely diverge, the domestic, aesthetic, and literary predominating in the woman's, and the public, civic, scientific, and technical sides be more, I do not say solely, emphasised in the man's.

The case for co-education, I confess, seems to me quite unbiological, though I am ready to change "this opinion if the evidence is forthcoming. It seems to depend for its influence on some rather dogmatic assertions of its value by co-educationists, which are not submitted to examination, and to the fact that it is cheap—a bad argument; and that classes are easier to manage—which is, if possible, a worse. The easy way in almost all pursuits is easy by avoiding, not overcoming, difficulties.

The mere facts that in America, even more than here in England, women are so often anxious to be like men, and so little desirous of disclosing the true glories of womanhood; that the great colleges like Newnham and Girton in England have teachers and principals who take little pains with the woman's home and domestic points of view, are almost proof to the scientifically trained biologist that something is wrong, as structure and function should go together ; a woman's body with womanliness and a man's with manliness. And as lecturer I know, what as biologist I look upon with great uneasiness, this fact, that there are extremely few women who glorv in womanhood or even take a pride in such an ideal. There are, it is true, few men who have really high manly ideals, but the majority really wish to be manly, even the feminine type of man. It is not so with women, and it is a pity and an error for our nation and civilisation.

Something such as the following is what is desirable biologically for healthy womanly and manly life :

The kindergarten system. Mother-trained and home-influenced for first five to six years. For boys and girls from about six to nine, under the guidance of women teachers.

Girls' schools. Nine to seventeen. Under the control of women teachers specially trained to sympathise with and draw out in healthy directions womanly ideals, and themselves of some feminine charm and insight.

College. Seventeen to twenty-two. Specialised studies, but domestic science taught to all. For the practical domestic teaching a woman lecturer, but for the theoretical a man. I am fairly convinced, just as women are adepts with children, and men in the early years of child life are very poor teachers, so for the final stages of teaching a man is a better and a more thorough guide than a woman.

This later college work might be combined with some practical occupation at a post in which hours were fight and work not heavy, and for those classes unable to afford full college work our national schools could be made use of. Examinations, except in the broadest spirit, I cannot myself accept for either sex, and while they seem unavoidable for men, but are none the less an evil, they could and ought to be dispensed with for women.

All girls could go through this training with advantage, and it would have this practical value, that no woman would be, as now almost all women are, unacquainted with all the many-sided demands and wonders of home life : child psychology; human physiology; dietetics and cooking; hygiene and house-cleaning; choosing a house; the ordering of a home; how a library may be acquired; pictures and their value; wall papers, furniture, windows, and how these can be hygienically and aesthetically treated; the stages of life; nursing and the management of disease. Such a course, rightly developed, would open out to woman what the domestic side of life could be, and it would fit her for what the majority of women become, wives and mothers, and what the nation needs as its greatest womanly asset. And this same course would teach women to understand the truth that, rightly appreciated, there is almost too much in the home and its requisites, and not too little, and good mothers and good wives would be seen to be, as they are, the women who realise their lives most fully and completely.

This college period of seventeen to twenty-two is the period when the majority of women become betrothed, and if a woman reaches twenty-two years without having met the man she is likely to care for as her future husband, it would be then quite time enough to open up the thought of the prospect of another kind of career. It is generally admitted in the practice of hospitals for nurses, and other similar institutions, that about twenty-three to twenty-five is a suitable vocational age for women ; and some spheres of life, such as music or art, which demand early training, might easily have been partially prepared for in the earlier stages. It is claimed that for no appropriate calling for women would this scheme of education be other than beneficial.

One word more ought to be said for the unmarried woman. She is sometimes the unchosen of her type and kind, and even as such may have a very useful and happy future ahead of her in literature, in music, or art, or in domestic pursuits, or in health visiting or similar occupations; but, as often, she is one who for the sake of a high ideal chooses celibacy rather than degrade it. Such women are apt to look on their lives as partial failures. It is not so. These are the women who elevate their own sex, teach the grandeur of womanly individuality, and lead men as well as women to a higher appreciation of womanly life and powers. The teaching to-day that action is for woman as for man the ideal, is a cruel and false doctrine, false by the record of all history as well as of biological thought. A woman may attain to greatness in literature or on the stage, the latter sometimes at the cost of her character; she may become a good musician or a good artist, a good nurse or a medical woman, but she is not primarily any one of these. A man's influence is small by the side of a womanly woman's, though his actions may be large, and it is the woman as she *is* that counts, not primarily what she does. But none the less I believe the day will come when by good motherhood the sexes will be equalised, or the excess even be on the man's side, and with a luster order of social life there will be few women who will not meet the men Nature has fitted them for. The call of sacrifice, however, may come to all, and perhaps in the final weighing up of things that man or woman, whether from the call of human love or for beauty or for truth, who holds up in his or her life the solitary ideal, may be the one who has really counted most in raising the standard of life. However this be, the teaching of biology, first and last, for woman and for man is to accept our natures, glory in them, and keep healthy what Nature has given us, making her vast possibilities real actualities by our lives. This can only be done for woman by being womanly, and for man by acting as becomes a man.

●●

14

Economics and Biology

Last century was an economic century, and a preparatory biological one. Smith's "Wealth of Nations" had prepared the way for Ricardo and Mill; and the first effect of Darwin's, Huxley's, and Spencer's work, but not its real final effect, being against religion, robbed religion of its strength to hold back the economic, rationalistic doctrines of supply and demand and a hard, rationalistic, unscientific view of life. It ought to have been a very obvious truth, one would have thought, that the laws which regulate money, prices, markets, and exchange of goods must be different laws from those which regulate a healthy blood supply in a human body; and that, whether one believes in an immortal soul and a destiny for individual man, or in a mind that disintegrates completely at bodily death, yet, while a human being lives, there are certain psychological or mind laws, certain mind feelings (appetites and emotions), certain other powers even beyond these, that require a knowledge of life which the science of life, biology, including, as it does, body and mind studies, could have supplied; and that, therefore, a completer view of society could have been obtained if biologists and economists had come together as social students to teach mankind its ideal of social life. Educational influences might in addition have been considered, as well as the geographical potentiality of the soil. It might have been thought that these would have been common-sense practical conclusions, involving no great or technical knowledge, and that a man trained to logic as Mill was would have seen such a simple, obvious, common-sense and necessary scientific proposition. As a fact, neither he nor his contemporaries except Comte saw anything of the kind. They saw men and women who could be reasoned, ignorantly, about; men and women, all alike, who in theory always obeyed rationalistic laws, who never suffered from disease, who never felt overstrain, who never felt a desire to do an act that could not be explained, justified, or blamed by the obvious reasons of a logician. Of course, Mill would have denied this attitude, had it been put to him. The fact remains, none the less, that there is not a single sentence, that I can remember, of applied biology, of the problems of human type and temperament of body and mind, of the problems of health and disease, in his work. He never saw practically the need to understand the biological sub-sciences, or even the practical economic study of prices of articles sold in the daily exchanges of life. He believed in a reasoned view of existence, quite apart from a study of it as a science, and hence his curious views about men and women and life generally. It was this unscientific, and in the larger sense illogical and unrational, attitude that justified Ruskin's strictures and Dickens's ridicule. Nevertheless, Mill is not to be too greatly blamed, for this blindness was largely an industrial attitude of the times, from which we ourselves have not even yet completely recovered; but it is not necessary to plead to-day that there is a biological aspect of life.

The Biological Demand

What are the biological demands which the biologist wishes to make of the economist in regard to woman ? They can be probably already foreshadowed by the reader.

The physiological needs of motherhood demand non-employment after married life, some would assert for those married women only who have children. This restriction is, however, unsatisfactory, as it might tend to discourage one of the most important aims of marriage, parentage. The married woman with a husband living and capable should not be a wage-earner for the following reasons :

1. After the third month of expectant motherhood, in some women earlier, slight and sometimes considerable interferences of health take place, and it is essential that for all women a composed, restful life, not idle, but with activities taken quietly, at the woman's own time and in the woman's own way, are essential for reasons. The home is the only place where this is possible.

   It is no longer arguable scientifically that the natural food of the infant, for its first nine months of life after birth, is its mother's, and that no artificial food can equal this from any point of view. Thus fifteen months' absence from factory or other occupational life outside the home is essential, not for the larger thought of motherhood only, but simply for the bearing and rearing of the child during this period.

   If we assume only three children to each family, this means on an average that in the first six years of married life the wife and mother would be precluded from industrial or arduous professional employment. But the matter does not end here, for those six years would be years in which a new attitude of mind would, or ought to have developed in the mother, and her fitness for her former work would for this reason have deteriorated.

2. For general reasons it is now granted that school is a mistake for children under five years of age, and there can be no serious question of the advantage of good home life, owing to less danger from infection; of the smaller stimulus and strain to the child's brain in the home if it is not taken out late and improperly

managed ; of the understanding and individual treatment that a mother can give her child, to say nothing of the feeling of love between them, or of possible bad habits that may be taught by a careless nurse or learned from another child of greater precocity, that the mother is the proper, sole guardian for her child during this period, assisted, of course, by the father. But this granted four or five years on to the six years already conceded takes the wife for ten or eleven years away from industry.

3. The majority of homes are servantless, the majority of servants are unsuitable as nurses, so that if boarding-schools are not to be accepted as a universal school custom and national ones established (and financial and biological reasons: could both be given against them), the child must be at home for fifteen years of its life. This makes twenty years' absence from employment almost a certainty.

4. Assuming a woman marries at twenty-three to twenty-five, the twenty years thus take her to forty-three to forty-five; would she be able to take up at this age her old pre-marital calling or a new one ? Obviously there is extremely little chance of this. A practical need at this moment creeps in which, though not of scientific- insistence, is one that can hardly be avoided. Assuming that fifteen years of age is the time a boy or a girl can begin to learn something of occupational life, an age thought to be two years too early by many authorities, these children will not, as a fact, in the majority of reasons, leave home immediately; in most instances they will remain until married, that is for another eight to ten years, and in the mere daily home needs of children and husband the wife will have her time fully

occupied. By the time the children begin to leave home a wife married at the biological age of twenty-three to twenty-five would be fifty to fifty-five years before her home would be free from children and her life less occupied. This is also about the period of the change of life in women, and most mothers would, I think rightly, consider that their active life was done, and that some leisure was due to them, so that the post-maternal part of a woman's life is unlikely to see her leaving home to take up either her old occupation she had practised thirty to thirty-five years earlier or a new one.

5. There remains the pre-marital stage of life. What is the young, unmarried girl to do before marriage ? I may remark in passing that if marriage were possible to men at twenty-three to twenty-five years of age, it would be fairly certain that the betrothal period would begin about eighteen months to three years earlier, so that for the majority of women the question would be what to occupy themselves with from the seventeenth to the twenty-third year. For those not marrying some other occupational solution different from the marriage one ought to be found. These questions come naturally into the subject matter of the next chapter but one. Thus on making two perfectly simple and scientific assumptions, one, that for the majority of women marriage and parentage are the normal, healthy destinies (and no sane, competent authority could question this), two, that the home must persist for the needs of the child, we see what common sense suggests as well, that marriage is an occupation in itself, and therefore excludes other occupations, and therefore for the married woman the wage-earning market must be closed.

I shall, of course, be told that this will bring into still more striking prominence the endowment of motherhood, but there are powerful objections to any proposition made on such a basis, *if the endowment is a teal endowment equivalent in kind and value to what a man earns by his occupation.*

It might be argued with much reason that the lazy wife's position ought to be legally punishable as well as the husband's, and it is, of course, needless to say that all celibate occupational positions should be gradually eliminated from social life.

Shortly, then, what the biologist demands is this: the abolition of all forms of child labour except those legitimately connected with the teaching of trades and professions to youth; the economic dependence of the married woman on the man—and women should remember that this only means the domestic dependence of the man on the woman—and the establishment of a man's mature marriageable living wage as the wage standard of the nation, the single woman and the single man being paid at the same hourly payment. It probably would be necessary to tax the single woman and man more heavily than the married man under these conditions, but as the single woman, better paid, ought not to work for such long hours (a great advantage to her health), and the single man would be mostly making preparations for marriage, the tax should not, in justice, greatly exceed the married man's.

This, then, is the biological demand, for a man's mature marriageable living family wage, varying, of course, for different occupations, as the standard payment for all in each respective employment, thus making juvenile labour impossible, and fixing all employment at the married man's standard.

How this is to be done, whether by law or trade-union pressure, how expeditiously it can be achieved, these and other questions must be left to the economist, but of the biological necessity of this standard for healthy national and individual life there can be little doubt; on this point biologists of the future will probably allow nothing in the nature of a compromise.

Yet I do not desire the reader to think that I am wishful to establish binding laws to which no individual exceptions are to be made. I repeat, I ask for. nothing else than this—that woman should recognise her own individuality and that man should recognise it also, in education, vocation, domestic life and national representation.

THE HOME AND MOTHERHOOD

T. Have said nothing so far about certain arguments that might be thought worthy of rather serious criticism. The fact, for instance, that in Lancashire, especially in many of the large towns, women have almost abandoned the home and work side by side with the men. Thus woman's economic independence may be said to be a fact accomplished, and that while this independence works badly in Dundee, it is fairly satisfactory in the cotton industry. The answer is simple; for the home not to be neglected some other woman than the mother has to keep it in order—why not the mother ?—and for expectant motherhood and for the child during infancy factory life is unphysiological. No one will seriously contend that the home under such conditions equals that of the better type of home-employed mother; and if such a contention were made, it could easily be confuted, for it is not the fact. The argument then appears to be this : because the best type of factory or professionally employed mother can manage to so control unphysiological methods of life, and by payment of others to work for her can keep a house in order, provided her children, who ought to be at home, are taken care of elsewhere, supposing this type of woman keeps up a condition of domestic life that, though defective, is yet better than the worst examples of home-employed motherhood, that therefore all examples of home-employed motherhood shall be swept away and the employment of married women can go on moderately unsatisfactorily and extremely unsatisfactorily as before. It is an argument worthy of a logician's analysis for exposition to his students, of faulty reasoning, but it is not worth the scientist's attention.

In all seriousness, what do such arguments amount to nothing. Supposing it could be granted that an expectant mother can do the same kind and amount of work as the non-expectant or the single woman without injury to herself or child, which it cannot; supposing it could be admitted that a modified cow's or so-called humanised milk could be prepared so as to suit the individual infant, and have the amount and quality changed with the infant's changing needs; and supposing a feeding-bottle could be made which automatically heated the milk up to body temperature, and kept it at that temperature, and never lower or higher, and, without destroying the living food substances in the milk good and necessary for the baby, could at the same time be kept perfectly sterilised; supposing this same feeding-bottle could be made so that the flow of milk could be properly regulated, and supposing you could guarantee that nurses who feed this little life shall not allow this very complex feeding-bottle to become dirty, as it easily might, and always obey exactly the regulations which would have to be sent out with it to keep it in order; supposing all this could be granted, would that justify an expectant mother living a factory life, or the nursing mother for her absence from her child ? Is there nothing in a mother thinking about the little life within her body and meditating upon it ? And what chance of meditation is there in the ordinary factory, or when the mother comes to her home tired (less her home, for it is managed by another woman), what chance is there for meditation there either ? A woman who would thus defend an industrial life after marriage is unworthy of marriage and of parentage.

Is the book that has been tossed off carelessly, typed by one hand, indexed by another, references made by another, and corrections by yet another, worth the same in value as the one-that is author-corrected, author-indexed, author-compiled ? No one in his senses would claim this. It would be pointed out that the care of the writer in his work would react on his mind, give him fresh ideas, enable him to link his chapters together and relate his thought, and make his hook a whole. And the old-fashioned mother at her best, who felt the presence of her child, who made its garments with her own hands, giving the little finishes that as a mother pleased her, who prepared for its birth, who felt its little fingers at her breast after it was born, and looked down with possession and protection on its little face, and cared for it herself until it had made a place in her heart mistakable by time or difficulty, does not such a mother represent the ideal of motherhood ? Is any sensible man or woman going to compare this woman, a mother, with that other woman who does none of these things, who simply bears the child grudgingly, and lets other hands minister to its wants and needs, when and wherever it is possible for them to do so ? That one who does, either has had no child or deserves none.

Is it necessary to carry the argument further, to suggest that bricks and mortar and pictures and furniture and food and knives and forks and a bed to lie on do not make a home ? That what is meant by home is as real and as spiritual as what is meant by beauty or truth and as difficult to define ?

The man or woman who has *felt* what the home means, is such a one going to be convinced by petitions or simple health arguments to abandon it for a life where meals are eaten at public places, where beds are hired and rooms purchased, when he or she has the chance of another mode of life, where the rule is affection, not finance, and privacy and individuality, not publicity and nonentity? To have your own pictures on the wall, your own books on their shelves, your own furniture, your own friends, your own fireside, and to weigh against these publicity and finance—as well tell an artist that photographs are cheaper, or a scientist that truth is only veracity and not worthy of the trouble spent upon it. Home as a positive, mental reality, motherhood and wifehood as fatherhood and husband hood, are things mental, spiritual, not material, as every one who has seen or had either knows, and to tell such a one that you could make a home by being absent from it and by doing little for it, and that it is not to be weighed by the side of industrial life, would leave such a person unconvinced.

The mere fact that such arguments are adduced demonstrates how far reason has usurped the place of feeling, and what an unworthy usurper it is ; how far low thoughts of trade have degraded life; how far a man or woman with natural manly and womanly, fatherly and motherly, feelings can lose these and be obsessed by a worthless shadow that has not even the form of the reality it counterfeits. I am not blaming the woman who has unconsciously made mistakes, for the character of the times has dehumanised our lives and affected women even more than men.

●●

15

Confusion of Thought of Times

I wish in this chapter, as I have to be unavoidably critical, to consider certain statements quite apart from the question of authorship ; but at the same time I shall try to use only those references that may be taken as being representative of widespread belief. I have, however, full authorities in my possession.

The Woman of the Past as she is Stated to have been as Compared with the Woman of To-day

> "... Sonte of us, perhaps, can remember a time when girls in the schoolroom were brought up upon text-books, in question and answer, that had to be learned by rote, such as 'Magnall's Questions' and 'Brewer's Guide to Science,' when Miss Corner's Histories were in fashion, when compound division was their extreme limit of arithmetic, and Euclid and algebra and Latin, and much more Greek, and even German, were not taught by governesses or included in school curricula. Both in limitation of range and want of thoroughness, the intellectual education of girls was sadly to seek."

This passage by a principal of an important ladies' college, though not intended to be disingenuous, could hardly be more so had it been a skilled, conscious, deliberate attempt at misrepresentation.

1. School text-books, whether for girls or boys, at this period were very defective; "Magnall's Questions " were not worse than many text-books read by boys;

2. While it is pointed out that girls did not learn Euclid, algebra, Latin, Greek, and German, the domestic training which they received, and, *for the time,* a not-to-be-despised training in music and art, is omitted. Thus the inferiority of the woman's side seems self-evident, when, as a fact, it was rather a different system of education than an inferior one which was practised.

Ruskin and many well-informed biologists are of opinion that in this respect the older thought was right for its time.

"The Bad Old Days."

"The women of our grandmother's days had few liberties and fewer rights. Their property and their persons belonged to their male relations, and they had little or no control over either. A father could dispose of his children, even after his death, without the slightest regard to the wishes of the mother. A man might legally beat his wife, and many men did so. Wives were put up for auction, and sold to the highest bidder. There were instances, though happily they had become rare, of the employment by husbands of ducking-stools, gossip-bridles, public whipping-posts, and stocks. Of social life women had none. Their outgoings were restricted to visits to church on holy days, and occasional rare journeys to market, wedding-feast, or death-bed. Such company as the master of the house permitted to cross its threshold was his company. It was the wife's duty to serve guests and then to depart; they were but added burdens in her dreary, colourless life."

This statement, made by one of the late leaders of the present suffrage movement, scarcely needs its fallacies pointed out.

Had such a state of suppression ever existed as *a world fact,* that fact alone would have proved the inferiority of woman, but the assertions are not accurate.

We are told that women of our grandmothers' days, that is to say from 1825 to 1860, had no social life, were sold at auction, were frequently beaten, had no friends of their own, and there were instances of gossip-bridles and ducking-stools and public whipping-posts being used. Not one of these practices was prevalent or existed at all in our grandmothers' days. They belong to mediaeval times, when the treatment of men was even rougher than that of women. There was one sale of a wife, a semi-humorous sale, in quite the early part of last century, which caused an *obsolete* law to be repealed ; as there was an obsolete law of trial by combat for men which had to be repealed nearly the same time.

Woman's lack of property and of rights to her children and other like defects, existed in our grandmothers' days as laws, and at times were tyrannous laws, but as marriage settlements and other legal contrivances proved, these were frequently evaded.

A picture such as this can only be dismissed from serious controversy, yet there are nine similar paragraphs in the article, and many women's thoughts are fashioned on such material.

Here is another extract:

> "Yet to-day, with liberty and training, women are proving their intellectual capacity; and their physical development is a joy to the eye of the beholder."

This reference to improvement in woman's physique is one that is frequently made without, so far as I am aware, one small shred of fact to support it. There are no large series of measurements of the bodies of men or women before 1880, no measurements of any kind comparing men and women together, and no records of the relative health of men and women in occupational life. How such comparisons as to the relative health of the woman of to-day as compared with the woman of the past have been framed, except from a few writers of nation, it is hard to surmise.

It would be easy to quote worse examples of incompetence, but I do not wish to make the picture too severe.

Such obvious bias, and such a seemingly deliberate attempt to palpably libel the woman of the past, cannot be regarded as being due simply to ignorance of social history, though no doubt such is partly the case; nor can it be thought of as a mere economic obsession, nor even as a means of crude propagandism, though something of each of these influences can be obviously traced. There is beyond this a conscious or unconscious animosity to the habits of the lives of our grandparents, of which it is difficult to explain the cause. At times, as one studies this aspect of the woman's movement, one is tempted to believe that a certain type of woman has been "educated" into a feeling of hostility to all things characteristic of woman, but no explanation is completely satisfying to the mind. One fact is, however, certain, that the economic demands of last century centred round one need, that of cheap labour, and that a convenient philosophy of life arose, which disregarded the real nature of womanhood and the healthy requisites of girl and boy life, and all the world over, no doubt unconsciously, encouraged all ideas that suppressed the demands of womanhood and parentage, and favoured an artificial and unhealthy life. No other view will explain the rapid spread of neo-Malthusian ideas, the rapid disorganisation of domestic ideals, and the rise of a type of woman and of man who favour factory employment outside the home for married women, artificial feeding of infants, creches, boarding-schools for quite young children, and who favour no legislative restrictions on the employment and for the protection of women and children.

The Anti-Woman and Anti-Home Policy of some Women Writers

The really serious extent to which this thought has become prevalent may be most easily seen if some attempt is made to co-ordinate into one whole the many various slipshod theories which have been formulated to attack the position that the womanly mind and body are unlike the manly mind and body, and need, therefore, different but complementary forms of activity.

The first and obvious difficulty that confronts even the superficial student is the ascendancy of man's influence in society ; the complete absence of first-rank genius, except in literature and acting, *in* women is so obvious, and has been so manifest for so many centuries, that some explanation, to hide the real facts, is required. Hence have grown up two curious ideas, both originating and flourishing mainly in the United States soil, but which have been transplanted to the more critical European climate: the one, the claim that woman at one time was the dominating influence in the world, and the other, which supports it, that early man had his industrial life organised by woman. These two ideas form the basis of a contention that beyond the patriarchal age was a matriarchal, and the argument one is invited to draw from this is that woman must recover the lost ground, and that the old matriarchy must be revived. But a few facts easily dispose of both theory and argument.

The assumption of a very early feminine ascendancy has no comparative evidence to support it. If early man had been dominated by woman, one would have expected that other related animals, such as the higher apes, would show evidence of the same influence; as a fact, however, over the whole mammalian and bird development of life, with two small exceptions in birds, the male is everywhere the stronger and the fighting creature, and the female the more passive ; and one has to turn either to the spider or a parasitic worm, themselves exceptions, for support in the animal kingdom for this matriarchal idea. Truly a thin thread upon which to try to suspend such a heavy theory.

In early man there is one support to this assumption of feminine ascendancy: in certain instances descent is traced through the female rather than the male line, but as maternity is an obvious fact, and paternity one that is much less certainly recognisable, it follows that maternal descent is much the more likely to be customary under early human life conditions.

The status of woman varies extremely widely under all social conditions, and although it has some relation to the degree of civilisation a nation attains to, rising with national evolution, yet no certain conclusions can be drawn. The Egyptians treated women less freely but more kindly than the Assyrians, yet the Babylonians, of the same race as the Assyrians, gave to their women citizens great licence. Sparta, less civilised than Athens, was yet more free in its treatment of women, and it would have been difficult to conceive of an emancipation movement among the Spartan women, so great was their liberty as compared with the men, though both sexes were subordinated to the state. The position of Roman women is often quoted, but their greatest period of licence was during the decline, not during the rise, of Rome, and to-day the different position of women in Germany, England, and the United States cannot, upon any sane estimate, be regarded as measuring the standard of civilisation of these three countries.

Even among savages the treatment of women is extremely various, and affords no satisfactory basis for any sound theory of national culture.

Finally, it is not true to assert that industrial life was organised by women under primitive social conditions, unless important qualifications are added, for early man had much to do with the pastoral side of life and cattle-rearing, and the specialisation was one of sex-capacity—the man doing the fighting and hunting forms of labour and the woman the more peaceful.

There is thus no satisfactory evidence for a matriarchy, as unquestionable authorities such as Wester-marck have pointed out, and if there were it would tell against the claims of womanhood, for in that case the status of the woman would have declined with advancing social evolution, instead of having, in some measure, advanced with it.

The second practical difficulty that the de-womanising emancipationists had to face was the obvious fact that woman in her nature is different *now* when compared with the man, the civilised woman being more differentiated from the man than the barbaric. If, therefore, it has to be proved that there is no such thing "as a female mind," one must assert that either the woman of to-day is "oversexed," whatever such an unscientific phrase can mean, and that the barbaric woman is the ideal woman, or that under civilised conditions a "neuter" sex is becoming manifested, a still wilder hypothesis, and that some women can discard their womanhood.

The word "oversexed " has no scientific meaning of any kind behind it, it is one of those pleasing words that seems to suggest something until it is examined, and then is found to be quite unreal and devoid of significance. The bodily cause of womanly and manly types depends primarily upon the activity of certain masculine and feminine glands, and if such an oversexed condition ever arose, it would be a state of actual disease that would need medical treatment. At present no such disease is known, and if it were it could have no direct relation to the woman's movement except in so far as something in our lives had affected woman hurtfully. An over- sexed woman, being diseased, could not work until her health was restored, either industrially or in the home.

The neuter sex idea is even cruder. It is an assumption that in man, a mammal, having a mammal's complicated organisation, obeying mammalian laws as to number of offspring born, a group of women and, presumably, men might arise in whom the call of parentage could be disregarded, and who could be compared to the neuter working bees. One has only to point out one fact to grasp the essential absurdity of this contention. The worker bee is recognisable as being different from the queen bee. Where are the men and women of the world whose bodily form as they walk up and down the streets permits us to assert that they belong to the undomesticated genus ?

Yet upon these three fallacies of the matriarchate, the oversexed, and the neuter types of women, all three of which logically destroy each other, as well as being the merest grotesques of serious thought, much of the modern woman's movement is built up.

From the oversexed idea we are told that woman is too much in the home, and that expectant motherhood can disregard the fact of unborn life for six to seven months after its beginnings; that the woman in the home is a worse, or, as some would put it, not a better, home-maker than the factory woman who neglects it, and that the state control and care of children is seriously to be discussed by the side of genuine, true, and worthy motherhood. That the very functional disabilities of woman that prepare for motherhood are expressions of disease, and that unmarried and married women must be free to work as they please under all conditions, and that divorce—as family ties are slight—should be easily granted.

The neuter sex idea has as yet had little practical application, but it should form the basis of a logical thought about co-education, for if co-education means what its name implies, it assumes that the girl and boy are so alike in bodily and mental characteristics during pubescence and adolescence that they can receive a similar education. Even on the other ground of different kinds of education for boys and girls associated together in the same classroom, co-associational, not co-educational, we see a strange disregard for the consequences of scientific thought. For many advocates of the co-association of children, and the co-association of women and men in industrial and cultural life-pursuits, advocate disassociational practice in the home, the husband and wife leading a dual life, with easy divorce laws, so that permanent co-association of the married man and woman will be difficult.

The aim in all, whether consciously or unconsciously, is to de-womanise the woman and destroy her real inborn individuality of body and mind.

The last of these unscientific assumptions is that of "economic independence." Sanely treated there is probably not a little truth in the idea ; a woman has a right—whether married or single—to the wages of her labour, and if some law could fix this right in statute form, so that a half of the husband's wages were regarded as legally belonging to the wife, I personally should have no objection to offer ; but to believe that either this or the franchise would make any serious difference to woman's domestic position is to openly disregard the teaching of fact and reality.

There are four great groups of citizens in the nation : the unskilled labourer, the skilled artisan or mechanic, the trader or shopkeeper, and the professional worker. If economic independence of women really counted in married life, as the customs vary so widely in these four groups, some real differences in the happiness of married women should be observable. What do we find ?

The labourer is frequently out of work, and apart from his periods of enforced unemployment is improvident, consequently, with one or two exceptions, the custom is for the wife to go out to work, and the better type of husband brings home his weekly wages to her when earning. The labourer's wife thus earns enough for her own keep and sometimes more, and has control of the larger part of her husband's earnings as well; she is thus not only economically independent, but economically is the controlling influence in married life. In other less favourable cases the husband earns little or nothing, and the wife is the sole bread-winner, and the husband is economically dependent on his wife. Any man or woman of real experience knows that the treatment of the wife will have practically nothing whatever to do with this economic relationship. Push the position one stage further. It is quite frequent that a mother or father or both are dependent on a daughter or a son. It will then almost entirely depend on the character of the parent and the child which of the following alternatives will be manifested :

Either the unselfish child will be sacrificed to a selfish parent, and the whole of the weekly wages will be absorbed by the mother or father who exacts it;

Or the parent will be treated badly at home or sent to the workhouse or an equivalent accommodation outside of the home;

Or, as more commonly happens, the parent shares with the child, and there is mutual understanding.

Among the labouring, mechanic, shopkeeping, and professional classes alike these alternatives disclose no relation at all, as far as I can discover, to the economic position of the child, or, within limits, the parent.

There are parents that exact from their children, and children from their parents, and this state of things exists in rich and poor and all classes alike.

According to the economic independence theory of woman, the labourer's wife should be the best treated in the nation, and it is needless to point out that this is not the fact; and there ought to be some relation between the treatment of parent and child to each other, varying with the monetary dependence and independence of the one on the other. It is remarkable how seldom this is the case. It is almost more true to say, though this is not a general truth either, that dependence of one human being on another makes for kindliness of treatment.

But, as if to demonstrate this point to the fullest degree, we see in the mechanic classes generally (there are some exceptions, as in the Lancashire cotton industry) the woman remaining exclusively at home, the husband bringing home his weekly wages to her, and the wife often giving him back for his pocket-money what *she* thinks the home can afford; and there is no happier nor better class in the nation, nor happier man and woman than the mechanic and his wife.

Finally, the larger shopkeeper and the professional man keep their earnings, make the wife a housekeeping allowance and a dress and personal allowance, and, as a whole, neither the shopkeeper's wife nor the professional man's is unhappy at the result.

I do not deny that there may be something to be said for a wife's independent economic position, but a custom which is so various (and besides class, national differences could easily be shown) has quite obviously little or no relation to the happiness or the unhappiness of the majority of women. The status of woman in regard to the man clearly does not depend upon economic financial conditions, but upon character reactions. There are tyrannous women and tyrannous men, and no law of any country can override Nature's law that in personal domestic relations of women with women, men with men, and women with men, it is character reactions, above everything else, that count. It is fortunate for human life that it is so, for the financial aspect has more than enough power as it is.

Here, then, is a strange position, which, in concluding this present chapter, let me summarise. From about 1830 to 1850 a type of woman, probably a product of an increasingly dewomanised educational system and of an economic social atmosphere adverse to human needs, began to arise, who, with increasing vigour, unreason, and unreality has spoken increasingly contemptuously of the home and of the domestic woman of the past; she has, with the help of men, formulated a number of crude and unsupported theories, such as the unhealthiness of the domestic, home and motherly type of woman; the supremacy of woman in early barbaric life ; the oversexed condition of the woman of to-day, and, when it is convenient to urge the conflicting hypothesis to that of woman's supremacy in the past, to refer to the neuter sex at the present time; when arguing about woman's work as compared with man's, claiming that a woman's work "is never done," and at other times that so much work has been taken out of the home that a woman ought to be able to seek employment outside it as well; when asking for such a reform as the endowment of motherhood, claiming that no work is higher than a mother's, and that, therefore, it ought to be well paid, invoking the fallacious assumption that the quality of the work is, or ever has been, in relation to money-payment, will yet in almost the same breath advocate the abandonment of motherhood and the home by maternity institutions, creches, infant schools, and boarding, co-educational systems, and a system of marriage that would abolish the disgrace of divorce and lead inevitably, if the nation accepted it, to a lowered parental responsibility.

For a natural, healthy-minded man or woman to hold such illogical views no explanation but that of a social obsession is possible, and it is discoverable in the economic demands of last century, which taught woman, and to some extent man, to believe that woman had no womanly individuality of mind, that mathematics, Latin, Greek, German, and logic were as much women's subjects as men's; that anyone could make and keep a home and be a mother, and that a lady clerk's calling of copying out dictated letters was intellectual in comparison to this; that a woman's gift of intuition was only instinct, and that a woman movement which was to emancipate her should in practice make her deny her bodily and mental personality.

●●

16

Female Crimes and Criminals in the Past

"It can hardly be said that crime entailing incarceration is otherwise than stationary among the women of India," is a line that I cull from the last-issued official report as to the gaol and criminal statistics of the dependency. The very small ratio of female to male malefactors is, however, one of the most remarkable and interesting aspects of the whole social system of the East from whatever point of view one regards it; while favourable to women as even the mere figures are, their statistical morality is placed even higher when certain facts concerning those who are classified as offenders are taken into consideration. First, however, it should be pointed out that crime among men shows a marked tendency to increase. In 1881, the number of male prisoners in gaol was 402,823, and ten years later those figures had jumped to 526,804, though better administration in Burmah may be held responsible for an appreciable percentage of this very large increase. In the corresponding years, of this number, only 23,718 and 24,933 were women; while in the intervening decade the total never exceeded the latter figure, nor sank below 21,794. This, for all practical purposes, places women convicts to men convicts in the proportion of 1 to 20.5.

Comparing this with our own ratio, I find in the corresponding British judicial statistics, that during 1891 the ratio of female to male offenders sentenced to penal servitude was 9.2 to 90.8, which is nearly double. It is true that 1892 saw these figures standing at 6.3 to 93.7; but the fluctuations in them during the past twenty years or so have been so marked that I fear, for the credit of my sex, the lower proportion is hardly likely to be maintained. The classification of the various headings of crime show a wider range to the Englishwoman's breaches of the law to that of her Indian cousin, and it is instructive to concerning those convicted in England during 1891:—

These proportions were somewhat diminished in 1892; but as I am unable to give the equivalent Indian statistics for that year, comparison cannot be instituted.

Recommitted is very rare among the Indian women, and with all save petty depredators the punishment of imprisonment exercises a deterrent effect. It is not so with ourselves, where the higher proportionate numbers of females frequently recommitted is always very noticeable. In 1892, I find that the males recommitted to English gaols were 41.7 per cent of the total number of males committed (exclusive of debtors and naval and military offenders); and the recommitted females (exclusive of debtors) formed 60.3 of the whole. In the preceding year the proportions were 42 per cent. with respect to males, and 54.6 per cent, with respect to females.

Now the first fact that tends to reduce the proportion of offenders among the average female population of India, is the existence of a thieving and begging caste. This is perfectly well recognized by those responsible for the administration of the law, and when I went through Agra gaol, where against 1900 men, there were only 66 women, no less than 11 belonged to this order, which is more or less nomadic, and goes by different names in different parts of India.

Secondly to be considered is the point, that an extraordinarily large number of the female offenders are in prison for receiving stolen goods. In this it is but just that the woman should be leniently dealt with, as in almost every case concerning which I made inquiries I found that she was more or less the tool of her husband or the men of her family. The stolen property was brought to her, and she was ordered to conceal it, a command which, with the submissiveness to those she has been taught are her lords and masters, as well as the possibility of *force majeure* if she had declined, she naturally obeyed. But surely, in such instance, it is fairer to judge her as a victim to her circumstances than as a lawbreaker on her own account.

The Indian female thief is as a rule guilty only of petty larceny, and minor depredations, such as a handful of rice from the grain-seller, or wood or charcoal from some wealthier neighbour's stores, or she may obtain possession by fraud of a kinswoman's jewellery; but she lacks the nerve, the readiness, and the resource for bolder efforts. Cases of assault rare comparatively rare, and I think indeed nothing shows more pointedly how thorough have been her life's lessons of discipline than this, when one takes into account the numbers of sisters and sisters-in-law, both married and single, who are to be found living in the one house, with a mother-in-law over them in supreme command and control.

The crime to be set down as the characteristic one of Indian women is infanticide. Not, be it understood, as it is with 11s, when it is generally the last desperate, piteous effort of a betrayed girl-mother to hide her shame from the world, but as an angry wife's most furious form of vengeance for a husband's coldness, neglect, or infidelity. Eliminating the female convicts under punishment for the offences I have named, it will always be found that fully four-fifths of the examining prisoners are undergoing sentence for this crime. The unfortunate infants may be strangled, deserted, poisoned, or thrown down wells; and the bitterness of the revenge is always enhanced tenfold if it be a little son whose life is taken.

In one case that I saw at Benares, the woman, who was awaiting trial, was accused of having left the baby upon the public highway to the endangering of its life. Her defence, however, was that she had only done it to bring her husband to a sense of his duty, as he was withholding adequate support from her. In the Agra prison I saw no less than ten women under life sentences for infanticide, and in two or three of the cases it had been done for what seemed absurdly trivial reasons, such as that a husband had commended the cooking he had seen at another house.

Murder among the women is very rare, and the only notable instance of it that I saw in the many gaols that I visited was at Madras, and it struck me as a rather tragic illustration of the way in which at times these women of the East view the domestic arrangements sanctioned by long custom in their land. This was the case of a young woman under sentence of ten years' "rigorous" imprisonment. She was unusually handsome, with a low broad brow, a wealth of coal-black hair, flashing brown eyes, and a tall lithe figure that would have served for a Venus in bronze. In a moment of mad jealousy she had murdered her sister, who was married to the same husband as herself. It was impossible to withhold a glance 'of pitying sympathy as her keen eyes rested upon mine while she grasped the fact that the wardress was conveying to me, in the little English at her command, the stormy story of her passionate love.

Madras was quite characteristic of all the other gaols that I saw, and though its male and female departments are actually within the same enclosing walls, and under the equal supervision of Mr. Macready, its kindly and courteous superintendent, the women's quarters are quite isolated, and under no circumstances whatever do the prisoners of the one sex see or meet with those of the other. A high wall and heavy iron-studded gates, similar to those characteristic of such establishments in England, have to be passed to gain admission; but, once inside, the gorgeous sunshine and the luxuriant ever-present flowering plants, which thrive in all corners and crannies, give a far less sombre appearance to the well-kept place than that of the grey, granite-flagged yards associated at home with prison life. Considerable enlargements and improvements were being carried out in the men's workshops, and when these are complete the prison will as a whole be one of the best equipped in the whole dependency.

On the day that I visited the Madras prison it contained 870 prisoners, of whom only 33 were women. This, Mr. Macready informed me, was slightly below the average number, which is about 40 ; a total rarely exceeded by more than two or three. A European matron and a native wardress—a remarkably intelligent young woman, who seemed not only to have the power of commanding respect and discipline, but also to feel a gentle feminine sympathy with her unfortunate charges—formed the whole staff necessary for the maintenance of good order, though over the prisoners themselves was appointed from their number a maestry, who was responsible to the matron for the execution of the tasks allotted to the prisoners. The woman in this position was a Hindu of the weaver caste, and was undergoing a sentence of seven years for infanticide, but her good conduct since her conviction had won for her marks enough to secure the remission of nearly a year of her time. The women sleep in a large dormitory, to each one being allotted a stone *piall,* or bed, the equivalent of our plank bed at home, a sleeping suit, a mat to lie upon, two blankets to cover her, and a pillow. This chamber is light, and particularly well ventilated—a very important point in any institution in the tropics. The dietary is the same as that of the men, only a little reduced in quantity, and gives them rice twice a week and raggi the remaining days, with curry, and a small quantity of meat or vegetable daily. Raggi, though highly nutritious, is not greatly enjoyed, and its use may be regarded as equivalent to that of oatmeal porridge in a London house of correction. It is a small grain, not unlike rape seed in appearance, and when ground fine produces a greyish flour. This is boiled with water and salt to a very thick batter, and is poured out into pound moulds, when it looks. like a rather stodgy chocolate pudding, and is served with about a third of a pint of thick and very savoury-smelling curry. All the cooking is done by prisoners of caste, so that no outrage is done to inherent prejudices on this point; and certainly in quantity and quality it seemed all that the most advanced humanitarian could desire. There is a small hospital set apart for the women, where iron pallet beds and mattresses are provided, while the food given them is according to medical orders. Two cases of slight fever were in it under treatment on the day that I was there, but as a whole the health throughout the prison—unless Madras should be visited by an outbreak of cholera, when it suffers proportionately—is very good. A kindly concession to maternal feelings allows any woman to keep her baby, whether born before or after conviction, with her until it reaches the age of two years, and a sufficient quantity of milk over and above the prison fare is allowed the mother for the baby's use.

All the jewellery, which is such a treasured evidence of social position to Hindu women, is of course taken off them when they pass behind the prison walls, and the only things they are permitted to retain are the symbols of marriage—usually a small gold charm worn suspended round the neck by a cord or beads, or the iron bangle, and the sacred cord which indicates certain Brahmin castes. The prison dress consists of a strong cotton unbleached or coloured cloth, which they drape round them in the manner they have been accustomed to wear it, covering the breast and left shoulder. Their hair is not cut off, and they twist it into a knot low down at the back of their heads.

The women, like the men, are put to varying employments in different prisons. One almost invariably, however, finds them set to clean and sort the grain, and afterwards pound it for the staple food of the gaol, this of course being labour to which they are quite accustomed at home. In many of the prisons, too, where carpet or other weaving is carried on, they are set to wind yarn, and in others basket and mat-making provides occupation for many more. In Madras the female prisoners themselves weave a broad webbing tape, which is almost all supplied to the army, who use it for tent fastenings and girthings, on account of its reliable strength and quality.

"Rigorous" confinement is the equivalent of our own hard labour; but I believe that women are not subjected to the additional punishments of "close" or "solitary" confinement. As one often hears exaggerated statements concerning the frequency and severity of this extra correction, I went at some detail into this question, and learnt that "close" punishment, which consists in keeping the prisoner alone in a cell, save for his daily exercise in company with other prisoners, can only be imposed at the following ratio to sentence: "Habitual convicts, if sentenced to less than two years, three months; two, and less than three years, four months; three, and less than four years, six months; four, and less than eight years, eight months; over eight years, twelve months; which must be served in two periods of six months, with an interval between of two months." The terms of "close" imprisonment for first or second time offenders are less in proportion. There are two grades also of "solitary" confinement which, under no circumstances, can be inflicted for more than seven consecutive days in a month, and which, with its accompaniment of lessened diet, is only resorted to in the extremest cases of refractoriness, insubordination, or violence to warders or fellow-prisoners.

Once in a way even now, there are instances in which settled law has failed to satisfy the instincts of the people, and since my return to England, I have had sent me the details of a luridly tragic story, which is surely one of the most notable instances of wrong-headed heroism and supreme self-sacrifice of modern days. It comes from Katthiawar, and to understand it, one must know that before law and order were introduced by us, *dharna* was a recognized mood of obtaining redress or compelling the payment of a debt. In this process the injured individual simply took up a position before his debtor's house and abstained from food, and religious ordinances compelled the debtor to do the same, and also to forego his usual amusements and pleasures. If the fast were continued until the suitor died, the debtor was held responsible for the death.

From this custom there grew up a caste of heralds known as *charans,* who made themselves responsible with their own lives for the fulfilment of public engagements or bonds, or important family contracts and bargains. The sign of their office was a dagger, which, in the event of their failure to carry out what they had undertaken, they would plunge into their own hearts. This form of duress was called *traga,* and if a herald feared that, in spite of the shocking odium which it brought upon a defaulter to have caused a herald's death, his own self-sacrifice would not suffice to overawe the wrongdoer, he would add to its weight by claiming also the lives of wife, children, or leading members of his caste. And in all these years the *charan* and *traga* have survived, and even yet vindicate sometimes their existence and principles.

In this particular instance, a banker had made a loan to a landholder in one of the native states, and took the precaution of securing the sign manual of the herald's dagger as a guarantee. When the time for discharging the debt came, the *charan* went and demanded payment, but the debtor was supercilious about old methods, and with a contemptuous laugh, referred his creditor to the machinery of the civil courts.

For these the *charan* had no particular respect, but his own honour and the fair fame of his caste he held very dear. He went home and talked the matter over with his aged mother and his brother, and the decision was taken. She would be the sacrifice to the solemn obligations of her race, and her life should be laid down in confirmation of her son's sacred bond. A last *sraddh* was performed, and the brave mother set out with her two sons to the defaulter's house. Again the demand was made, "Wilt thou pay or not ?" and this time the debtor was not sneering, but rather conciliatory. The mother unfalteringly knelt, and bared her head and neck of the draping sari. The debtor understood the grave reality now before him, and said, "I will pay as soon as the wheat-is in-gathered," while the old woman's head was unflinchingly bent. Once more the request was peremptorily repeated for instant discharge of the loan, and in abject terror and confusion the debtor made some too-prevaricating reply. Then the stalwart herald's heavy Rajput sword fell, and with one sweeping cut his mother's head rolled in the dust at his feet. The brothel's then inflicted wounds upon the awe-stricken defaulter, for the formal purpose of having his blood to blend with that of their own sacrificed victim to sprinkle upon the doorposts of his hated house. The police were quickly brought, and the prosaic procedure of ordinary justice was invoked to finish this fierce, chivalrous, barbaric drama; and the son, for whose pledged word his mother had given her own life, was sent into transportation over seas for life. But the debtor, knowing full well the withering infamy in which public opinion would henceforth hold him, starved himself to death for very shame.

And yet there are English people who will assure one that truth, honour, and heroism are not to be reckoned among the attributes of Indian women!

●●

17

Death and Funeral Customs

"A band Of waiting people: foremost one who swung An Eastern bowl with lighted coals; behind The kinsmen shorn, with mourning marks, ungirt, Crying aloud, ' O llama, Kama, hear! Call upon Rama, brothers;' next the bier, Knit of four poles with bamboos interlaced, Whereon lay stark and stiff, feet foremost, lean, Chapfallen, sightless, hollow flanked, a-grin, Spriukled with red and yellow dust—the Dead, Whom at the four went ways they turned head first, And crying, ' llama, Rama!' carried on To where a pile was reared behind the stream. Thereon they laid him, building fuel up. Good sleep hath one that slumbers on that bed! He shall not wake for cold, albeit he lies Naked to all the airs—for soon they set The red flame to the corners four, which crept And licked and flickered, finding out his flesh, And feeding on it with swift, hissing tongues, And crackle of parched skin and snap of joint, Till the fat smoke thinned, and the ashes sank Scarlet and gray, with here and there a bone White midst the grey—the total of the man."

Sin Edwin Arnold, "The Light of Asia."

Over marriage, with its joyous symbolism of new life, the Hindu lavishes all the ceremonial and rejoicing that he can command; over death, with its solemn mysteriousness, he is restrained and simple. In the Indian funeral customs there are scarcely any survivals of barbaric forms, and indeed the Rig Veda itself inculcates ideas by no means distant from those of Christianity, and sings—

> "Depart thou, depart thou to the place whither our fathers have departed. Meet with the ancient ones: meet with the Lord of death. Throwing off thine imperfections, go to thine Home. . . . Let him depart to those for whom now the rivers of nectar. Let him depart to those who, through meditation, have obtained the victory, who, by fixing their thoughts on the unseen, have gone to heaven. Let him depart to the mighty in battle, to the heroes who have laid down their lives for others, to those who have bestowed their goods on the poor;" while a somewhat later canticle in the "Atharva Yeda" carries on the idea with, "May the water-shedding spirits bear thee upwards, cooling thee with their swift motion through the air, and sprinkling thee with dew. Bear him, carry him; let him, with all his faculties complete, go to the world of the righteous. Crossing the dark valley which spreadeth boundless around him, let the unborn soul ascend to heaven. Wash the feet of him who is stained with sin; let him go upwards with cleansed feet. Crossing the gloom, gazing with wonder in many directions, let the unborn soul go up to heaven."

Speaking generally, it may be said that the Hindus of the Brahman and higher castes dispose of their dead by burning, while the Mahommedans and Hinduized aborigines and the non-Aryan tribes resort to burial. The funeral observances of the Hindus are simple, and there is very little to be added in description of them to Sir Edwin Arnold's lines with which this chapter is prefaced. Before the corpse is taken out of the house a *sraddh* or ceremony of offering and propitiation of departed ancestors takes place, and rice, oil, spice, and the usual objects of sacrifice are presented. Among the Rajputs this *sraddh* is performed on the thirteenth day after death, and another, known as the *barki sraddh,* takes place on the anniversary. The extremely orthodox of these people impose upon the sons a daily offering of water, but if there were no boys in the family, the *sraddh* and *barki* do not lose efficacy if carried out by the daughters, and I may mention that the Rajput women have what is known as a *Tihi Puja* (held on the 15th day of Asin, at the end of December), when they make offerings of cakes and oil to the souls of their mother-in-law, grandmother-in-law, and great-grandmother-in-law, in gratitude, it is averred, for the good husbands with which they are blessed.

The Eautias of Chota Nagpore are particular that the body of a married woman should be bathed, anointed with oil, and dressed in a new sari, the two latter details being omitted in the case of a widow. When the corpse is laid upon the pile, the head must be to the north, and the nearest relation takes a torch, which must be made of five dry twigs of bel soaked in *ghi,* walks seven times round the pyre, and touches the mouth of the corpse with the torch before setting the wood alight. Before this, however, a small piece of clothing is taken from the body, and in it a knife or bit of iron is wrapped. For ten days this must be carried about by the chief mourner and placed beside him when he sleeps, while he must also daily make libations of water or milk during the same period to the ashes which have been collected and placed in a new *ghauti* or earthen vessel.

To the strict Brahman, and all who are truly orthodox, burning on the shores of the Ganges is the most desirable method of disposal. Like the majority of travellers, I had a somewhat morbid desire to see the much-talked-of burning ghats of Benares; but I am bound to say that there is nothing particularly gruesome about the place of incineration itself, unless perchance one sees the unceremonious manner in which the body is doubled and crushed up to fit upon the pile of wood. The bodies, tightly swathed in cotton cloth, which must be white for a man and red for a woman, lie for one hour upon the water's edge, where they are just lapped by the stream, and the pyre is lighted by a near male relation from a sacred fire, the monopoly of which is held by a man of the servile dome caste. The scene is neither impressive nor repulsive, and as a spectacle may take rank among one's disappointments of travel. One may see as many as three or four fires alight at once, and unless the breeze happens to puff a smoky heavy odour of burnt fat in the direction of the boat, which may be moored as closely up to the scene as desired, there is absolutely nothing to tell one that the cremation of human remains is going on.

It is of course only the wealthy who can take their dead to Benares, or the almost equally sacred Gaya, to be burned, and so the scene may be witnessed in any town or village that one looks for it. Indeed the Malabari Brahmans have an axiom that the corpse of a man or woman should always be burnt in their own compounds. But it may be possible even to the poorest to be able in time to cast the ashes upon the broad bosom of Mother Ganga, or in the sanctified branches of the Kaveri at Birunelli in the Wynaad, and Perur in Coimbatore, and, until opportunity offers, the remains can be piously preserved in an urn at home. The advantage, according to Brahmanical ideas, of casting the ashes upon a sacred stream, is that a body, provided all orthodox prayers have been recited, passes into the keeping of Badra (one' of Siva's many forms), and his cares cease when the burning is complete. All that is" left after the incineration is pure, and therefore belongs of right to another of Siva's incarnation, Paramesvaran, who is reached through the holy waters. I heard in Calcutta of a curious instance of the way in which the orthodox are beginning to adapt the resources of Western innovation to the assistance of their religious rites in a carefully elaborated plan which a Brahman laid, in all seriousness, before the Postmaster-General for a system by which the ashes of the holy might be sent by parcels post, to be thrown upon the regenerating flood at the specially desirable seasons. Thus, at Calcutta or Bombay, and in fact wherever Hinduism flourishes, from Cape Cormorin to Beloochistan, there the place of burning will also be. And the widows go to make lamentation with their bereaved friends, and one of the most dolorous spectacles of which I have the recollection, was the sight of some five and twenty of them seated upon their heels and clad in dull ashen grey, which was not far removed from black, in a dreary upper room in one of the many-storied houses of Bombay, and monotoning the while a wailing, melancholy dirge.

Among the non-Aryan, but wholly or partially Hinduized races there are a few interesting survivals in burial customs, but, as a rule, a woman's remains are disposed of with less ceremony than those of a man. Some of the Mahilis, for instance, bury their dead face downwards, while the Paus, Males, Bagdis of Orissa, the poorer Goraits of Bengal, and the Koras, among many more, are careful that the head should be towards the north. Burial customs of certain castes often differ in localities, but the Jugis, who rank among the very lowest, are invariable in their methods of interment. They make a circular grave, often as much as eight feet deep, and a niche is made to receive the corpse in a sitting posture, the face being to the north-east, the quarter of the Sivaite paradise. A new cloth is wrapped round the body, and in a bag over the shoulder four cowries are placed to pay, as in pagan mythology, for the ferry across the gloomy waters of Yaitarani. When the grave is filled up, food of various sorts is placed upon it to appease the wandering spirits, and a few cowries are left as offering to the earth-god, whose space has thus been taken up.

Money again enters into the funeral observances of the Mangars, a fighting tribe of Nepal. Almost as soon as the breath has left the body, the corpse is tied to a bamboo pole and taken to the grave, where it is dressed in a new cloth, and sectarial marks are put upon the face. The money, however, is put by the Mangars into the mouth of the dead, together with a piece of coral, to which all sorts of talismanic virtues are ascribed. Then, a near relation, who should be a maternal uncle of the deceased if possible, after sundry minor rites of touching the lips with fire have been performed, lets down a piece of board in which nine steps or notches have been cut, the idea of this being a ladder to help the spirit to the regions above, while every one present also cuts a nick in another similar length of wood, which is afterwards broken in two. These people have another oddly reasoned custom, in that of placing a barrier of close-set thorn bushes across the path leading to the house of the dead. Beside this stands one of the chief mourners with a censer filled with an aromatic incense. Each one must step over the hedge and through the smoke, as the spirit then could not force its way through the thorns, nor could it be carried over on any one's shoulders, as smoke is anti-pathetic to it. Thus it is prevented from annoying the living in its former haunts.

With the Oraons—who usually burn and not bury their dead—the women of the village are expected to do the chief part in the outward evidences of mourning. They first loosen their hair, and then by their loud lamentations let their kinsfolk and acquaintance know thal the sad event has occurred. In an Oraon family the task of laying out the body devolves solely upon the 'women, and a wife is expected to set alight the funeral pyre of her husband, her female friends uttering piteous dirges the while.

Every separate tribe and caste has its distinctive days for feasting, purification, and *sraddh,* or propitiatory offering to deceased ancestors. These details occur earlier with some than with others, but I know of none who dispense with them entirely, nor of any who do not at one period or another consider a banquet as essential. Still, the true Hindu, orthodox or not, does not spend anything like the money upon funerals that he does upon weddings; and in that respect, as well as in a good many others, he sets our own working classes an example worth imitation, for "a gude solid burying" seems hardly to recommend itself as a popular recreation on sanitary or aesthetic grounds. But that is the light in which the British middle and lower orders regard it.

There is very little variation in the Mahommedan observances, and it is only in minor details that a woman's burial differs at all from that of a man. In theory, hope is never abandoned, however certain death appears, as a good Muslim argues that to count upon the end is reckoning that the Omnipotent could not, were He so willed, perform a miracle of saving. Therefore, though the house may be filled with the near and the distant relations, no preliminary steps may be taken towards funeral necessities, and the *rafan,* or shroud, may never be ordered until life is undoubtedly extinct. The *rafan* must never be cut with knife or scissors, nor may it be touched with a needle.

The corpse is washed, and laid in the new cloth, which is tied at the head and feet with slips torn off it. When the grave is nearly complete, the *janaza,* as the bier is called, is brought to the house, and the women, if *purdah,* look upon their relative's face for the last time, which they do with every sign of deep grief, and the recitation to one another of the good and womanly qualities she possessed.

If a bier is not obtainable, then an ordinary *charpai,* or bed, can be used to convey the body to the cemetery, to which it is carried at the usual walking pace on men's shoulders, and it is an Islamic command that if the number of bearers appears insufficient, or they show the slightest signs of fatigue, any passer-by, even though a complete stranger, must lend his aid. This task, wherever possible, and especially for a woman, should be done by the nearest relations, and there are a few small signs by which the members of the faith know whether the corpse is that of a married or unmarried woman. The *kalima,* or confession, is repeated by all as the procession moves along.

There is almost invariably a mosque, small and humble as it may be, within every cemetery, and to this the body is taken, and *namaz-i-janaza,* or the funeral office, consisting of portions from the Koran, is recited. As soon as the body has been lowered into the grave itself, all the relations present repeat a short but important chapter, called *Kul-liaivallah,* from the same sacred book thrice, and cast earth upon the remains. Then the face is uncovered, and a last look taken, and it is, the final tribute of respect to the strictly kept *purdah* of a well-born lady, that no man except her father, brothers, husband, sons, or the few more distantly removed relatives who could see her in life, should look upon her after death. It is a touching little proof, I always think, of how intensely strongly is the theory of a woman's non-existence for any save her own kept up in tradition and practice.

Boards are then laid above the corpse, and the grave is filled with a tenacious mud, and if the family is wealthy enough to command such a religious luxury, a *haftz-i-Koran, i.e.* one who can repeat the whole book by heart, is appointed to recite this at the grave for the benefit of the dead. It is an invariable rule that liberal alms shall be given to the poor after a funeral has taken place.

Muslim hospitality in India commands that all who attend the funeral shall be received at the house of the deceased for at least three days afterwards. At the end of that time *tija* or *suam,* a gathering of friends from different parts, is held in the family mosque early in the morning, and prayers for the souls of all the faithful departed are offered, and there follows a distribution of a particular form of confectionery known as *chani,* and *batashi,* a sweetmeat into whose composition sugar and dates enter largely. This does not, however, end the funeral feasting, as on the tenth and fortieth days after the death numerous dishes, for which special and costly ingredients are required, are prepared, and are sent to all who were present at the previous ceremonies. Commemorations of the departed one also take place six months and a year after death, and the same dishes are again served at these.

A Mahommedan woman's tomb is easily distinguishable from that of a man by having a small semi-circular elevation upon it. This is soon learnt after a sight of the Taj at Agra, in which I was prepared to be disappointed, for one has high expectations where almost all men speak well. But surely one's eyes would be wanting in some quality of artistic appreciation did not one submit from the first moment to its unutterable charm of form and brilliancy. My first view of it was under the waning sun, when a soft rosy glow lay upon its glistening whiteness, and there was a quiet hush upon its gardens, deserted save for two or three native students who looked at it with reverence and almost awe. No photograph does it justice, for this cannot convey the marvellous charm of colour of its inlay work, where choice stones have been lavished with unsparing hand, or the delicate fineness of the marble carvings outside, assuming now, under the hand of age, which is dealing very gently with the whole, the creamy richness of old ivory. The screen round the tomb and the doorways conveyed the idea to my mind of petrified lace, while the quotations from the Koran are engraved in black marble with a grace of curve and flourish that our stiffer letters could never possess. There are some who profess to find a "weakness of femininity," as they are pleased to express it, about the Taj. I would rather see in it Shah Jehan's discriminating sense of what his loved wife, Urjumand Banu, to whom it is the memorial, would herself have admired most, and respect him for having given to a woman the most beautiful monument in the world.

Curious in contrast is the simple grave at Delhi to Jehanara, the good and beautiful and virtuous daughter of Shah Jehan, which is a plain headstone, bearing at the top the words, in Arabic, "God is the life and the resurrection;" while over the grave itself grass, always kept green and fresh, is growing, in obedience to her wish, recorded in Persian, upon the stone :—

> "Save the green herb, place naught above my head, Such pall alone befits the lowly dead. The fleeting, poor Jehanara lies here. Her sire was Shah Jehan. . . ."

It might indeed be a grave in a country churchyard; and strange in truth is it that the daughter of her over whom one of the wonders of the world has been reared should thus have chosen so modest a memorial.

Lastly I come to the funeral rites and ceremonies of the Parsees, which are perhaps the most curious in all India. The Parsees have no reticence whatever about their strange customs, but explanations to understand them thoroughly are long, and few, I think, trouble themselves to do more than look at the "Towers of Silence" of Bombay and other places in Western India.

Precisely the same observances are carried out for a Parsee woman as for a man, and indeed the equal rights of women are put forward in the Zoroastrian books with considerable insistency. The death preparations begin, unlike the Muslim practices, from the moment that the case is pronounced hopeless, and priests are sent for to recite the *patet,* which is a prayer of repentance, and a complete robe of white, in which the dead body is to be clad, is washed by a near relation. The *kusti,* or sacred thread, which every adult

Parsee wears, is tied after death round the waist by a relative, and after that the care of the corpse passes to the professional watchers by the dead.

Then is performed the *sag did,* or "seeing of the dog," an office that I do not attempt to explain, nor in truth do the Zoroastrian authorities agree in offering any solution of the idea. A dog, however, at certain intervals of the day, is brought to where the body is lying, but whether with any belief that it will indicate whether life be really extinct, or as the symbol of the destroyer of the sensual passions, avarice and pride, it is impossible. to say. A brazier filled with sandal-wood, frankincense, and other aromatic substances is then kindled in the room, this being solely based upon reasons of sanitation, which is a guiding principle of all these special funeral rites. Meanwhile a priest sits beside the name and recites portions of the Zend Avesta till the body is removed, which *must* be done in full daylight.

About an hour before the time fixed for the removal of the body to the tower, two corpse-bearers, clad in pure white, come to the house. They bring with them an iron bier, called *gehan,* on which to carry the corpse, and it is a curious fact that every detail of a Parsee funeral must be done by people in couples. Even the mourners must come in pairs, and walk holding a white handkerchief, or *painand,* between them, the idea being that mutual assistance and consolation is derived from company. After certain offices have again been said, the friends and relations take a last look at the deceased, and the procession sets out. The mourners are enjoined to walk at least thirty paces behind the bier, and the men must be clothed in white.

The Bombay towers occupy the loveliest site-on the very crest of the Malabar Hill, commanding a marvellous bird's-eye view of the great busy city, with its tall factory chimneys, its streets, churches, and public buildings, while southward lies the open sea of sapphire blue. There are five towers, the oldest of them having been built in 1669, and the newest only a few years back. They are surrounded by all the gorgeous luxuriance of splendidly kept tropical vegetation, and flaming crotons in their metallic glories of gold and bronze, purple and crimson, lovely waxy oleanders, pink and white, and feathery palms ; and the simple structures themselves would not attract much notice, perhaps, but for what Professor Monier Williams has aptly described as " an extraordinary coping, which instantly attracts and fascinates the gaze. It is a coping formed, not of dead stone, but of living vultures. These birds, on the occasion of my visit, had settled themselves side by side in perfect order, and in a complete circle, around the parapets of the towers, with their heads pointed inwards; and so lazily did they sit there, and so motionless was their whole mien, that, except for their colour, they might have been carved out of the stone-work." Hut with the exception of the corpse-bearers, who form a class apart, none may see more. Even the priest may not approach within thirty yards ; and the body, according to the directions of the Zend Avesta, is carried in naked, and laid upon clay bricks, stone, and mortar. What the formation is we know from official description, and this I give in the words that were furnished to me.

> "The circular platform inside the tower, about three hundred feet in circumference, is entirely paved with large stone slabs well cemented, and divided into three rows of shallow open receptacles, corresponding with the three moral precepts of the Zoroastrian religion — 'good deeds,' 'good words,' 'good thoughts.'
>
> "First row for corpses of males."
>
> "Second row for corpses of females."
>
> "Third row for corpses of children."

"Footpaths for corpse-bearers to move about. A deep central well in the tower, about 150 feet in circumference (the sides and bottom of which are also paved with stone slabs), is used for depositing the dry bones. The corpse is completely stripped of its flesh by vultures within an hour or two, and the bones of the denuded skeleton, when perfectly dried up by atmospheric influences and the powerful heat of the tropical sun, are thrown into this well, where they gradually crumble to dust, chiefly consisting of lime and phosphorus. Thus the rich and the poor meet together on one level of equality after death."

"There are holes in the inner sides of the well through which the rain-water is carried into four underground drains at the base of the tower. These drains are connected with four underground wells, the bottoms of which are covered with a thick layer of sand. Pieces of charcoal and sandstone are also placed at the end of each drain, which are renewed from time to time. These double sets of filters are provided for purifying the rain-water passing over the bones, before it enters the ground—thus observing one of the tenets of the Zoroastrian religion that ' The mother earth shall not be defiled."

To Western ideas the system seems repugnant, and yet the most prejudiced leaves with a feeling that nothing to be seen outrages in any way the dignity and solemnity of death. There is nothing at all revolting or repulsive in the quiet scene, and the ill-favoured birds are merely performing nature's purpose in nature's own manner. They nest within the grounds, and scarcely ever take a circling flight of wider sweep than that enclosed within the boundary walls.

A Parsee woman's prayers are six fold. While she is a girl she is taught that she may ask for a good and a worthy husband—no unfitting thing surely, even though a European mother might forbid it among that "little hoard of maxims preaching down a daughter's heart"—and on engagement she asks to be permitted to retain her husband's full love, confidence, and respect. On marriage she beseeches the inestimable: joy of maternity, and at the prospect of this her prayers are for safe delivery, to which she couples a formula begging that the child may be naturally intelligent, healthy, strong, one that shall grow up to lead a virtuous life, able to enter into the deliberations of men, and "one that shall add to the glory of his family, to the glory of his street, to the glory of his city, and to the glory of his country." Lastly, her prayer is for milk at her breasts to nurse her child, for a woman who is unequal in this respect is, according to Zoroastrian tenets, to be classed as a maternal failure, who has not done her duty in preserving the purity of her own and her husband's race.

All these facts bear upon the Parsee doctrines as to the future state, in which for the first three days after dissolution the woman's soul remains within the limits of this world in the care of the angel Srosh, but on the third night it goes to the gates of the Great Bridge. There stands the grim judge, Meher, with the angels Astad and Eashne, who symbolize Truth and Justice. Meher weighs the actions good and bad against one another in his scales, and the woman who can throw in obedience to her husband, and the meritorious act of having thrice daily experienced the desire to be one with him in thoughts, words, and deeds, has a heavy weight of virtue to cast on the side of her own advantage. For if the good deeds outweigh the evil ones, even by the smallest particle, the soul may cross the bridge to the paradise beyond; but if the balance is on the other side, the erring soul is hurled into the yawning abyss of hell below. For those whose virtues and vices make a perfectly level scale, there is a place called Hamast Gehan, which appears to offer a refuge for all too bad for heaven and too good for hell.

Nothing, I think, is a more impressive evidence of the immense diversity of racial modes of thought and custom than the variations in burial rites. The conditions of soil and atmosphere, important considerations in the disposal of the dead, are common to all, yet each great race, nay, rather each tribe, caste, and subsect, has observances peculiar to itself. So far, English rule has been to allow all liberty and freedom in matters of domestic habit, and the result has been that the Hindu has not interfered with the Parsee, the Mahommedan has not troubled the non-Aryan, and all has worked well. How long this will continue, if every officious busybody who scampers across in three weeks from Bombay to Çalcutta is permitted to dictate what he (or, worse, she) thinks should be done, it would be rash to predict. In following the Indian woman's life along its successive stages and concerns, I have tried to show that its present conditions are the result of countless generations of hereditary influences, and that the separate elements which go to form the vast empire are only to be welded together by the most judicious handling. The policy of interference and innovation only introduces further items of discord which, under the existing order, it should be our utmost care to avoid.

> "We bestow a great deal of pity upon the Indian woman." We might give it where it would be more useful and more appreciated. The tone we have adopted towards her and her prejudices, customs, and theories of life, derived, be it remembered, from a civilization that was old when our own began, has savoured too much of patronage, and a forgetfulness of that eternal truth, *Ce que femme veut, Dieu le veut.* She has now before her all the possibilities of' education, though truly she shows no exuberant enthusiasm to accept them. Having laid these within her easy reach, let us now leave the situation to its own development, helping, as with medical aid, to those things which without us she could not enjoy, but

not forcing upon diverse races and peoples one stock pattern of conventional European ideas. It will be, perhaps, to some a lamentable suggestion of non-progressiveness to venture to remind the rough and ready exponents of new methods, new views, new" woman, and much more that is rash and crude, that social systems which have endured through the centuries, and survived in face of political revolutions and changes, cannot be without recommendations to their particular needs and environments, even though the Western mind fails to grasp what these may be. It is part of the charter by which we rule India that private freedom in matters of faith and conscience shall be fully respected, and we are only fulfilling this while we recognize that any demands for change in the domestic conditions of the people must come from within, rather than forcing upon them artificial reforms from without.

●●

Index

K

L

M

N

P

R

S

T

V

W